THE **PEN** AND THE **PAN**

THE
PEN
AND THE
PAN

FOOD, FICTION AND HOMEGROWN CARIBBEAN FEMINISM(S)

Robyn Cope

The University of the West Indies Press
Jamaica • Barbados • Trinidad and Tobago

The University of the West Indies Press
7A Gibraltar Hall Road, Mona
Kingston 7, Jamaica
www.uwipress.com

A catalogue record of this book is available from the
National Library of Jamaica.

ISBN: 978-976-640-860-2 (print)
978-976-640-861-9 (mobi)
978-976-640-862-6 (ePub)

Cover art: Samere Tansley, *And the Shadows of Twilight Grow Broader and Deeper upon the Understanding* (46" x 72", acrylic on linen, 2008–2012), www.sameres gallery.com. (The title of the painting is taken from the words of Henry Wadsworth Longfellow: "I venerate old age; and I love not the man who can look without emotion upon the sunset of life, when the dusk of evening begins to gather over the watery eye, and the shadows of twilight grow broader and deeper upon the understanding.")

Cover and book design by Robert Harris.
Set in Scala 10.5/15 x 24

Printed in the United States of America

FOR CARIBBEAN WOMEN,
INSIDE AND OUTSIDE THE ARCHIPELAGO

CONTENTS

ACKNOWLEDGEMENTS

YON SÈL DWÈT PA MANJE KALALOU . . . some things can only be accomplished by working together, and this book is one of those things.

I am deeply grateful to Sandra Casanova-Vizcaíno and to Marda Messay, who had the courage to let me into their worlds, and the grace to set foot in mine.

Special thanks to Martin Munro for his early input and guidance on this project, to Angel de Armendi and Manosky Sarrette for their language skills and cultural insights, to Dana Stewart for fighting for me when it really mattered, and to Diana Gildea for organizing a writing group to keep us moving toward our dreams, one pomodoro at a time.

I would like to acknowledge the various sources of institutional and organizational support that afforded me the time and money to develop this project: the Winthrop-King Institute and the Florida State Graduate School, Harpur College and the Institute for the Advanced Study of the Humanities at Binghamton University, and my brothers and sisters of the United University Professions in New York State.

Much appreciation to Althea Brown, Shivaun Hearne, Nadine Buckland, Joseph Powell (may he rest in peace, I will not forget his kindness) and the whole team at the University of the West Indies Press. Likewise, I thank Robert Harris for the book and cover design and the anonymous external readers for their insightful comments. My sincerest gratitude to Samere Tansley, who generously granted permission to use her beautiful art for the cover.

Bloomsbury Academic has kindly allowed me to reuse here some portions of my essay "Scattering and Gathering: Danticat, Food and (the) Haitian Experience(s)", which first appeared in *The Bloomsbury Handbook to Edwidge Danticat*, edited by Jana Evans Braziel and Nadège Clitandre, in 2021.

Finally, I wouldn't have been able to persevere to the end of this project without the affection and encouragement of friends like Susannah Fleming, Ray Montalvo, Bill and Mary Oliver, Astrid Gonzalez and Cezar Georgescu, Bryan Kirschen and Blake Schmutz, Omid Ghaemmaghami and Vida Rastegar-Ghaemmaghami. I am thankful for my daughter Sophie's example of grit, my son Adrian's sense of humour, and my aunts' and sister-cousins' unconditional love, always only a phone call away. Most of all, I couldn't have done it without my husband, Tarek, who has been and remains my sounding board, intellectual partner and soulmate.

FOOD, FICTION AND HOMEGROWN
CARIBBEAN FEMINISM(S)

WHENEVER SHE SERVES A MEAL TO GUESTS, literary giant Maryse Condé always makes the same joke, and nobody ever finds it funny. In the preface to her 2015 food-focused memoir *Of Morsels and Marvels*, Condé describes her guests' response: "'I know you'll love it! I'm not sure I'm a good novelist, but I'm convinced I'm a great cook!' Nobody laughs. Not one. It's because my guests are shocked. What sacrilege! they think. How can she be so bold as to compare cooking with literature? It boils down to mixing sheep with goats, jute with silk."[1]

The trouble, of course, is that Condé's guests fail to see her work in the kitchen as cerebral or creative or *feminist*. But Condé's cooking, like her writing, is all of those things. Writes Condé in *Of Morsels and Marvels*, "Together with literature, it [cooking] had been my dominant passion for years. . . . I realized that both passions could not be radically dissociated. They discreetly share common ground."[2] In fact, Condé is one of a number of Caribbean women writers who have combined food and fiction to showcase homegrown Caribbean feminisms. Authors such as Gisèle Pineau, Edwidge Danticat, Lakshmi Persaud, Shani Mootoo and Maryse Condé have used food, which is quotidian, personal and concrete, to navigate the political and the abstract. Over the past quarter-century, the culinary has emerged as a significant subversive discursive stream in both Afro- and Indo-Caribbean women's writing – a compelling means of telling women's previously unheard stories of oppression and resistance, thus engendering Caribbean history.

As this volume will show, culinary fiction by Guadeloupeans Maryse Condé and Gisèle Pineau, Haitian Edwidge Danticat, and Trinidadians Lakshmi Persaud and Shani Mootoo contests the partiality of colonial and neocolonial versions of Caribbean history, the reductive tendencies of masculinist cultural theory and the prescriptive impulses of a single monolithic Feminism, even a regional one. This comparative study of contemporary food-focused fiction from the francophone and anglophone Caribbean exposes the genre's potential for laying bare intra-Caribbean power dynamics, including those between women, and for promoting coalitional homegrown feminism(s), figured by the central trope of the shared meal.

Food imagery is a logical vehicle for expressing the quest for and shifts in identity that are so characteristic of Caribbean and diasporic people. As Richard Wilk puts it, "Food is more than nutrition or physical substance that flows through the economy. Food is packed with meaning, as well as vitamins, carbohydrates and protein. It satisfies needs beyond those of the body and the pocketbook. Food is a medium to build families, religious communities, ethnic boundaries and a consciousness of history."[3]

Food is also an archive of cultural memory and of history – for example, it charts and memorializes the movement of Afro- and Indo-diasporic Antilleans from one continent to another over centuries. Food can be used to create or cross boundaries, to assimilate or to hold on to the past, to reject or to affiliate oneself with groups. Food, as a site where people and cultures mix and overlap, can be a symbol of *creolization* – a mixing of identities, languages and cultures that goes beyond mere hybridity to create something new – or an emblem of *creoleness* – an Afrocentric Caribbean identity born of cultural confrontation in the plantation space. (As we will see, callaloo, a stew that is supposedly the universal culinary symbol of a proudly creolized Caribbean, can be problematic for people of East Indian descent, who see Caribbean society as "tossed salad", even if in some ways they are in fact "living callaloo".[4]) Food, like literature, is a material embodiment of Caribbean worldview(s).

People negotiate their identities through food: both personal identity (it is the site of many power struggles between women, especially between mothers and daughters, a conflict that is central to many of the novels discussed here) and group affiliations, whether ethnic, linguistic, geographic, cultural, religious or political. It connects body and mind, for it "is both a physical substance and a vehicle for the imagination, something that nourishes the body, but also fascinates and moves the mind".[5] It can symbolize survival in hard times and in faraway places.[6] Where there is no food, hunger can be weaponized, harnessed as a tool of exploitation and control. And food is a primarily feminine domain. Food, like fiction, is a tool that is accessible to women, who use both the pen and the pan to navigate structures that have left them out or shut them out.

CARIBBEAN HERSTORY

In her introduction to *Food and Literature* (2018), Gitanjali Shahani identifies a number of key questions for the emerging field of literary food studies: What do food words and scenes do for the literary text? How does food function as a literary device? How does eating work in the text and how do we, as readers, consume the process of eating in the text? Why is food studies considered a natural fit with women's studies? What can writing about food teach us about changing postmodern identities, selfhood and nostalgia, and about the colonial encounter and its aftermath? In the end, asserts Shahani, literary food studies is most interested in "recovering important stories and histories that cannot be told without food".[7] In *The Culinary Imagination*'s twist on Brillat-Savarin's "Tell me what you eat: I will tell you what you are", Sandra Gilbert says it best: *"Tell me what you read and write about what you eat, and I shall tell you more about what you are. Tell me how you envision food in stories and poems, memoirs and biographies, films and pictures and fantasies, and we shall begin to understand how you think about your life."*[8]

Unsurprisingly, in the Caribbean, where history has been shaped by colonial and neocolonial appetites, both literal and symbolic, metaphors of food and consumption have been an important trope in Caribbean "writing back" to (neo)colonialism, not only in the novels I examine here, but in a wide range of Caribbean writing throughout the twentieth century.[9] Because of the prominent role food has played in the colonial and neocolonial history of the Caribbean, food is a useful lens through which to consider (or reconsider) the Caribbean past. For centuries the voracious European appetite for sugar drove the massive Caribbean economy of trade in people and goods. Staggering numbers of enslaved Africans and indentured East Indians were brought to the Caribbean to do the backbreaking labour of producing sugar. Under the plantation system, the commodification of sugar (and other agricultural products) for large-scale export was mirrored by the commodification of human beings for mass import.[10] And Caribbean land and ecosystems were also commodified as the expansionary logic of global capitalism pushed the "commodity frontier" of sugar production ever farther from global centres and deeper into global peripheries.[11] Cultural chauvinism, including culinary chauvinism, justified these Eurocentric systems of economic, political, social and ecological domination.

Neocolonial North/South power relations still perpetuate these colonial patterns of exploitation and peripheralization, and neocolonial relationships continue to undermine not only local food culture but also local food security and food sovereignty in the Caribbean. Lack of access and restricted access to food propel Caribbean poor and working-class people into the city, across the border, to another island or into the Global North that started it all, in an endless cycle of orchestrated hunger and forced dependence (as we will see in chapters 1, 2 and 5). Meanwhile, where there is blind complicity or outright collaboration with neocolonial powers, upper-middle-class Caribbean entrepreneurs and professionals fill their bellies respectively with food and self-satisfaction (see chapters 3 and 4) while Caribbean elites nourish insatiable appetites (see chapters 2, 4 and 5).

The authors featured in *The Pen and the Pan* use food to illustrate women's experiences of those colonial and neocolonial pressures, and to show how women respond to those demands. In this body of writing, food discourses and practices are put forth as woman-centred potential avenues for countering hegemonic (neo)colonial structures and discourses. *The Pen and the Pan's* target literary corpus, published between 1990 and 2015, centres women's experiences and tells their untold stories, a project that runs parallel to contemporary changes in academic historiography, which aimed during this period to incorporate gender into historical narratives, both thematically and as a conceptual lens through which to read history.

During this period, historians expanded and made more inclusive the previous reductive narratives of the Caribbean past, which had centred on colonial perspectives, systems and institutions. A representative sample of twenty-first-century "brief" and "general" histories of the region[12] shows that new histories supplement the former colonial histories with accounts of the experiences of the colonized, as well as alternative economic, agricultural and social models. Stories of the arduous Middle Passage balance "discovery" tales; accounts of spontaneous human cooperation and solidarity accompany the history of inherited coercive labour; depictions of small-scale polycultural farming producing food for local consumption stand alongside reports of the monocultural, export-focused plantation system; portraits of maroon communities and a multiracial peasantry complete oversimplified accounts that reduce Caribbean society to the white enslaver class and the black people they enslaved. This new form of historiography shifted the focus from chronicling the mechanisms of centuries of brutal colonial control and neocolonial dominance to relating the means of Caribbean survival and resistance. The incorporation of a wider spectrum of Caribbean experiences unquestionably provides some insight into the formation of a Caribbean worldview(s). However, because of extreme colonization and erasure in the Caribbean, historians cannot hope to do this work alone.[13]

These same concerns are reflected in the set of novels examined here, which embody the changes in how history is told. And the novels are themselves history, for although they are fictional, the fictions they recount are true. As Marie-Sophie, the Martinican heroine of Patrick Chamoiseau's *Texaco*, hears from her grandfather Esternome and records in her notebook, "In what I tell you, there's the almost-true, the sometimes-true, and the half-true. That's what telling a life is like, braiding all of that like one plaits the white Indies currant's hair to make a hut. And the true-true comes out of that braid. And Sophie, you can't be scared of lying if you want to know everything."[14] As we will see, the Caribbean history and cultural theory produced and imagined by men has left out whole swathes of female experience and ways of knowing. In contrast, the body of historical culinary fiction written by women that has coalesced over the past quarter-century makes practical and real – that is, it puts into practice – concurrent scholarly efforts to engender Caribbean history.[15]

In "Writing Gender into History", an essay in the edited collection *Engendering History: Caribbean Women in Historical Perspective*, Patricia Mohammed explains that it is not enough simply to add women to historical accounts without challenging the gender-biased theoretical framework that excluded them in the first place. To engender history, she asserts, one must address how hierarchies of gender are constructed and legitimized, as well as how they are consciously contested in specific historical contexts. In this volume I use the term *engender* in two senses. I simultaneously embrace both Mohammed's definition – to add gender sensitivity and specificity – and a second, performative sense – to cause or give rise to something. In both these ways Caribbean culinary fiction engenders Caribbean history, for it both articulates women's experiences and brings a new kind of Caribbean history into being.

According to Edouard Glissant, "History is a highly functional fantasy of the West, belonging precisely to the time when it alone 'made' the history of the world."[16] For Glissant and for other twentieth-century Caribbean cultural theorists, history is a construct of the colonizers, a distortion that can be remedied only by reconstructing history itself. Glissant argues that these decolonized histories cannot be separated from literature, for it is the fiction writer who most effectively reconstitutes the Caribbean past: "Because historical memory has too often been crossed out, the Caribbean writer must sift through this memory, beginning with the sometimes hidden traces that he has discovered in the real world."[17] But much of twentieth-century French Antillean cultural theory, aimed at liberating the French Antillean psyche from race-based frameworks of thought, was framed around men and men's experiences. It thus enacted some of the violence Glissant saw in Western histories, this time ignoring the contributions of women rather than the contributions of the colonized. As James Arnold has observed, influential Caribbean cultural theory before 1994 replicated oppressive gender roles in its engagement with the "erotics of colonialism" of Western imperial discourse. In this framework, the European colonizing power or people are cast as the assertive virile male, while the colonized territory or people are assigned the role of submissive, accommodating female – a dynamic that is used to justify subjugation.[18] As a result, much of twentieth-century French Antillean cultural theory, like the history it purports to complete, is not only masculine but masculinist, diminishing, dismissing or erasing altogether Caribbean women's experience.

For example, in the French Antilles, female voices of the Négritude movement, such as Suzanne Roussi and the Nardal sisters, have been largely eclipsed by their more famous male contemporary Aimé Césaire. And although Césaire's vision of Négritude in the seminal *Notebook of a Return to the Native Land* (1939) laid the foundation for a transformative reappropriation of African and Afro-diasporic history and culture, the poem's phallogocentric discourse posited psychic liberation in terms of salvatory maleness.[19] A decade later, Frantz Fanon's influential *Black Skin, White Masks* (1952) convincingly deconstructed racialized essentialism, unveiling race as a social construct and understanding racism as a collective mental illness. However, Fanon's sharply gendered heteronormative approach to Martinican identity effectively silenced his female contemporary, Martinican author Mayotte Capécia, and rejected out of hand the possibility of Martinican male homosexuality.[20] A quarter-century after that, Glissant's *Le discours antillais* (1981) shattered the myth of a univocal Caribbean experience by foregrounding the heroic maroon, the archetypal masculinist figure of Caribbean resistance and revolt,[21] and ignoring women's role in resisting colonialism. And while Jean Bernabé, Patrick Chamoiseau and Raphaël Confiant's *In Praise of Creoleness* (1989) aims to transcend ethno-class limitations, widen the master narrative of Caribbean experience and elevate the status of Caribbean oral history, it also ignores gender, focusing on the male *conteur* as the ancestor of all creole culture and the *marqueur de paroles* as his contemporary heir, thus eliminating women's contributions to oral history.[22]

Likewise, with the notable exception of Marie Vieux Chauvet, a long line of Haitian women writers such as Ghislaine Charlier and Jan Dominique[23] were often similarly overlooked in a canon whose centre of gravity was occupied by male authors and cultural theorists, from the indigenist Jean Price-Mars (whom Senghor called "the father of Négritude") to the Marxists Jacques Roumain and Jacques Stephen Alexis and the spiralist Frankétienne. Meanwhile, among Indo-Caribbean writers in the English-speaking Caribbean, where V.S. Naipaul loomed large, women's writing was so thoroughly suppressed and for so long that Mariam Pirbhai hails Lakshmi Persaud (see chapter 3) and Shani Mootoo (see chapter 4), writing in the 1990s, as "pioneers of the Indo-Caribbean women's novel".[24]

In the introduction to her 1990 edited collection, *Out of the Kumbla: Caribbean Women and Literature* (with Elaine Savory), Carole Boyce Davies calls out George Lamming, along with other prominent male critics and cultural theorists across the archipelago, for their wilful blindness to the contributions of Caribbean women writers and thinkers, attributing it to their prioritization of the politics of decolonization over women's emancipation struggles.[25] Masculinist literary and cultural criticism, she notes, tended to boil down Caribbean thought into three elements: anti-colonial and post-colonial nationalism, Black Power and Négritude, and Marxism–Leninism. Proclaims Davies, "It is time to argue that a fourth ideological formulation – feminism – now is being seriously articulated."[26] She celebrates the "flowering" of Caribbean women's writing in the 1980s, both within the Caribbean and in diaspora in Europe and North America. Among those writers, a handful of English-speaking Afro-Caribbean women writing in diaspora can and should be seen as precursors to the authors featured in *The Pen and the Pan*, a ground-breaking first wave of Caribbean women writers taking back the kitchen.

KITCHEN TALK

In the late 1970s and the 1980s, a handful of English-speaking Afro-Caribbean women writers in diaspora in North America staked a claim on the kitchen as a site of both their repression and their resistance. Antiguan-American Jamaica Kincaid's well-known poem "Girl" (1978) was a series of instructions in acceptable female behaviours with regard to food, in the kitchen, at the table, in the garden and at the market, interspersed with a handful of other suffocating expectations around female sexuality and self-expression, a theme we will see echoed in Edwidge Danticat's and Lakshmi Persaud's writing (see chapters 2 and 3 respectively). Meanwhile, in Barbadian Audre Lorde's semi-autobiographical *Zami: A New Spelling of My Name* (1982), the narrator subverts her mother's culinary and sexual control, taking sensual and sexual pleasure in the spice grinding she is commanded to do,[27] an approach we will also find in Shani Mootoo's writing (see chapter 4).

In her iconic essay "From the Poets in the Kitchen" (1983), Barbadian-Grenadian-American Paule Marshall writes of the women she knew as a child: "Indeed, you might say they suffered a triple invisibility, being black, female and foreigners. They really didn't count in American society except as a source of cheap labor. But given the kind of women they were, they couldn't tolerate the fact of their invisibility, their powerlessness. And they fought back, using the only weapon at their command: the spoken word."[28] Marshall credits those women with her "first lessons in the narrative art", attributing the best of her own work to them, declaring it "testimony to the rich legacy of language and culture they so freely passed on to me in the wordshop of the kitchen".[29] Pineau's and Danticat's culinary fiction reflects a similar indebtedness to black women's storytelling (see chapters 1 and 2).

In the 1990s and 2000s, Jamaican-American Opal Palmer Adisa's culinary poetry included "Senses Related to the Nose" (1996), in which Caribbean fruits such as mango, star-apple and naseberry symbolize Caribbean women, "crated and cargoed", "consumed and discarded",[30] themes we will encounter in Condé's *Victoire* (see chapter 5), and Adisa's "Poui" (2000), in which the tongue is a site of both culinary and sexual pleasure, and memories of the heat of Caribbean foods accompany recollections of conflicted female desire, a theme both Persaud and Mootoo explore (see chapters 3 and 4 respectively).[31]

Like their Afro-Caribbean counterparts from the English-speaking Caribbean, Condé, Pineau, Danticat, Persaud and Mootoo directly challenge reductive discourses of Caribbean resistance, replacing masculine archetypes with feminine ones. In their novels, the rebel and the maroon are replaced with the quietly courageous domestic servant and the cook; the maternal grandmother, not the paternal *conteur*, is the repository of oral history and folk medicine; the manly *marqueur de paroles* is replaced as oral historian by the female narrators. These authors assert their right not only to record and reflect upon the Caribbean past and present, but also to imagine and shape the Caribbean future. The target corpus passes over the public geography of male defiance in favour of the more private terrain of female intransigence – the courtyard, the kitchen, the cookpot, their own bodies. Above all, this representative sample of the past quarter-century of Caribbean culinary fiction sidesteps the prescriptive trappings of sweeping masculinist rhetoric and an ideology that limits itself to the colonizer–colonized binary. Instead, these works offer a blueprint for intersectional epistemologies based on women's lived experience that acknowledges both inter- and intragroup conflict in the Caribbean and its diaspora.

Like their historian counterparts, the authors featured in this volume revisited pivotal moments and movements in Caribbean history, bringing fresh awareness of gender to familiar terrain that had been read by male theorists and writers only in terms of race and colonization. These women's original renderings of both well-known and lesser-known topics in Caribbean history – including the Duvalier dictatorship and its aftermath, the Parsley Massacre of 1937, the wave of Antillean immigration to mainland France in the 1960s, post-indentureship Indo-Trinidadian identity politics, the post-abolition period in Guadeloupe, and the Caribbean diaspora in North America in the twenty-first century – incorporate gender not only as a theme but also as a conceptual foundation. They ask new, gender-sensitized questions and provide gender-informed perspectives on major aspects of twentieth-century Caribbean life, including autocratic rule, demographic diversity, mass migration and the ongoing process of decolonization and psychic liberation. And they do it, in part, through their depictions of food – of women's everyday domestic worlds.

Culinary fiction's keen insight into intragroup dynamics largely preceded and foretold twenty-first-century developments in theoretical engagement with post-coloniality and hybridity in the Caribbean. In 2006 Silvio Torres-Saillant warned that reductive, unequivocal symbols of resistance to colonial and neocolonial exploitation from the outside (the "cult of the Maroon" as he calls it) only feed into a Caribbean mindset that justifies or obscures internal abuses.[32] Meanwhile, in 2004 Shalini Puri pointed out that discourses of hybridity have distracted from and obscured rather than resolved gender and class inequalities in the Caribbean.[33] Indeed, Caribbean women creative writers outpaced cultural theorists, exposing the practical shortcomings of those overly broad concepts. Unlike their male contemporaries, these female authors of culinary fiction, a subset of what Odile Ferly terms "millennial writers", fully engage with the problems of present-day Caribbean societies rather than glossing over them because of their potentially divisive effects.[34] Their varied depictions of women's lives in the Caribbean fly in the face of any simplistic representation of the Caribbean freedom struggle as entirely reducible to the quest to free oneself from (neo)colonial domination. My reading of food in the fiction of Pineau, Danticat, Persaud, Mootoo and Condé engages with Caribbean women authors' gendered perspective on all these intra-Caribbean relationships, illustrated by the way they play out in the kitchen and at the table, and on coalition-building, figured by the central trope of the shared meal.

Culinary fiction is an ideal medium for what have become "classic" Caribbean questions of rootlessness, assimilation and belonging. After all, food has always been an important means of cultural retention and innovation for members of the African and South Asian diasporas in the Caribbean, as well as for their descendants in the Caribbean diaspora.[35] In the Caribbean and its diaspora, culinary culture is a medium for memory, longing and nostalgia, and a symbol of national identity, ethnic pride and group belonging.[36] However, as my reading of these novels demonstrates, the significance of food practices cannot be reduced to their role in retaining African, South Asian or Caribbean cultures in diaspora. In fact, at times the culinary fiction of Pineau, Danticat, Persaud, Mootoo and Condé questions whether nostalgia is compatible with growth, innovation and inclusion. The "authentic", as my reading of this food-focused fiction demonstrates, can be both a source of pride and inspiration and a tool of exclusion and control. In the end, women pay a disproportionate price for nostalgia and "authenticity". In the same way, Caribbean food culture cannot be defined solely in terms of anti-colonial cultural resistance; any reading that does this oversimplifies and obscures the part which food plays in intra-Caribbean relationships. What these authors do is more complex than that. By retelling Caribbean history from the perspective of Caribbean women, who bear the brunt of oppression and violence in these novels, the target corpus offers a window into women's particular experiences of trauma and violence.

Food practices are also intimately connected to a multitude of intragroup dynamics – to interactions among generations, cultures and ethnic groups, social and economic classes, religious and political affiliations, and sexual identities. These novels show how women themselves use food to both exclude and affiliate. Moreover, because of women's centrality to food production, preparation and consumption patterns, food-focused writing necessarily addresses questions of gendered labour and place, evoking the potential for gendered epistemologies arising out of women's work and woman-centred spaces. In the Caribbean (as in the rest of the world), nearly all women spend a significant portion of their day working with or thinking about food, and food becomes an integral part of women's identities. Food is therefore logically a tool both of the exploitation and oppression of women and of their resistance.[37]

HOMEGROWN CARIBBEAN FEMINISM(S)

If we are to think of the novels contemplated in *The Pen and the Pan* in terms of Caribbean feminism, it is most useful to do so as a mosaic – a loose coalition of diverse types of Caribbean feminisms, each of which is separate from but intimately connected to the others. These works acknowledge that there are many distinct Caribbean contexts, each with its own particular type of oppression and resistance to that oppression. These feminisms work independently and together to foreground Caribbean women's experiences, situating them both within the legacy of race and colonialism and amid the intricacies of intragroup conflict, both in the archipelago and within its diaspora. These Caribbean feminisms might be called "postcolonial", "standpoint", "intersectional" or even "indigenous", but I argue that the historically inspired literary feminisms of Pineau, Danticat, Pineau, Mootoo and Condé can best be described as *homegrown*. This term captures something of the spirit of this body of work that escapes those other classifications.

Some might question the appropriateness of *homegrown* in relation to a group of women writers who work, live and resist in the diaspora. However, recall that the writing of Pineau, Danticat, Persaud, Mootoo and Condé has deep roots in and a commitment to the Caribbean. Whether their characters are inspired by their own grandmothers, mothers or selves, or whether they are based on a more general sense of Caribbean women's everyday experiences of oppression and resistant response, these authors have something meaningful to add to the archives of homegrown Caribbean feminism(s). And as we will see in the chapters to come, they are prepared to earn – write – their place at the table. What follows is not intended to be an exhaustive history of Caribbean feminist and women's activism in the Caribbean.[38] Rather, it is a brief contextualization of the target corpus within contemporary debates about more inclusive, coalitional Caribbean feminist theory and practice at the turn of the twenty-first century (recall that ten of the eleven works were published in the 1990s and 2000s) and about the overlapping (and still current) emphasis on rooting Caribbean feminisms in Caribbean history and Caribbean women's everyday lives, establishing the continued salience of the target corpus moving forward. I hope the discussion below will provide a useful basic framework for understanding my preference for the term *homegrown* as, in the chapters to come, I delve into Afro-Antillean, Haitian and Indo-Trinidadian women writers' depictions of women's everyday freedom struggles.

In the years leading up to the publication of the target corpus of this study (the 1980s and early 1990s), many theorists explored the intersections of feminist and post-colonial criticism. Feminist perspectives exposed some of the unexamined assumptions within post-colonial discourse, while post-colonial criticism interrogated the limitations of Western feminism in non-Western circumstances. The idea that women in formerly colonized societies were "double colonized" – by both imperial and patriarchal ideologies – became a familiar paradigm.[39] For example, in 1984 Chandra Mohanty contested Western feminist discourses that portray the Third World woman as sexually constrained, ignorant, poor, uneducated, tradition-bound, domestic, family-oriented and, above all, victimized, while the Western woman is depicted as educated and modern, with control over her body and sexuality, and free to make decisions.[40] Mohanty warns of the dangers of a discursive consensus, complete with assumed sociological and anthropological universals, that presumes gender difference to be the origin of oppression. In this flawed mode of thinking, she argues, one specifies the context of the oppression only after the fact.

Building upon Mohanty's concerns, Uma Narayan cautions that post-colonial feminisms must avoid homogeneous characterizations of heterogeneous non-Western peoples whose values, interests, ways of life, and moral and political commitments are internally plural and divergent.[41] She also admonishes those who equate with "the preservation of culture" women's conformity with culturally dominant practices that adversely affect women. In this way, she points out, feminist challenges to norms and practices affecting non-Western women are framed as "cultural betrayals" and non-Western feminists as "stooges of Western imperialism".[42] Ahistorical essentialist pictures of non-Western cultures obscure the fact that what constitutes a given culture – and, therefore, what must be central to projects of "cultural

preservation" – changes over time. What doesn't seem to change, notes
Narayan, is that it is women who are saddled with the primary responsibility
for cultural preservation.[43] The most powerful feminist perspectives can
come from simultaneously criticizing the effects that certain "traditions"
have on women and questioning the timelessness and centrality of the traditions themselves.[44] As we will see, the fictional writing of Pineau, Danticat,
Persaud, Mootoo and Condé also strives to look beyond assumptions about
non-Western women to scrutinize internal differences, problematizing "authenticity" and "cultural preservation". Yet despite these shared concerns,
"post-colonial" risks painting the feminisms they portray with too broad a
brush.

Elsewhere during the late 1990s, scholars of the Caribbean were asking
similar questions in a Caribbean framework. Rawwida Baksh-Soodeen traced
the evolution of "second-wave" Caribbean feminism, from post-independence
feminist discourse that conflated (black) race, (working) class and nation
throughout the 1970s and 1980s to a general shift away from ideological
dogmatism and towards standpoint feminism in the 1980s and 1990s.
Afrocentric theory and practice, she writes, dominated second-wave feminism
in the Caribbean. Feminist organizing, she notes, was viewed as largely the
domain of Afro-Caribbean women, while women of Indigenous, East Indian,
Chinese and other origins were left out of the process.[45] Matrifocality and
female-headed households became associated with black or creole culture,
while poor Indo-Caribbean people were supposed to live in three-genera-
tion extended families and the nuclear family became the domain of white
people only.[46] This narrative left no room for the emerging black educated
middle class or, indeed, for the very rapid social mobility that was typical
of some Caribbean societies post-independence. As Baksh-Soodeen points
out, during the decades following independence, many women were able to
move out of their class of origin through education.[47] A "third wave" of more
standpoint-oriented feminist theory, she contends, will have to account for the
ever-shifting structure of Caribbean societies at the turn of the twenty-first
century, while new feminist practice will need to become a space in which
women of different racial, cultural and sexual identities interact. Echoing
Baksh-Soodeen's concerns, the authors I examine in the chapters to come
clearly demonstrate that a disinterested, impartial "view from nowhere" is

simply impossible. Their female protagonists' socially situated knowledge and ways of knowing align themselves thoroughly with the principles of standpoint feminism.

Although the term *intersectional feminism* is highly visible not only in academic circles but even in popular culture today, Kimberle Crenshaw's ground-breaking "Demarginalizing the Intersection of Race and Sex: A Black Feminist Critique of Antidiscrimination Doctrine, Feminist Theory, and Antiracist Politics" first appeared in 1989, just one year before the novels I examine in this volume began to emerge. Crenshaw argues that if we begin by addressing inequalities at the intersection of race and gender and within the most marginalized groups, all those who are singularly disadvantaged will likewise stand to benefit. In her reflections on the legacy of twenty-five years of "intersectionality as a method", Catherine MacKinnon highlights its exceptional value in holding abstract, dissociated academic theory account-able to the reality it models itself after. "Intersectionality begins", stresses MacKinnon, "in the concrete experience of race and sex together in the lives of real people".[48] Another of intersectional feminism's strengths, she asserts, lies in the fact that it advocates for universal change not by hiding, disavowing or omitting particularity, but rather through embracing individual experiences.[49] She concludes, "Capturing the synergistic relation between inequalities as grounded in the lived experiences of hierarchy is changing not only what people think about inequality but the way they think."[50]

Although the term is imported from North America, one might certainly ask, as Elie McDonald does, if intersectionality in the Caribbean didn't prefigure Western thinking on the subject.[51] In any case, intersectional feminism's principles permeate the Caribbean women's writing I examine in this volume. The writers in question resist additive notions of identity, emphasizing the inseparability and non-hierarchical nature of their forms of belonging, uncovering hidden forms of collusion between resistance and dominance.[52] However, neither *standpoint* nor *intersectional* fully captures how deeply rooted *The Pen and the Pan*'s target corpus is in Caribbean history, culture and society.

In her 1998 essay "Towards Indigenous Feminist Theorizing in the Caribbean", Patricia Mohammed uses *indigenous* to describe the direction she prescribes for accessible and applicable Caribbean feminist activism and discourse. Citing what she calls "an unrelenting dialogue about what constitutes Caribbean manhood and masculinity and womanhood and femininity",[33] Mohammed describes a number of very different Caribbean experiences of femininity throughout the archipelago and over the course of the twentieth century. In the Indo-Caribbean communities of Trinidad, she explains, ethnic allegiance was encouraged through the Brahminic model of ideal womanhood, Sita. Indo-Caribbean women were expected to be like the ancient queen – the virtuous, long-suffering, faithful bride of Rama – in order to negate "westernizing" influences.[34] To fail to behave like Sita was to betray one's ethnicity and one's very womanhood. Meanwhile, in the Dominican Republic, where *nation* was equated with European filiation, Trujillo's regime adopted a "patronizing patriarchal attitude" that made some symbolic concessions such as women's suffrage, a protective labour code and pensions for prolific mothers. However, notes Mohammed, the regime suppressed any truly revolutionary tendencies among women, including multi-ethnic coalitional feminism.[35] Finally, she observes, the entire region has inherited a stereotype associated with Afro-Caribbean culture – that of the matrifocal, or mother-centred, society. *Matrifocal*, she argues, is often confused with *matriarchal* and *matrilinear*, neither of which actually applies to Caribbean society.[36] Truly indigenous Caribbean feminist theory, it follows, needs to engage with a range of competing loyalties, pressures and understandings of gender itself.

Unfortunately, as Rhoda Reddock observed in 2001, throughout the twentieth century Caribbean women faced many obstacles to constructing broad alliances and coalitional feminisms. Caribbean women's common cause faced opposition from both conservative and progressive elements of Caribbean society. Within the region, women had long been used as markers of racial, ethnic and national difference.[37] During the 1960s and 1970s, Caribbean feminism took a back seat to activism centred on race and ethnicity, especially Black Power and black consciousness. Then, in the 1970s and 1980s, increasingly influential socialist and anti-imperialist movements dismissed feminism as "bourgeois", "foreign", "irrelevant" and "potentially divisive".[38] In addition to these challenges emanating from overlapping movements, the practice of feminist organizing itself was problematic during the 1980s and in the decades that followed. Caribbean feminists had failed to address the power relations among women, thereby tolerating the continued (conscious and unconscious) domination and exclusion of some women at the hands of others.

By the turn of the twentieth century, points out Andaiye, it had become clear that Caribbean feminism would not succeed in transforming the power relations between women and men if it ignored the power relations between women.[59] In 2002 she identified the women's movement in the Caribbean as Afrocentric, "with Indo-Caribbean women in a small minority and little or no connection with indigenous women, the poorest in the region, with working class women of all races/ethnic groups forming another minority".[60] At the time, Eudine Barriteau[61] echoed Andaiye's concerns about inclusiveness, identifying the "failure to grapple with our ambivalence to power" – whether it be with regard to women's economic hardship or to lesbianism and homophobia – as the single major challenge confronting contemporary feminisms in the Caribbean.[62]

In the midst of that very unease about Caribbean feminism's inclusiveness, Patricia Mohammed voiced a different sort of anxiety, pointing out the difficulties of enacting change in the twenty-first-century Caribbean, where feminism is no longer a concentrated set of ideas shared by specific groups and individuals. Instead, wrote Mohammed in 2003, feminism had dissolved, "like sugar in coffee", throughout society. While younger feminists had internalized a certain gender consciousness, she insisted, they would need to move towards a feminist consciousness if they were to work actively and consciously at solving problems instead of just acknowledging them.[63] Twenty years on, Caribbean feminisms are still alive and kicking, even if this particular question remains an open one. However, this snapshot of a moment in time illustrates two important challenges for Caribbean feminism that remain salient today: first, the perpetual problem of deciding what can or should be called "feminism" in the Caribbean, and second, the difficulty Caribbean women so often experience in seeing Caribbean women (both themselves and others) *as* feminist.

Although "indigenous Caribbean feminisms" seems to articulate the geographical specificity of Caribbean feminism at the turn of the century, another descriptor has better stood the test of time: "homegrown Caribbean feminisms". The term *homegrown* first appeared in Lizabeth

Paravisini-Gebert's essay "Decolonizing Feminism: The Home-Grown Roots of Caribbean Women's Movements" (1997). Paravisini-Gebert criticizes totalizing European and US theories of feminism and gender relations, ascribing to them "good internal logic, but low external reliability".[64] She urges against blanket statements about feminism in the Caribbean, pressing instead for recognition of women's individual choices and strategies, which respond to their particular historical and material conditions. Paravisini-Gebert especially objects to what she perceives as the individualism of US feminist theory, which she claims does not apply in the Caribbean, where female heroism is most often in service of the community.[65] The phrase "homegrown Caribbean feminism" has resurfaced in recent years and seems to have caught on. Amílcilar Sanatan, for example, embraced *homegrown* in 2016, asserting that "indigenous feminism" is an inappropriate misnomer that displaces Indigenous people. Following a brief history of "homegrown" feminism in the region, including a good deal of intra-regional cooperation, Sanatan exhorts Caribbean women to embrace the legacy of their solidarity: "This feminism is we own ting! Claim it!"[66] Alongside theoretical work by Paravisini-Gebert, Sanatan and many others, the creative writing featured in this volume urges recognition of homegrown Caribbean feminisms past and present, visible and (especially) invisible, as an important step in the liberation process.

In a 2015 post on her blog at grrlscene.wordpress.com, Gabrielle Hosein also emphasizes that Caribbean feminisms have nothing to do with Europe or North America, for their roots are in the plantation economy and colonial history. Hosein places Caribbean feminisms, both Afro- and Indo-,[67] at the heart of the Caribbean freedom struggle. "Women's struggles are a continuation of the long struggle for emancipation", she writes. "Every person who came here as enslaved or indentured dreamt for the right to equality, to fairness, to justice, to freedom, to peace and feelings of personal safety and security." Hosein identifies two central aims for Caribbean feminism(s) going forward: (1) we want to root Caribbean feminisms in our own struggles against slavery and indentureship and come to understand how those set the terms for what women are still struggling with today; and (2) we want to see those struggles as still continuing and not yet resolved. As my reading of the past quarter-century of food-focused Caribbean women's writing has shown, in many ways contemporary culinary fiction has been an ideal mode for conceptualizing and articulating the ideas Hosein identifies as key to the future of Caribbean feminism(s) – an understanding of the region's history and a vision for its future.

During a 2015 conference at Barnard College titled "Caribbean Feminisms on the Page", Haitian-American author Edwidge Danticat used the term *homegrown* to describe the kind of Caribbean feminism she witnessed as a child:

> In Haiti, I grew up mostly around poor women who were in my family, who I thought were feminists. You know, they weren't theorizing feminism, but they were living their feminisms. They were central to the community, they really believed in justice. Even though they were looked down on because of their place in society they were very . . . I don't want to say "strong women" in the blanket way, but they were living a feminism. And of course, their lives and their manner of feminism was influenced by the fact that there was a thirty-year dictatorship, there was a lot of migration. . . . They were dealing with a very specific situation from which their kind of feminism emerged. That's not splitting hairs or trying to divide feminism. I think we have to think about also these homegrown feminisms and how they are manifested. It was very liberating for me, too, to realize when I came here [to the United States] and started studying textbook feminism that it had always been in some way in my life.[68]

As Danticat illustrates, homegrown feminisms – *lived* feminisms of the kind one might witness every day – have a special power to inspire. Rooted in the soil of Caribbean culture and history, they have developed resistance to regional political pests, local economic conditions and the choking weeds of neocolonial influences. Like the creole garden, homegrown feminisms are a product of both inherited know-how and a willingness to improvise. They are the fruits of Caribbean society itself. Unsurprisingly, it is in homegrown feminisms that Caribbean women can most easily see themselves and their own possibilities for resistance.

Using women's relationships to food, Pineau, Danticat, Persaud, Mootoo and Condé tease out the intersectional nature of Caribbean women's problems and highlight the need for homegrown solutions. Many of the female characters in this body of fiction are stigmatized and excluded because of their illiteracy, colour, illegitimate children, menial work or foreign status, or simply because they cannot or will not adhere to gender expectations for their ethnic group or social class. These characters' gendered strategies for resistant response are recipes for homegrown ways of handling the challenges Caribbean women face in daily life.

Caribbean feminism faces multiple challenges in the twenty-first century, and creative writing such as the culinary fiction I treat in this volume helps to address them. First, women must learn to trust their own life experiences as valid ways of knowing,[69] and these novels advocate for women to examine their daily reality and compare it to the ideal of a just and robust society. Second, feminists must recognize power relations between women as a first step towards coalitional feminism, and these novels attend carefully to intragroup conflict among Caribbean women. Third, Caribbean feminisms must be rooted in Caribbean history and have a vision for a Caribbean future, and these novels offer new generations of Caribbean women historically based models for feminisms that begin at home and reach out to pursue unexpected solidarities.

In many ways, culinary fiction is an ideal mode for planting the seeds of feminist – especially coalitional feminist – sentiment. This highly marketable genre is well placed to reach a broad female audience. Food is simultaneously the most and least accessible feature of these texts, seducing the outsider but speaking intimately and exclusively to the insider. And because these works elude fixed interpretation, they likewise escape full commodification, exportation and appropriation. Leveraging the "exotic sensuality" of Caribbean food culture, this group of Caribbean women authors has harnessed the enormous power of the corporate publishing world to disseminate some fairly radical content.[70]

Each of the authors in this study puts forth her own particular models for homegrown feminist response or resistance. Thanks to these historically inspired fictional grandmothers, mothers and daughters, Caribbean women can not only identify but also identify with women's gendered freedom struggle and homegrown feminist responses within their own communities. However, as my comparative reading will demonstrate, Caribbean women might also use contemporary culinary fiction to recognize women's oppression and homegrown feminist responses within other Caribbean communities (including the diaspora), a foundational step in coalition-building among Caribbean women. And those local and regional solidarities, of course, are only the beginning.

These women authors have successfully mined the Caribbean past for examples of homegrown feminism by shedding what María Lugones calls "arrogant perception" in favour of "loving perception",[71] which enables them to perceive resistance in what might otherwise appear to be inaction, disengagement or nonsensical behaviour.[72] Arrogant perception can see resistance only as *reaction* (a simple no), but loving perception understands that resistance is *response* – devious and insightful behaviours.[73] Lugones argues that while the oppressed cannot exercise agency, they can practise active subjectivity; what matters is not *what* women do, but *why* they do it. And the only way to find that out, she explains, is by travelling epistemically, which enables one to know not only what others know, but *how* they know. Lugones challenges women, especially mainstream women, to put aside their blind assumptions about other women's wrongheadedness or passivity. When women stop forcing one another into neat categories, argues Lugones, they will discover sisters in struggle with resistant strategies and a vision of their own.[74]

But these resistance understandings cannot easily be communicated across social barriers, and it can be challenging for women to grasp other communities' resistant logic.[75] One significant impediment to such awareness is tradition: "When tradition seems a haven from cultural and psychological devastation, it is hard to honor critical stances as it is hard to see the dangers of orthodoxy and conservatism from within and under siege. Yet those of color who are culturally homeless understand that orthodoxy in itself is dangerous, a form of self-destruction, an ossification of culture that aides the ethnocentric racist push towards culture as ornament."[76] In other words, Pineau, Danticat, Persaud, Mootoo and Condé may have accomplished the shift from arrogant perception to loving perception, thanks to their "cultural homelessness" – their outsider status, diasporic or otherwise. As these authors imagine and reimagine their homelands from a distance, they are uniquely positioned to rethink the power dynamics between women, including women's inability or unwillingness to perceive one another's response to oppression as a form of resistance. In this loving perception, passed on to the reader in the Caribbean, its diaspora and beyond, one finds a powerful call to understanding, to solidarity, to coalition – to the table.

STRUCTURE OF THE STUDY

Chapter 1, "Gisèle Pineau: Cooking Creole in the City", analyses *Un papillon dans la cité* (A butterfly in the city; 1992) and *Exile According to Julia* (1996), two novels that use food imagery to portray French Antillean women's particular experience of the ongoing Caribbean liberation project, in this case expanding its geography to include Paris, a major European centre of Caribbean migration. Pineau's food-focused novels portray multiple generations of French Antillean women in diaspora in urban spaces of France in the 1960s and 1980s, respectively. In these novels (one autobiographical and one for young adults), where creole cooking meets French food and North African fare, the author injects gender specificity into the history of French Antilleans' late-twentieth-century circular movements between the Caribbean and Europe. Drawing on H. Adlai Murdoch's *Creolizing the Metropole: Migrant Caribbean Identities in Literature and Film,* this chapter argues that Pineau's food-focused writing shines a light on the unseen challenges and relationship-based survival strategies of "Negropolitan" girls caught in the middle – too black for Paris and too Parisian for Guadeloupe. For Pineau, food is a lifeline that both anchors her female protagonists to their native Caribbean land and ties them to others in their adopted European land as they eat and write their way from painful exile to a more empowered errantry.[77] Pineau's coalitional vision is of a potluck world to which everyone would make their unique contributions and whose richness would lie precisely in its diversity.

Chapter 2, "Edwidge Danticat: The Hunger to Tell", focuses on how *The Farming of Bones* (1998), *Breath, Eyes, Memory* (1994) and *The Dew Breaker* (2004) break the silence about the impact of political violence on Caribbean women on the island of Hispaniola. Danticat's *The Farming of Bones* depicts Haitian migrant workers in the Dominican Republic, victims of a 1937 ethnic cleansing at the hands of Trujillo's national and nationalist army, the Ejército Nacional. *Breath, Eyes, Memory* and *The Dew Breaker,* meanwhile, contemplate the transgenerational nature of trauma inflicted by François Duvalier's terrifying secret police, the Tonton Macoutes. Building upon Michel-Rolph Trouillot's *Silencing the Past* (1995) and Myriam Chancy's *Framing Silence* (1997), this chapter asserts that Danticat's food-focused writing injects gender specificity into the history of dictatorship and political violence in the Caribbean. In all three of her testimonial novels, I argue, food imagery helps to tell the too-often untold story of Haitian women's trauma, their silencing and their healing. Danticat's coalitional prayer is for a welcome table where all will be nourished, safe and heard.

Chapter 3, "Lakshmi Persaud: Forbidden Fruit", examines *Butterfly in the Wind* (1990) and *Sastra* (1993), two novels that interrogate the interactions among gender, class, religion and ethnicity in the Caribbean *vivre ensemble*, examining the Indo-Trinidadian experience of exile and assimilation via the clash between Afro-Caribbean food traditions and Hindu dietary laws. Informed by Shalini Puri's *The Caribbean Postcolonial: Social Equality, Post/Nationalism, and Cultural Hybridity* (2004) and Gabrielle Hosein's "Modern Navigations: Indo-Trinidadian Girlhood and Gender-Differential Creolization" (2012) – and more generally by Hosein and Lisa Outar's edited collection *Indo-Caribbean Feminist Thought* (2016) – this chapter illustrates that for Indo-Trinidadian women, the stakes of culinary assimilation are high. Persaud's characters must balance the potential gains of creolization with its known dangers as well as with the religious duty to adhere to strict dietary laws. As this chapter shows, Persaud explores how some women, the guardians and reproducers of culture, police both moral and culinary boundaries by regulating other women's behaviour, asserting a cultural and culinary traditionalism. Meanwhile, others commit acts of culinary rebellion that undermine stereotypes of past generations of Indo-Caribbean women, engaging in post-colonial nation-making through commensality.[78] Read as a pair, Persaud's first two novels chart a new direction for Indianness in the Caribbean, in which female self-determination and multi-ethnic coalitions are no longer forbidden fruit. Lakshmi Persaud's coalitional meditation identifies the kitchen as a site of divine connection across harmful economic, religious and ethnic divides.

Chapter 4, "Shani Mootoo: Kitchen Indians", scrutinizes *Out on Main Street* (1993) and *Valmiki's Daughter* (2008), a collection of short stories and a novel that deconstruct class, race, ethnicity, gender and sexuality in contemporary Trinidad and its diaspora. Mootoo's short stories and novels, loaded with food imagery from India, Europe and Trinidad, depict "kitchen Indians" – women whose Indianness has been so eroded within the Indo-

Trinidadian double diaspora (here the move is from India to Trinidad and then to Canada) that they find themselves lost among the unclassifiable, facing identity crisis. These women's homosexuality and nonbinary gender expression further alienate them from what many perceive as their "authentic" South Asian roots. Mootoo uses food to expose all these categories as constructed, remnants of the colonial era; gender, sexuality and national/ethnic identity are all cultural and psychological aspects of the devil's bargain that Norman Girvan terms the "Independence Pact". Read together, *Out on Main Street* and *Valmiki's Daughter* unmask both the performativity and the interconnectedness of colonially imposed categories and identities, an insight that paves the way for true independence through cultural and sexual self-determination. Engaging with Amar Wahab's "Homophobia as the State of Reason: The Case of Postcolonial Trinidad and Tobago" (2012), my reading focuses on Mootoo's commitment to radical solidarity. Mootoo's incendiary coalitional reimagining brings sexual minorities to the table with economic and racial underclasses, for their mutual liberation.

Chapter 5, "Maryse Condé: The Pen and the Pan", reads together *Victoire: My Mother's Mother* (2006) and *Of Morsels and Marvels* (2015), two works that tease out hidden interdependencies between the creative feminine endeavours of writing and cooking (the pen and the pan) as it explores the relationship between the individual and the group – how an individual balances meeting her own needs with her responsibility to the group. For Condé, cooking and writing are acts of individual pleasure and at the same time acts of self-sacrifice. This is the same dynamic that underpins her examination of race in the post-colonial, post-slavery Caribbean, for her characters are torn between racially determined forms of belonging and the individual longing to be themselves. Condé thus uses these novels to work through the tensions between essentializing theory and the complexities of lived experience. *Victoire* and *Of Morsels and Marvels* provide a blueprint for disrupting masculinist theories of Caribbean liberation and fossilized attitudes and ideas about freedom and sovereignty. In dialogue with Yarimar Bonilla's *Non-sovereign Futures: French Caribbean Politics in the Wake of Disenchantment* (2015), this chapter draws meaningful parallels between invisible forms of feminine resistance among newly emancipated people and among contemporary political actors working within and against the constraints of post-colonial sovereignty. For Condé, the tools of art, mutiny and political movement include both the pen and the pan. Condé's coalitional dreams are of people everywhere sharing one another's cuisines and one another's struggles without losing their individuality – of *liyannaj kont pwofitasyon* ("coalition against exploitation").

Both the content and the form of *The Pen and the Pan* embrace a spirit of coalition, simultaneously marking racial, ethnic, linguistic, class, religious and sexual orientation differences and transcending those very differences. On the one hand, each author-specific chapter analyses a different community's unique female perspective on Caribbean history, culture and politics. Individual chapters thus provide valuable insight into the role of context in Caribbean women's experiences with (neo)colonial and intragroup oppression, including the power dynamics between women. At the same time, my reading gathers these five authors into a temporary alliance (albeit a largely unwitting one) united in the interest of engendering Caribbean history in all its complexity. By reading these authors as a mosaic, both with and against one another, I construct a more nuanced and complete picture of the range and diversity of Caribbean women's ongoing struggle for freedom. *"Yon sèl dwèt pa manje kalalou"*, proclaims the Haitian proverb: "You cannot eat okra with one finger." In other words, some things can be accomplished only by working together.

CHAPTER 1

GISÈLE PINEAU

COOKING CREOLE IN THE CITY

Bondye fè nou retounen an Gwadloup![1]

BETWEEN 1963 AND 1980, IN RESPONSE to the complementary economic dilemmas of underemployment in the French "overseas departments" of Martinique and Guadeloupe and a labour shortage in the European territory of France, BUMIDOM[2] organized 160,000 migrations from the French Antilles to the European territory of France.[3] French immigration policy and discourse framed Martinican and Guadeloupean migration as an intranational movement no different in kind than the relocation of so many other French provincials from Bordeaux or Marseilles to the country's capital in pursuit of economic betterment during the *"trente glorieuses"*.[4] BUMIDOM promoted immigration as a path to social ascension, a voyage to the promised land, creator of wealth, a place where workers could put food on the table for themselves and for their loved ones back home. However, in its mechanical analysis of economics and employment, French immigration policy neglected to address key psychological and cultural factors that were rooted in the history of colonialism and racialized slavery in the Caribbean.

Gisèle Pineau's culinary fiction, inspired by her own life experiences, challenges the "myth of non-separation from France"[5] with which she and her family had been inculcated back in the islands. Instead, her writing captures the disappointment of Afro-Guadeloupeans in the European territory of France who found that their French citizenship was second-class, overshadowed by racial discrimination. Funnelled into low-ranking government and private-sector jobs, resented and rejected by the majority white population, these former colonial subjects and descendants of enslaved Africans became disillusioned. Given the hostility of the environment, republican rhetoric about national solidarity could do nothing to save the false narrative of France as the "mother country".[6] Instead, French Antilleans and their European territory of France-born children began to assert the value of creole culture, including creole cuisine, and to dream of a return to their own native land – the Caribbean.

In Gisèle Pineau's culinary fiction, food imagery illustrates French Antillean women's continuing freedom struggle in Paris, a city sometimes dubbed "the third island" because of the large number of French Antilleans who have migrated there. Set in the 1960s and 1980s respectively, the autobiographical *L'Exil selon Julia* (1996) and the fictional *Un Papillon dans la cité* (1992) depict multiple generations of diasporic French Antillean women and girls living, cooking and eating in the European territory of France. In Pineau's writing, food practices reflect "third island" social realities, from the creative contact between creole, European French and North African peoples and cuisines to the circular movement of foodstuff and human beings between the Caribbean and Europe. Most importantly, Pineau's culinary fiction gives voice to the unique challenges faced by "Negropolitan"[7] girls, too black for Paris and too Parisian for Guadeloupe. Their relation-based survival strategies include using food to hold tight to their Caribbean origins and to reach out to others in Europe. Thanks to the culinary and to the literary, Pineau's female protagonists transform themselves from victims of exile to agents of errantry.[8]

CREOLE IN THE CITY

In the decades leading up to the publication of *Un papillon dans la cité* and *Exile According to Julia*, Martinican cultural theorist Edouard Glissant[9] and self-proclaimed *"créolistes"* Patrick Chamoiseau, Jean Bernabé and Raphaël Confiant[10] elaborated a creole model of Caribbeanness born of radical displacement, the colonial encounter and the plantation space. "Neither European, nor African, nor Asian",[11] creoleness, which included creole food, was something entirely new. Characterized by movement, mixture and transformation, diversity, syncretism and hybridity, creoleness, they insisted, is a distinct worldview and way of life. However, owing to the prolonged disempowerment and extreme colonization of creolized peoples in the Caribbean, for centuries creole culture and experiences had been largely ignored.

When large numbers of French Antilleans moved to Paris, in some ways history repeated itself. Already the product of extensive creolization in the Caribbean, this population underwent a re-creolization in diaspora in the European city, redefining the limits of Caribbeanness in the process.[12] In the HLMs[13] of the Parisian *banlieues*,[14] second- and third-generation French Antillean children interacted with other children from the mixed immigrant communities as well as from underprivileged "native" French classes, such that a great deal of mutual borrowing and cultural swapping (including culinary exchange) occurred. In many ways more integrated into mainstream French culture than their parents because of the daily exigencies of work, school and recreation, they grew up alongside post-colonial peoples who fell outside the France–Antilles colonial binary, including (and especially) those of Maghrebi descent, popularly known as *beurs*.[15] Thus, in diaspora in Paris, their already hybridized creole identity was further hybridized in new and distinct ways.[16]

Unfortunately, cultural exchange was not the only element of history that repeated itself. The same white supremacist ideology that had enabled and rationalized colonialism and racialized slavery continued to manifest itself in the European territory of France through racial discrimination and social and economic exclusion. Although this came to be common knowledge and an everyday lived experience for French Antilleans in the European territory of France, the French state turned a blind eye to racially motivated injustices. Fearing the perceived threat of *communautarisme*,[17] both the political right and the left refused to acknowledge the growing existence of ethnic and cultural differences on the ground.[18] In the service of a lofty republican universalist discourse that defied reality, demographic records that distinguish Afro-Caribbean migrants from the rest of the French population were not (and are not) officially compiled by the state. This ideologically inspired denial had very real consequences for Caribbean people in diaspora: "The supposed incompatibility of republican values with a vigorous antidiscrimination policy, including arrangements for measuring differences in the treatment accorded ethnically defined groups, has created a void in which, over a long period, everyday acts of racial and ethnic discrimination have gone largely unchecked, breeding enormous frustration and discrimination in the banlieues."[19] So, just as the French Empire's history[20] had failed to record their enslaved African ancestors' persecution (much less their defiance), republican universalist History erased the diasporic French Antilleans' day-to-day encounters with injustice, and their resistant response.

Recall that Glissant problematizes historical knowledge itself. History, he insists, is a highly functional Western fantasy, a distorted colonial construct that can be reconstructed.[21] He argues, then, that we can read Caribbean history through literature, which tells truer stories – stories as they were perceived by non-colonizers, stories that were rendered invisible by the prominence of the colonizers' versions. For Glissant, breaking down the barriers between history and literature can remedy Caribbean peoples' lack of historical consciousness, and it is the fiction writer who most effectively reconstitutes the Caribbean past. In order to accomplish this, the Caribbean writer must excavate a largely blacked-out memory, making use of those traces of the past still found in the present.[22] And so it is that the Guadeloupean author Gisèle Pineau, in the service of personal and collective memory, records the ways in which French Antillean women were and are marginalized in the European territory of France and articulates the specificities of homegrown Caribbean feminist response in the city.

WRITING AS LIFELINE

"*Bondye fè nou retounen an Gwadloup*", little Gisèle used to pray with her Antillean grandmother, even though the author herself was Parisian-born. For a long time, explains Pineau, she resented her parents for her Parisian birth, which resulted in her exclusion from both European French and French Antillean society. "When I was in France, people rejected me because of my black skin; when I arrived in the Antilles, I was also rejected because I was a 'Negropolitan': This Guadeloupean woman is black, but she speaks very bad Creole, rolling her r's. So, I was never at the right time, never at the right place, always a misfit."[23]

Pineau describes herself and her siblings as "children who grew up away from the island, who didn't know the games they play there, who could not speak Creole".[24] The main goal of her culinary fiction – engendering the "Negropolitan" history of migration and alienation – is therefore rooted in Pineau's own experiences of "vicarious exile"[25] or "exile by inheritance".[26] Writing, she explains, has been a lifeline and a consolation for the heart-breaking difficulties of everyday life.[27]

As has typically been the case for French Antilleans for the past half-century, Gisèle Pineau's geographical trajectory has been a circular one, in which years spent in the islands alternated with time spent in the "third island", Île-de-France.[28] Born in Paris to French Antillean parents in 1956, Pineau lived on the French Caribbean island of Martinique from 1970 to 1972, and then in her parents' native Guadeloupe, where she arrived just in time to begin high school. She returned to Paris for her university studies in 1975, then went back to Guadeloupe in 1979, where she worked for the next twenty years as a psychiatric nurse and wrote much of her early fiction. Over the past two decades Pineau has continued her rotational pattern of displacement, living and writing in Paris and in Marie-Galante, Guadeloupe. Between 1987 and 2018 she published eight novels for young adults, including *Un papillon dans la cité*; ten novels, including *L'exil selon Julia*; eleven short stories; two coffee-table books; and a number of critical essays. In 1998 her commitment to engendering French Caribbean history found a new iteration in the collaborative reference work *Femmes des Antilles: Traces et voix; 150 ans après l'abolition de l'esclavage.*[29] Pineau has won ten literary awards, including the Prix Terre de France and the Prix Rotary for *L'exil selon Julia*. Along with fellow Guadeloupeans Maryse Condé (the subject of chapter 5) and Simone Schwartz-Bart, Gisèle Pineau is one of the most well-known, oft-studied and highly influential women writers of the French Antilles.[30]

Literary critics have most often classified Pineau's writing as a literature of migration,[31] diaspora[32] and exile,[33] dominated by questions of memory and trauma,[34] alienation and melancholia.[35] Pineau explicitly identifies as a woman writer who bears witness to women's suffering[36] and a feminist writer who gives a voice to women.[37] However, her principal self-identified standpoint has most frequently been that of a black person writing in a white country. The author cites African-American literary influences, including

Richard Wright, Toni Morrison and Maya Angelou, to emphasize her main perspective as an excluded, derided minority pursuing self-affirmation, wholeness and belonging.[38]

While her work deeply engages with creoleness, Pineau does not self-identify primarily as a *créoliste*. The author has no desire to act as standard-bearer or to speak for "the people", nor to belong to a particular school or movement. Instead she asserts her right to create as an individual, from the perspective of a Parisian-born person of Antillean descent.[39] Maintains Pineau, "I don't follow recipes. Here's the recipe for the Creole novel: a dash of Creole dialogues here, sprinkles of coconut trees and small hills there ... no. I write with my heart and I want to give my readers a land to be seen, a land to be felt. ... I want to make beauty. I want to create art."[40]

Pineau credits the *créolistes* Patrick Chamoiseau, Jean Bernabé and Raphaël Confiant with elevating French Caribbean literature above regionalism, but she insists that their preoccupation with the distant past and Caribbean island space is too limiting. "As for me," the author insists, "I want to write about today's Antilleans." Thousands of those Antilleans, she points out, live in and around Paris and travel the world. Asserts Pineau, "I do not want to force them back into the corner of their island. For me, that's not reality."[41] True to her own Parisian experience of creoleness, Pineau's artistic standpoint is that of a creole in the city.[42]

Creoleness in its original French Caribbean form – that particular combination of cultures that emerged from the colonial encounter and plantation space – suffuses Pineau's culinary fiction, which explores the relationship between Guadeloupeans and the European French. The author connects creole food with the Creole language, examining how both contribute to preserving Caribbean identity and culture among Guadeloupeans who emigrated to France in the mid-twentieth century. At the same time, Pineau uses food imagery to portray the re-creolization of French Antilleans in Paris, depicting both their assimilation into mainstream European French culture and their cultural mixing with the *beur* immigrants who largely share their predicament. Throughout both novels, the search for self pivots on culinary difference; food choice is a feminist resistant response, an assertion of creole identity that is both generally post-colonial and uniquely French Caribbean/European French.

In *Exile According to Julia* and *Un papillon dans la cité*, food tells the story of the formation of that multifaceted identity. It serves as a kind of historical archive, charting and memorializing the movement of Afro-diasporic Antilleans from one continent to another, as well as a site of personal and familial affective memory and connection. In Pineau's work, food from home is not only useful for feeding the exiled heart; it can also help emigrants preserve home cultures, assimilate into new cultures and build a new, broader community, joining together the minority ethnic groups living in the urban spaces of the European territory of France. The author thus uses food to illuminate the nourishing ties that exist between Guadeloupeans on the island and those in the "third island", and the beneficial ties that *could* exist among the diverse peoples formerly colonized by the French.

DREAMING OF HOME

Pineau's *L'exil selon Julia* draws upon her own family's experiences of exile and return, especially the seven years (1960–67) when her paternal grandmother came from Guadeloupe to share the family's small apartment in Kremlin-Bicêtre, a southern suburb of Paris.[43] Man Ya, as her grandchildren called her, was a storyteller and a source of what was still, as Glissant famously theorizes, an obscured Caribbean history of pain and overcoming, an inspiration for little Gisèle, who began writing at a very young age. Recalls Pineau, "In that little apartment, there was all the magico-religious that came in: the she-devils, the blood-sucking hags, and also History, she talked about slavery. . . . She had inherited stories from her mother, from her grandmother, whereas my parents wanted to get rid of that cumbersome past and didn't answer my questions."[44] *Exile According to Julia* is autobiographical fiction, drawn from those truest, most formative aspects of Pineau's personal history – the ones that left significant traces to be excavated.

Exile fictionalizes the episode of Man Ya's residence with Pineau. It tells the story of a young Guadeloupean girl, Gisèle, who lives in the European territory of France. Her father, Maréchal, brings his mother, Julia, to live with him and his family in France in order to "save" her from her abusive husband, Asdrubal. Maréchal is fully dedicated to the French nation, both as a career solider and as a man. But although Gisèle was born in the European territory of France, she is rejected by her racist white peers and teachers, for whom she will never be truly French by dint of her black skin. Julia fosters a sense of cultural belonging in her French-speaking grandchildren by teaching them her native Creole, oral Caribbean history and an appreciation for Guadeloupean food.

When Julia eventually chooses to return to Asdrubal in Guadeloupe, Gisèle writes her letters, letting her grandmother know that she is still using food to remember Guadeloupe. Since Gisèle knows that the cruel Asdrubal will never actually read them to the illiterate Julia, the young girl's letters are really to herself – a means of negotiating and recording her evolving sense of creole identity. Then Maréchal is transferred to Martinique. After years of dreaming of "home", Gisèle and her siblings discover that in many ways they are strangers to the Caribbean. The children must adjust to everything, from mosquitoes and hurricanes to the Creole language and a highly racialized and colorized social hierarchy chock full of internal divisions, that sometimes treats them as "Negropolitan" foreigners. But because Man Ya maintained their ties to the Caribbean "over there" in the France of their birth, the children are unshakeable in their determination to reintegrate the French Antillean "back home" of their hearts. Gisèle vows that if the Antilles will teach her their secrets, she will write them, inscribing them in History through her art. When the children are finally reunited with Man Ya in Guadeloupe, they get a chance to witness her competence and appreciate her food-based folk knowledge. It is the memory of this version of Julia, happy and capable on her own turf, that stays with Gisèle, affirming her for the rest of her life.

The figure of Man Ya also appears in *Un papillon dans la cité*, in which Pineau recreates a novel she wrote at ten years of age. If *Exile According to Julia* relates the painful realities of the doubly exiled girl child Pineau actually was, *Papillon* tells the story of the little girl Gisèle wished she could be: born in the islands and therefore wholeheartedly accepted there, but also gifted with a happy French Caribbean/European French hybridity and supportive relationships in the European territory of France, and therefore at home there too.[45]

Un Papillon dans la cité tells the story of young Félicie's journey away from and return to her Guadeloupean home. Félicie joins her mother, Aurélie, in the housing projects of the Parisian *banlieues*. She leaves behind Man Ya, the maternal grandmother who raised her, in Guadeloupe. Aurélie is estranged from Man Ya and from her Guadeloupean roots; the young woman is fully invested in assimilation into white European French society. Félicie, on the other hand, is torn between the need to adapt to her new life and her longing for home. Taking comfort in the Guadeloupean foods her grand-mother sends her and drawing resilience from the memory of her *nèg mawon* ancestors,[46] she works hard at school and at home to build a new life and new relationships in Paris. Those relationships include a friendship with Mo (Mohammed), a classmate and neighbour whose post-colonial experi-ence of racism in France is not unlike her own, and whose family invites Félicie to partake of their North African culinary heritage. While Félicie is academically brilliant, Mo succumbs to his feelings of alienation and begins skipping school to spend time with much older boys who seem headed for trouble. When Ms Bernichon, Félicie and Mo's teacher, announces that she will take the whole class to Guadeloupe for a *classe de mer*,[47] Mo agrees to return to school. Once they are in Guadeloupe, Félicie delivers a letter from Aurélie to Man Ya asking for reconciliation between the two. Mo sheds his disaffected persona and discovers a passion for the sea and an appreciation for Guadeloupean food. For her part, Félicie admits that her fervour for writing is another meaningful way of preserving cultural ties and reaching out to make new ones.

Pineau's protagonists' longing for Guadeloupe reflects the *Zeitgeist* among people of French Antillean descent in the last decade of the twenti-eth century, when both of these novels were published. While in 1960, six hundred thousand French Antilleans in the Caribbean were dreaming of the European territory of France – of a better life for themselves and their children – by 1990, four hundred thousand French Antilleans in Paris were dreaming of the Antilles. They wanted to go back to the land of their birth (or of their parents' or grandparents' birth), a place they did not know at all.[48] Pineau's accounts of culinary return to Guadeloupe thus mirror the literal geographical return of many Antilleans and their children; a 1978 decree guaranteed Antilleans a periodic return to the Antilles every three years, as a form of enhanced leave.[49] During the 1980s a whole nation returned home. Not coincidentally, Antilleans in France also began demanding their right to cultural self-determination. The path forward was thus nourished and informed by this reconnection with the native land.

Alain Anselin describes the complexity of this "return" thus: "Against his will, the French Antillean leaves the land where his ancestors arrived against their will, to put down roots in a country that he doesn't know, but that is his, and which he leaves in order to return to his home, where he wasn't born."[50] Some Antilleans (like Pineau in real life) thus returned "home" to discover that, in the islands, others saw them as French. At the same time, like those real-life "third island" Antilleans, it is actually in Paris that Pineau's protagonists learn to claim and take pride in their Caribbean identity, perhaps even because of the distance from their home islands.

Mariana Ionesco illustrates these contradictions using the Creole deictics *là-bas* ("over there") and *ici-là* ("over here"). For Antilleans in the islands, she explains, the *là-bas* of France is utopian and idealized.[51] However, once they arrive in France, the illusory *là-bas* is demystified. As France becomes *ici-là*, it reveals itself to be unhospitable, alienating, riddled with its own social problems.[52] Meanwhile, the Antilles now assume the role of the dreamed-of *là-bas* whose nostalgic memory promises fulfilment and deliverance.[53] Ionesco argues that Pineau brings together these two irreconcilable spaces via a third space, the space of memory and writing.[54] As we will see, in Pineau's culinary fiction that third space also includes food.

FOOD AND MEMORY

Food has been used to sustain memory in the Caribbean from the earliest days of colonization. Europeans carried delicacies from home to the furthest reaches of their empires, at great cost, in order to maintain European culture in the Caribbean – to help European emigrants and even the generations born in the Caribbean to "remember" what they were supposed to think of as home.[55] In a reversal of this culinary imperialism, in Pineau's novels the Caribbean characters and other post-colonial subjects practise this same sort of remembrance when they leave their homes behind for Europe. According to Valérie Loichot, "In these two texts, the act of tasting, smelling and savouring is the most direct path to remembering the homeland and cooking is the most direct path to actively recreating it."[56] Similarly, Brinda Mehta recognizes the way that Pineau's novels "highlight the historicity of foods",[57] using food to contain and convey the history of the people who eat them. *Un papillon dans la cité* and *Exile According to Julia*, then, use food imagery to help do the work of remembering, on both the individual and collective levels.

In *Papillon*, island-born Félicie's best memories of Guadeloupe are anchored in food and a strong sense of community, and her memories of culinary pleasure make her memories of Guadeloupe itself sweet. "I imagine Laurine climbing up the mango tree in the courtyard to collect tons of perfectly round *mango-pomm*. I see her mouth smeared with their good orange juice, thick and sugary. . . . We used to put our pocket money together to buy a big bottle of orange Fanta or Coca-Cola, After the bath, we used to take turns drinking it, holding down the elbows of the greediest drinkers."[58] Félicie's memories of tropical mangos create a strong sense of place and of insider experiential knowledge. However, though she retains the untranslated Creole "*mango-pomm*" in the main body of her text, the author adds a footnote with the French *mangue-pomme*. In this way Pineau foregrounds the islander's perspective without excluding others. Likewise, the sensory imagery surrounding the fruit ("perfectly round"; "good orange juice, thick and sugary") will be familiar to those who have lived in or spent time on the island. Their own memories will be activated by this evocative depiction, for they know exactly what mangos look and taste like and what it feels like to have their tasty, colourful juice running down your chin. At the same time, this vivid visual, tactile and gustatory description also speaks to outsiders – those who have never been to Guadeloupe. Thanks to Pineau's writing, they can imagine what they have never actually encountered in the flesh. The bottle of Fanta or Coca-Cola will be familiar to all, but the way the neighbourhood children buy and drink it together foregrounds the roles of cooperation, sharing and togetherness in Guadeloupean culture. Countering narrow economic stereotypes of "miserable" Guadeloupe, the author depicts a wide range of normal human emotions: pleasure, anticipation, inclusion, greed, impatience, *fun*.

For Félicie, food is not just a tool of individual memory. Excluded for centuries from French History, French Antilleans transmit collective historical memory through food rituals. Félicie recalls Guadeloupean Christmas culinary traditions and how they function simultaneously as community builder and historical archive:

> All year long, Robert fattened a pig for Christmas. . . . In Guadeloupe, our tradition is to eat the pig in a ragout with pigeon peas and tender yams. All day was spent in the excitement of the meal preparation. But it was when the *tanbouyè* [drummers] arrived, their *ka* [drums] on their back, wearing the halo of glorious self-confidence as the authentic descendants of the *nèg-mawon*, that the celebration of Christmas really started. We served them, with deference, heaping plates of pigeon peas, yams and pork. We placed a bottle of rum next to them. . . . Christmas is for singing about the coming of Christ, Man Ya used to tell me. But it is also for enjoying, eating your belly full, drinking, laughing, dancing and forgetting the bad times. (49–50)

Each culinary element of the Guadeloupean Christmas is a repository for collective Caribbean memory, encoding the history of Félicie's enslaved ancestors, celebrating their resilience and resistance.[59]

Pork, for example, was introduced to the Americas by Europeans as part of the colonial project: pigs were favoured for their willingness to eat anything, their capacity for rapid reproduction and weight gain, and their easily salted and preserved meat. But this important tool of colonization was reappropriated by enslaved Afro-Caribbean peoples and their descendants and repurposed for their survival.[60] Because the heat-resistant creole pig can be raised even by very poor people, using nothing but kitchen scraps and by-products of the garden, it remains a symbol of regional adaptation, survival and latent possibilities for Caribbean food sovereignty. Pineau retains the untranslated Creole *roussi*, thus emphasizing the cultural specificity of the spicy pork ragout that is emblematic of Guadeloupean cuisine. Pigeon peas and yams, meanwhile, were brought to the Caribbean from Africa during slave times.[61] Together they are a culinary record, an encoded history that identifies Félicie as a Guadeloupean and Guadeloupeans as part of the African diaspora.

An essential part of this ritual is the reverence shown for symbolic representations of the *nèg-mawon*, rebellious enslaved people who would not bend to subjugation and humiliation without a fight. Every Christmas, through food, their descendants hold tight to the memory of them, drawing strength and courage from it. For Guadeloupeans, drinking rum is an identarian act. Not only does rum implicitly distinguish itself from imported French wine, it also plays an important symbolic role in Guadeloupean spiritual and religious practice. Ritualistically served and shared among men as part of rituals, rum is also used to offer libations to the ancestors. Finally, traditional Guadeloupean food offers consolation for the hardships of the past and present, and strength to face the difficulties of the future.

In the Caribbean diaspora in Paris, food and memory work together to provide a sense of belonging in a space of alienation. During Félicie's first Christmas in France, for example, her mother, Aurélie, gives her a blond Barbie as a gift. Félicie does not dare to object to a doll that does not look like her, for Aurélie insists that every little girl in France dreams of having one just like it. In the midst of Félicie's feelings of unease and non-belonging, Man Ya's Christmas package arrives from Guadeloupe. Man Ya's gifts include food that is intended to evoke memories of home, food that will keep Félicie emotionally connected to the Caribbean: "In any case, in my package that smelled good like Guadeloupe, there were: a flask of castor oil for my hair, a white lace underskirt (sewn by hand by Man Julia), an envelope with a gold chain and a medallion in the shape of a map of Guadeloupe, wrapped in a page of France-Antilles, two vanilla pods, a stick of cinnamon and three nutmeg seeds" (93).

The contents of the package emphasize and valorize the young girl's island roots. The flask of castor oil, for example, is intended to nourish and strengthen her African hair, the norm in Guadeloupe. Its inclusion emphasizes Félicie's belonging to the Afro-Caribbean community as well as her ethnic minority status in the European territory of France. The lace underskirt, a key element in Guadeloupean traditional dress that dates back hundreds of years, is a product of the long history of Afro-Caribbean people on the island and of their unique relationship to the colonial past. The medallion, shaped like Guadeloupe itself, is to be worn close to Félicie's heart, a constant reminder of where to find home. Meanwhile, the newspaper is a reminder that Guadeloupe doesn't just exist in the past; life goes on there despite the absence of Félicie and all those in the diaspora. But above all there is an intentional gift of culinary memory aimed at keeping Félicie's ties to Guadeloupe strong. In vanilla, cinnamon and nutmeg – the mainstay spices of Man Ya's everyday cooking but rare in the European territory of France – Man Ya intentionally encodes the memory of home.

Man Ya is not the only one who understands the importance of maintaining a lifeline to "back home" in the Parisian diaspora. Félicie's friend Mohammed's Algerian grandmother, Fathia, who lives with him in France, leverages culinary tradition in similar fashion. Although the boy naively insists that France is his country, Fathia knows from personal experience that cultural and economic insertion won't be so easy. Mohammed's two aunts, for example, have never found work in France. Dejected and depressed, they spend their days in bed, eating Arabic sweets and living in the past. Fathia doesn't want Mohammed to settle for culinary escapism and impotent reminiscence, the only recourse at his foreign-born aunts' disposal. Instead, she urges French-born Mo to actively harness food and memory, drawing strength from his ancestors' example: "Your father and mother's ancestors were the Tuareg of the Hoggar mountains. . . . They ate *tadjellas* (flatbreads) and kept their water in goatskins, and raced through the desert, superb riders on their Azelraf camels. . . . Go right ahead! Tell about your French relatives since you say it's your country!" (60).

Mohammed, as his grandmother reminds him, is made of heroic stuff. His ancestors were nomadic Berbers whose foodways, from the unleavened flatbreads they made under the open sky to the goatskins that held their water, reflected their ingenuity, their adaptability and their ancient way of life. Alongside the dishes the Tuareg prepared in the harsh environment of the Sahara Desert's Hoggar Mountains, Fathia lists their heroic physical exploits and skill in animal husbandry. Mo's people did not always languish away in a tiny apartment in an HLM, culturally devalued, economically discarded and dependent. On the contrary, his Tuareg inheritance is self-sufficiency and freedom itself. Fathia knows that Mohammed's ancestors were not Gauls and that the key to his survival is not to pretend that they were. Perhaps counterintuitively, Mo will be best equipped to endure the French "desert" if he remembers where he came from.

In *Exile According to Julia*, "third-island" French Antillean Gisèle's earliest memories of Guadeloupe are of the simple pleasures of transgenerational belonging and unconditional love enjoyed during family visits. In one particularly vivid memory of the "back home" she knows only through vacations, five-year-old Gisèle and her siblings huddle together with the many children taken in by their maternal grandmother (three orphaned grandchildren, the children of a poor relative, and the neighbour's poverty-stricken brood) to watch Man Bouboule make chocolate custard:

> We watch her hands, which proceed with a deference mingled with certainty. She measures out without weight or scale. First she takes down a saucepan without a handle, with a blackened bottom, a bit of zinc pierced with holes, rusted, black. She grates the chocolate, adds a trickle of water, and then slowly stirs. An old biscuit tin holds cinnamon, nutmeg, vanilla. She breaks a piece of this, sprinkles a pinch of that. With her sharpened old knife, she peels a lime, drops the peel into the mixture . . . continues, imperturbable, stirring gently with her big wooden spoon, adding little by little water, French flour, until the cream thickens. At last she taps the spoon gently on the heel of her hand, tastes with her tongue, and then bends over to put out the fire. This last gesture gives us permission to take one step into the kitchen.[62]

Gisèle's memory preserves bits and pieces of a particular Caribbean place and time, an entire way of life that exists outside of History and may someday be lost to the world. Her loving perception honours her grandmother's competence, her bodily way of knowing and her personal qualities. Man Bouboule's hands, for example, seem almost to have a mind of their own. She is certain in her movements and acts based on long experience and instinct: they measure without weight or scale; she adds ingredients little by little, using her judgement; she makes decisions by taste. Defying the capitalist French ideology of personal vanity, mindless speed, rote repetition and endless accumulation, the narrator celebrates the cook's humility, her patience (she stirs with no hurry, carries on undaunted no matter how long the process takes), and her satisfaction with the old (the knife) and even the worn-out (the blackened saucepan with no handle). Like Condé, who assigns aspects of her own artistic rebellion to the grandmother she imagines (as we will see in chapter 5), Pineau finds something of her own will to resist assimilation and economic coercion in the grandmother she remembers.

Deeply scarred by the dysfunctionality of post-colonial race relations in 1960s France, where her family found racial and ethnic difference paradoxically both erased and used as a rationale for exclusion, the adult narrator

Gisèle draws solace from positive childhood memories of togetherness in Guadeloupe. In Gisèle's memory, while Man Bouboule's cooking is a lesson in humbleness and patience, her way of serving is an education in living together in community:

> We assemble on the table earthenware bowls, jugs, china cups, mugs, goblets, tin cups. No two bowls are alike, but we are confident. Man Bouboule has a secret measure in her eye. She gives to each according to the size of his stomach and not the hunger in his eyes. . . . The one who has been good all day long earns the favor of scraping the pot. Man Bouboule gives it to him or her solemnly, like a real monstrance, holding the sacred host. . . . Out of Christian charity – and because Man Boule is watching – the chosen one furiously spoons into bottomless mouths a scraping of the delight, so that he can be left in peace. (28)

The Man Boule of Gisèle's memory uses the chocolate custard to inculcate the children with an appreciation for each one's individuality – no two bowls are alike; each receives according to the size of his stomach; the one who has been good is singled out – and a sense of unconditional communal belonging and sacred human worth. In this light-hearted juxtaposition of the spiritual and the physical, the metaphor of Christian Communion, in which individuals are united as a single "body", unifies the middle-class "third-island" children and the island children, the more modest blood relatives and the desperately poor neighbours, asserting the value of each. Furthermore, the passage's liturgical allusions – the pan as monstrance; the burnt chocolate as sacred host; the unspoken *Do this in remembrance of me*[63] – announce food's potential for carrying memory through time and space, which is soon developed as one of the most significant themes of the novel. This memory of a diverse but united community in "communion" with one another nourishes and sustains Gisèle in Paris, where racist white people see all black people as the same: foreign, undesirable, undeserving, less than human. As we will see, Gisèle portrays herself as her Antillean grandmothers' "disciple", modelling her relationship to memory and story-telling after Man Ya and answering Man Bouboule's "Who will remember the rest of us?" with "I, I will remember, Man Bouboule!" (31).

Cautioning the reader against a narrow, paternalistic interpretation of this food-focused recollection, Pineau asserts the right to cultural and artistic self-determination, assigning herself sole responsibility for recording and interpreting her account:

> The attachment to scraping out the saucepan does not proclaim a longstanding daily hunger on the part of the heirs of slavery. Earning the right to scrape the bottom of the dessert saucepan – corn, vanilla, or chocolate custard – shows that life can satisfy itself with simple pleasures. This one, you cannot weigh in gold or silver, at best you may be able to trade it against two coconut sugar cakes, a share of *doukunnu*, the first steps in a sweet dream. . . . . For, when all is said and done, the custard chilled in bowls, that everyone – big and small, ignorant and wise – eats at dinnertime cannot be compared to the exquisite *crème brûlée* at the bottom of the saucepan. (28–29)

Just as Condé refuses to imagine her grandmother Victoire's cooking as nothing more than menial labour (as we will see in chapter 5), Pineau rejects remembering the children's attachment to the burnt chocolate as the pure product of financial need. The children do not, as outsiders might mistakenly imagine, clamour after what sticks to the bottom of the pan because they are hungry; they fight over the burnt chocolate because it is the most delicious part of the dish! Pre-empting any tendency to collapse the complexity of Guadeloupean family life, oversimplifying and reducing its workings to the inevitable result of post-slavery economics, the narrator consciously re-members a community with its own set of autonomous values. Within this alternative economy, she insists, one can no more commodify the culinary (the burnt chocolate, coconut sugar cakes, *doukunnu*) than the imaginary (the first steps in a sweet dream), or, indeed, happiness itself. Presaging Gisèle's later assertion that she is like Tom Thumb, who "preferred all the same to have nothing to eat rather than to end his days far from his own" (130), the narrator elevates the relational over the fiscal as the truest measure of worth.

For Gisèle's grandmother Julia, whose son has brought her to France and keeps her there against her will, escape into memory becomes a survival mechanism, her only possibility for feminist response where outright resistance is impossible. Although Julia longs for home from the beginning, the real turning point comes the day she is arrested while going to get her grandchildren at school, for wearing Maréchal's military uniform coat in public – in a way, for impersonating the "real" French. As the old woman speaks Creole, not French, and is unable to explain herself, her body yields to the police officers while her mind retreats into the safety of another time and place. Even the officers can see that Julia's body is an empty shell:

> They can just feel that this lady is no longer there, with them. Her eyes are looking inward to another world. Her spirit is brooding over thoughts of another time. . . . Man Ya walks along like a zombie, her eyes staring straight ahead. She does not walk like someone who knows where she is going. She puts one foot in front of the other mechanically, while her spirit floats about, like debris from a shipwreck. (52)

In the European territory of France, Julia's relationship to Guadeloupe mirrors her enslaved ancestors' ties to Guinen ("Guinea"). In forced diaspora in the Caribbean, enslaved Africans dreamed of a future return to Guinen, which was at once the physical Africa that preceded their capture and deportation into slavery and a spiritual Africa, a heaven of sorts, where they would go once death released them from servitude. In either case, to set one's mind on Guinen was to mindfully divorce oneself from the intolerable conditions of the here and now. Allusions to French Caribbean *zombis* further reinforce this parallel between Julia's predicament and that of her African ancestors in Guadeloupe,[64] including the mechanical way their bodies performed unthinking labour while their traumatized minds, as battered as debris from a shipwreck, sought refuge in Guinen. For her part, Julia adopts the only feminist response at her disposal: she sends her mind and spirit to the Guadeloupe of yesterday and the Guadeloupe of a hoped-for tomorrow, as a way of surviving the unbearable exile of today.

Finding herself traumatized and trapped, Julia longs for home all the time. Whether she merely endures the empty space, dresses it up or nurtures it, there is no denying the pain it causes. Cooking creole in the city feeds those feelings of nostalgia and frustrated longing, making them more intense:

> Nourishing this longing means buying freshwater fish in France, soaking it in imitation brine – there are neither limes nor bird peppers here. Fry tomatoes and onions gently in an ounce of Masclet red butter out of a package from the Antilles. Put in the fish, let it cook, then eat it. Take note of the offense. Then, think about Home. In your memory, go in search of odors and the joys of tasting.

> Reinvent a Caribbean Sea. . . . Later, close your eyes, suck a fish head from a
> red snapper, crush a thick slice of breadfruit in the *court-bouillon* sauce, sweat
> from the heat of the pepper. Relive all those tastes. Breath in and belch. (89)

For Julia, creole food in Paris is a poor imitation of home foodways, rife
with deficiencies for which a few authentic elements from home simply
cannot fully compensate. At the end of what should have been a satisfying
meal, she can only take note of the fact that it was not quite as good as she
had imagined it would be. On the other hand, creole cooking stimulates
the memory, and the *memory* of food never fails to appease. In the nostalgic space of diasporic consciousness, Man Ya unfailingly finds the best of
Guadeloupean fare in all its appealing specificities. Her culinary dreams
of home (unlike reality) always end in a peaceful breath and a satisfied
belch. Moreover, Man Ya's attitudes about Caribbean food figure her (and,
increasingly, her granddaughter Gisèle's) relationship to Back Home, a place
that looks ever more perfect through the rose-coloured glasses of distance.

When Julia returns to Guadeloupe, leaving Gisèle behind in Paris, the
former's homesick yearning for Back Home translates into the latter's sentimental pining for Julia herself. Conflating her beloved grandmother, creole
cuisine and the island itself, Gisèle, like her grandmother, attempts to use
her senses to revive memories of safety and belonging in the unwelcoming
diaspora. She seeks out the smells of Man Ya's garden among the spices in
the kitchen, but the connection lasts only as long as she can hold her breath
(106). She envisions the archipelago among the scattered lentils on her plate,
but her musings are interrupted by anxious thoughts of how few memories
she actually has of Guadeloupe, and how incomplete they are (110).

Modelling herself after her grandmother Julia, Gisèle endeavours to use
food to induce a trance-like state where memory and imagination meet:

> We got the cinnamon, the curry powder, and also the cassava flour. The very
> same day, Manman made a chicken curry with rice. . . . After the curry, I did
> not brush my teeth, to keep a little of the taste in my mouth. I closed my eyes,
> and I saw you in your garden, in the middle of all your tall trees. . . . I said,
> "Man Ya! Don't forget me!" You looked at me and you said: "*Pa pé a yen! Ou ké
> sové*. . . . Don't be afraid! You will be safe!" So, I opened my eyes and I went to
> do my writing. And I felt full of energy thanks to your words. (112)

Three generations of Antillean women thus participate in the process of recreating the homeland using food: Man Ya sends spices and foods from Back Home to her children and grandchildren in the diaspora; Gisèle's mother, Daisy, cooks creole in the city using those raw materials; Gisèle ingests that cuisine, using it, just as her grandmother did before her, as a catalyst for memory. Consciously conjuring up images of her grandmother in Julia's own Caribbean environment, Gisèle realizes that she lives with twin fears: first, that she will forget Back Home; second, that Back Home will forget her. But because her grandmother tells her not to be afraid of *anything* –in Creole, *a yen* (the above English translation is incomplete) – Gisèle knows she can overcome both of these fears by using the pen.

WRITING BACK HOME

Like Maryse Condé (see chapter 5), Gisèle Pineau draws parallels between the culinary and the literary. In Pineau's case, in *Un papillon dans la cité* and *Exile According to Julia,* she portrays both food and fiction as valuable historical archives and transmitters of culture.[65] As Pineau explained in a 2007 interview, "Creole cuisine creates deep links to the island. When Antilleans prepare Creole dishes here, it's a way for them to maintain a relationship with the land, and I think that cooking allows one to plant roots in the land, even for those who can't travel often or can't go back home every year. Thanks to the cuisine, they call themselves Creole."[66] Likewise, in her food-focused writing, Pineau shows that writing, like food, can help young members of the Caribbean diaspora born and raised outside the archipelago to connect with older generations and their heritage. From penning heartfelt letters and journal entries to inscribing oral history and lived experience into History, Pineau's protagonists write to anchor themselves to Back Home and to the past.

The more time Gisèle spends away from Guadeloupe and the longer she is separated from Man Ya, the more tenuous the girl's connection to the island becomes. Over time, Gisèle is left with nothing but increasingly fragmented and insufficient memories – "scraps of memory" (127); "thoughts that are trying to put themselves in order" (127); "bits of your memory . . . scattered pieces . . . vague memories, creamy chocolate. . . . Sorry visions, rehearsed over and over again, hackneyed, worn out" (130). It gradually becomes clear to Gisèle that if she wants to continue to belong to Guadeloupe and wants Guadeloupe to continue to belong to her, she will need more than the pan alone; she will also need the pen. In this she will both diverge from and follow in the footsteps of the illiterate grandmother she adores.

Amalgamating the written word with colonization and racialized slavery, Man Ya is understandably sceptical of it. Not so long ago, French writing had freed the enslaved Afro-Antilleans – "They were being told that they had French law on their side. Signed and sealed" (81) – only to enslave them again.[67] The old woman, born only a few decades after abolition, wonders, "Who knows if one day soon, some law won't put the blacks back in chains? The law on paper, stamped, makes all men bend, pretty writing and violet ink" (83). Neither Asdrubal's handsome French uniform nor his love letters, full of pretty French words and empty promises, protected her from his physical and verbal abuse when he came home from the war (71). Even her own son uses the written word against her, tricking her into making an X next to her name in her passport, then forcibly removing her from the only home she knows, "for her own good" (21). Julia's disillusionment with her husband and her son feeds into her disenchantment with French writing, for it proves just as mendacious in the personal as it has been in the political.

For her part, the adult narrator Gisèle understands that the colonizer's written History can indeed be as treacherous as French law, Asdrubal's letters and Julia's X-mark signature. She knows that French Antillean truth resides in the Guadeloupean folk tales and oral history that Julia passed on to her grandchildren. The narrator is convinced that these stories, like the Creole language and Guadeloupean food that the old woman shares with her descendants, are the most reliable vectors of French Antillean culture and most honest repositories of collective memory. But thanks to her voracious reading – everything from encyclopaedias to the French literary canon (43) – the narrator also knows that literature can undermine society's dominant narratives, exposing their underbelly and reversing their power dynamics. If *Dangerous Liaisons* could protest social rot in pre-Revolution France and Baudelaire could expose the hollow dullness of nineteenth-century bourgeois sensibilities, surely Pineau can write herself and her people into

History. Over time she reappropriates French writing, diverting it from a tool of occlusion, division and oppression into a means of enlightenment, connection and liberation.[68]

When schoolgirl Gisèle's teacher verbally and physically abuses her, then emotionally mistreats her by pretending that she doesn't exist, the girl dreams of being immortal, visible and influential like the characters in the books she reads: "I say to myself that the Marquise de Merteuil and the Princess of Cleves have et cetera of time to live. . . . Death is nothing to them. So, even if this teacher doesn't see me, I do believe that others will see me, will hear me, will love me" (43). She fantasizes about taking control of the teacher's own handwriting, repurposing its elements to defend herself against the merciless woman and the institutional power she represents:

> The dictation written on the blackboard is under my orders. At my command, the words fall apart. Each letter becomes a weapon, an instrument of torture. The *l*s are lassoes. The *i*s fire their dots like cannon balls. The *t*s are sharp knives. The *u*s, latrines that have not been emptied for a century of time. A band of *a*s, holding each other by the hand, form a chain around the witch's neck, haul her in, and then cast her into the filthy waters of the *u*s. (44)

The dictation, a classic French pedagogical exercise, is an exercise in pure obedience and mimicry, the ultimate symbol of linguistic imperialism and prescriptive cultural domination. In a nod to her own slippery, subversive creole heritage, wherein elements of the French language have been deconstructed, repurposed and reassigned to contain and convey a new culture and worldview, the narrator imagines using one of the teacher's favourite means of control against her. Challenging its inherent legitimacy, logic and integrity, the girl bids the French written word to split wide open, fall apart, expose its changeable nature. If, in the violence of the narrator's revenge fantasy, the reader can suppose something akin to an opposite and equal reaction, then one glimpses the depths of the psychic violence and deep humiliation that have been visited upon the little girl. Moreover, the "latrines", which have not been emptied for "a century of time", contain more than just the "filthy waters" of the girl's own personal degradation; they hold the dishonour of generations. As we will see, building upon these early instincts towards weaponizing writing, the narrator will eventually subvert the dictation exercise entirely. Instead of transcribing imposed French mainstream narratives, she will write Man Ya's stories . . . and her own.

Once Julia returns home to Guadeloupe, leaving Gisèle in Paris without her, the girl suffers intensely from her grandmother's absence. Homesick for Man Ya's voice – her sighs and her prayers, her stories and her comforting Creole words (*"Pa pléré ti moun* – don't cry little one" [104]), haunted by memories of rejection – "Go back to your country, *Bamboulas*! Go home, to Africa!" (104); "Go back to your own country!" (105, 106) – Gisèle dreams of being delivered, like Julia, from a France that does not want her:

> I want to leave this land that rejects me. So I become someone who writes in the afternoons, a midnight scribbler, a scribe in the wee hours. Write to invent existences for yourself. Migratory pen, magic ink, wizard letters, which take you back every day to your dream country. . . . Write the burned bottom of a saucepan of chocolate custard, memories of kites, children dancing in the rain across from a blue savannah. (105)

In the range of French terms she uses to describe her identity as a writer, the narrator charts the evolution of her relationship to writing. "Someone who writes" (*écriveuse*) implies a penchant for and a pleasure in writing. The *écriveuse* is a relational being who writes daily letters to Man Ya in Guadeloupe. "Midnight scribbler", meanwhile, encodes the creative impulse that cannot be contained within the waking hours or inside recognizable forms of expression. The scribbler writes the stuff of dreams, the urgency of the unconscious at the magic midnight hour. Last, the narrator serves as a "scribe of the wee hours" (*scribe du petit matin*), our clearest indication that her writing records collective history for the greater good. In the French *scribe du petit matin*, moreover, we find an echo of Aimé Césaire's "Au bout du petit matin", the first and repeated line in the seminal *Notebook of a Return to the Native Land*. *Exile According to Julia*, like *Notebook*, records the French Antillean experience and shares it with the whole world. Pineau's special insights into French Antillean realities, like Césaire's, spring from the act of leaving and coming back to the Caribbean.

Gisèle's pen records what has been and what is and imagines what could be. In "invent existences for yourself" there is the sense that the narrator is inventing alternative existences for herself, but also that she is inventing exis-

tences period, for in the European territory of France, the girl feels so invisible
it is like she does not exist at all. Gisèle's pen, like Julia's pan, is "migratory"
and "magic", whisking her away to her "dream country" (*pays rêvé*), which in
French connotes not so much an ideal country as a dreamed-up country – a
creation of the narrator's active memory and imagination. The dreamed-up
country is sewn together out of recognizable elements of Caribbean childhood,
from the culinary (chocolate custard) to the cultural (kite flying), from the
meteorological (tropical showers) to the geographic (the savannah). In the
final image, that of the "blue savannah", we find a gesture towards Edouard
Glissant's reflections on French Antilleans' first wave of experiences with
atavistic memory and the impossible return. Afro-Antilleans, asserts Glissant
in *Poetics of Relation*, could know what was lost from Africa only through
the Africa-shaped hole that it left in their lives: "a reverse image of all that
had been left behind, not to be regained for generations except – more
threadbare – in the blue savannahs of memory or imagination".[69] In much
the same fashion, Pineau's writing reconstitutes Guadeloupe by studying
the contours of the empty space the island's absence leaves in her life. As
her writing inscribes French Antilleans' second diaspora into History, the
text rescues memory from the blue savannah's haze for generations to come.

When at last Maréchal and his family return to the Caribbean, thirteen-
year-old Gisèle is thrilled to finally go where "blacks are at home", where they
have the right "to be proud, just as whites are proud of themselves", where
there are books about black people, full of tales in which "all the heroes are
blacks" (125). Thanks to Man Ya's cooking and Gisèle's writing, thanks to
Gisèle's writing about Man Ya's cooking, Gisèle feels as attached to Back
Home as ever. But in all her enthusiasm, the young woman still fears that
the islands she has pined for may not see her as one of their own:

> Here I am! I am bringing my arms to build this country with you! Tell me
> the true story; I will write it for those who are to come. Tell me over and over
> again about the intertwined lives of the living and the dead; I will give life to
> the words and put old fears to death. I will make myself paper, ink, and pen to
> enter into the flesh of the Country. (125–26)

Here the narrator directly pledges to write in the service of her people, like
the "scribe in the wee hours" she became in Paris. She promises to record

the stories History has forgotten; she swears to preserve truth for generations to come. Gisèle will legitimize the French Antillean relationship to
time and space by writing the ways in which the past haunts the present.
She will take possession of the written word, harnessing its power such
that Man Ya's people will never again fear its potential to re-enslave them.
In her ecstatic imagining, the narrator de-personifies herself, giving up her
selfhood in order to become a mere instrument of the writing. Meanwhile,
she personifies Guadeloupe, endowing it with living flesh. Gisèle is prepared
to do whatever it takes to belong to that place where she was not born but
has always lived in spirit. If her people bring their stories, the narrator vows,
she will bring her pen, and indeed her whole self. And together, in potluck
fashion, they will write Back Home.

A POTLUCK WORLD VISION

In a 2007 interview, Pineau used the word *potluck* to describe the "world
vision" she tried to capture in her later novel *Fleur de Barbarie* (2005), which
at the time she believed might be her last: "It was a [last will and] testament in
which I wanted to put everything: all my themes, my world vision. A potluck
world to which everyone would contribute: this one would bring his Sarthe
rillettes [potted meat], that one would bring his Creole *boudin*. I dreamt of a
world of peace. . . . I wanted to show that the world was beautiful and diverse,
that the richness of the world lay precisely in its diversity."[70] This dream of a
potluck world also inhabits Pineau's *Exile According to Julia* and *Un papillon
dans la cité*. While in the former a "potluck" approach to multiculturalism
is most conspicuous in its painful absence, in the latter the possibility of
such a world expresses itself through the culinary.

Both *Exile* and *Papillon* depict three generations of French Antillean
women. Each generation has a different relationship with assimilation,
and those differing attitudes manifest themselves at the table. Both Man Ya
grandmother characters, as we have seen, resist assimilation entirely, using
Guadeloupean food to preserve ties to the island. The mother characters,
Daisy and Aurélie, on the other hand, are completely invested in assimilation into a mainstream European French way of life: "'Children! There is
nothing, absolutely nothing good for you Back Home,' the grown-ups would

say. 'Long ago it was a land of slavery, which no longer has anything good in it. Don't think about the past! Take advantage of France! Take advantage of the luck you have to be growing up here!'"[71] No sensible person, they insist, would look back on the miserable Antilles with fondness or nostalgia; only an ungrateful child would look upon the French promised land with anything but untempered appreciation and admiration. What Daisy asserts by using words, Aurélie espouses by using food. As we will see, Aurélie, whose motivations are both economic (like Daisy's) and emotional (because of a rift with Man Ya), insists on a wholesale adoption of European French foodways, to the exclusion of Guadeloupean fare. The granddaughter characters, however, demand the right to love their grandmothers' Guadeloupe, including the island's food culture, and the right to claim it as their own.[72] The Gisèle narrator – more closely based on the real-life young Pineau – is deeply wounded by her experiences of racism and rejection in the European territory of France, and thus she understandably turns to Guadeloupean foodways for self-affirmation and healing. The Félicie character, on the other hand – based on the girl Pineau wished she had been – is more at ease as a creole in the city, enjoying a happy hybridity that manifests itself most clearly at the table.

In *Un papillon dans la cité*, when Aurélie is ready to send for her daughter to join her in France, she asks her friend Marie-Claire, who has travelled from France to Guadeloupe in order to visit her own mother, to go and fetch Félicie from Man Ya's house. Finding the girl's suitcase heavy, Marie-Claire asks Félicie what Man Ya has put in it. "My clothes, ma'am, and also my notebooks, and yams and sweet potatoes, and a little breadfruit, I think", answers Félicie. These foods, like the girl's clothes, are necessities and, like the girl's notebooks, are deeply personal and filled with meaning. Anticipating that yams, sweet potatoes and breadfruit will be hard to come by in the European territory of France, Man Ya sends some along with Félicie. In so doing, the old woman validates the girl's need for and right to a continuing connection to Guadeloupe and to her enslaved ancestors, who survived the planters' greed by growing yams and sweet potatoes in secret provision grounds, and her maroon ancestors, who prized breadfruit as a means of survival. The suitcase, it seems, is filled not only with food but also with the weight of the history it holds.[73] In addition, because Man Ya is illiterate, she cannot send a letter with Félicie. The only way she can communicate her deep affection and continue to care for the girl is through food.

Emphasizing Man Ya's ignorance, Marie-Claire, who is of the same pro-assimilation generation as her friend Aurélie, shows total disdain for Man Ya's food-based love language: "Your grandmother is crazy. You'll have to leave all that at my mom's" (20). Later, Marie-Claire can't resist emphasizing her own sophistication as an émigré, contrasting it with Man Ya's naive inexperience as someone who has never left Guadeloupe and, most especially, has never been to the European territory of France. Marie-Claire regales first her brother, then the rest of her family with the story of the suitcase full of yams and breadfruit. While the relatives mock Man Ya in order to distance themselves from the island's low cultural status (well beneath that of the esteemed mainland), Félicie remains loyal to her grandmother, to Guadeloupe and to its food. Although she is in no position to contradict these adults whom she barely knows, the young girl imagines that her grandmother would chastise them for their guffaws, shutting them up with "Enough of this nonsense!" (21).

As Félicie sits down to her first Christmas dinner in the European territory of France, her mother insists that the whole family must embrace French holiday traditions and adapt to French customs. As she serves a traditional French meal with raw oysters and a big turkey (46), complete with a white tablecloth, porcelain plates and real silverware, plus chocolate cake and champagne (51), Aurélie feels confident that the material abundance her daughter enjoys in France will easily outweigh the girl's sentimental attachment to Guadeloupe. Indeed, the contrast between France, the land of opportunity, and Guadeloupe, the land of scarcity, is striking:

> No lie, it was the first time I had seen a whole turkey. Man Ya has never seen one either. Back home, we only know turkey wings. You find them in all the shops. They are frozen, sometimes with big white feathers still on them that you have trouble pulling out and that prove that they belong to the poultry family. In Guadeloupe, they are the meat of people without much in their wallet. They sell them for 8 or 10 francs a kilo. Sometimes, in the shop that was close to our house, Man Zizine had to separate the wings that were frozen together by hitting them with an old hammer before throwing them on the scale plop, plop, plop! (46)

In this passage, Guadeloupe's inferior position on France's periphery is painfully clear. The island's inhabitants are a second-class sort of French, the kind who are lucky if they get the European territory of France's leftovers, which are nearly unrecognizable in their great difference from what those on the mainland enjoy. Despite Guadeloupe's political status as a theoretically equal overseas department, Félicie's life testifies to the island's neocolonial predicament, a situation whose hallmark is unequal exchange. In the girl's personal experience, while the island sends its best to the mainland – her young, able-bodied mother and stepfather as consumable exported labour, and the bananas Man Ya packs in the warehouse as agricultural exports – in return, the mainland delivers only unappetizing scraps.

Although she enjoys the meal, Félicie remains unswayed by this flashy show of affluence. She retains her attachment to a Guadeloupean model of celebration, where people enjoy one another's company and each person is free to relax and express themselves: "We spent so many Christmases together, without a turkey, without oysters, without chocolate . . . but what Christmases they were! Without snow, without a decorated Christmas tree, without shiny ornaments . . . but we never stayed, sitting stiffly with our legs together, in a living room with silence as our only party guest" (48). Awkwardly inhabiting the materialistic, ahistorical mimicry of French culture that Aurélie has imposed on her family, nobody knows quite how to behave. In contrast, back in Guadeloupe, the girl recalls, nobody needed high-status French foods or decorations to have a good time. In their end-of-year celebration of the baby Jesus and their own nèg-mawon ancestors, people felt good in their own skin, connected to each other and to their ancestors.

Despite Aurélie's unwelcome pressure to assimilate, *Un papillon dans la cité* includes many positive interactions between French Antilleans and the white European French people who share their schools, their neighbourhoods and, in some cases, their homes. Experiencing and sharing food is one of the things that makes Félicie feel at ease in France and among the French; she absorbs their culture with their food. At Christmas she does enjoy the turkey with chestnuts, the *bûche de Noël*[74] and champagne, all European French holiday traditions (51). Later her family's vacation on a farm in the Sarthe region is filled with delicious *produits du terroir*[75] and the pleasure of sharing them with the people those products "belong" to: "The farmer treated us to a round of cider. . . . We drank fresh milk every day, we ate vegetables, fruit, and nice fatty *rillettes* [potted meat]"[76] (75). Far from being reactionary or closed-minded, Félicie demonstrates at the table that she is neither afraid nor even reluctant to embrace the good things that her adoptive country has to offer. She is a transnational being, re-creolized in Paris, and her transnationality includes a part of her that just wants to be French on her own terms.

French food culture holds the notion of *terroir* in very high esteem. Even the average European French person recognizes on some level that there are no truly national cuisines. Instead a cuisine possesses essential ties to a given region and its resources, such that the basic unit of cuisine is the region.[77] The European French attachment to the notion of *terroir* acts as a culinary trace of the diversity within the country, a last bastion against complete regional cultural erasure within the framework of a national republican universalism that has largely wiped out local languages and histories. No one would accuse a Sarthois[78] of *communautarisme* because he preserves traditional regional methods of cider or *rillettes* production. On the contrary, he is celebrated for his continuing contributions to the diversity of French cuisine(s). By focusing on this aspect of French food culture, Pineau portrays a France where unity in diversity is possible. Instead of being negated, French Antilleans could be celebrated for what they bring to the table.

Acceptance and openness at the table also help the white French characters of *Un papillon dans la cité* to more easily accept the immigrants who have come into their city, their family and their lives. When French Antillean Marie-Claire marries Bernard, her white French fiancé, the wedding is a transcultural affair where European French white people and French Antillean black people dance Kassav's "Zouk"[79] (86) and eat a *pièce montée*[80] (87) together. Félicie is thrilled to see how much Bernard's family enjoys the Antillean aspects of the celebration: "They were having a good time after all, especially after drinking a couple of rum punches and burning their tongues on the spicy sausage's fire" (86). Both the *ti punch* (rum punch) and the *boudin pimenté* (spicy blood sausage) are emblematic of Guadeloupean food culture. The Guadeloupean *boudin*, made with rum and local spices, is a creolized version of the original French blood sausage that dates back to enslavement times and the colonial encounter. In the context of Marie-

Claire and Bernard's wedding, the dish comes full circle: the original culinary imperialism is transformed into a culinary exchange. In this hopeful scene, which (as we will see) resembles the "last supper" of Condé's *Victoire: My Mother's Mother*, food imagery figures a creole-style integration through inclusion instead of a universalist French republican assimilation through erasure, bringing all the parties together in a conciliatory mosaic version of Frenchness.

Félicie is particularly struck by food's power to connect people when she shares food with her friend Mo's family. When Mohammed offers her some of his grandmother's *loukoum*,[81] Félicie immediately sees both the woman and the candy as stand-ins for her own grandmother, Man Ya, and her cooking: "Once more I saw Man Ya making a big *doukoun* [cake]. *Loukoum* and *doukoum* sound alike, they rhyme, they are related. I couldn't resist helping myself" (56). The coincidental linguistic similarity between the names for Caribbean and North African sweets opens Félicie's mind to the possibility that she and Mohammed might have a lot in common after all.

Félicie's mouth waters at the prospect of eating Fathia's *loukoum*: "My saliva ran down my throat like candy syrup" (57). The family's couscous titillates her senses – "the rich smell of meat in sauce that was floating through the whole apartment" (60) – and stimulates her imagination: "I could already see myself with my mouth all red with sauce" (58). Once she actually tries the *loukoum* she does not hide her pleasure, much to Mo's delight: "A delight. With each mouthful, a fine film of sugar coated my lips, which I carefully licked and licked again to make the pleasure last" (59). Félicie's attitude toward Mo's culinary traditions draws a distinction between passive tolerance and active mutual affirmation, an essential element of effective coalition-building.[82]

When Mo visits Guadeloupe, he reciprocates his friend's affirmation: "Mo, who had never tasted the tiniest bit of crab claws, greedily asked for more. It didn't surprise me. He fearlessly threw himself on everything that came out of Man Ya's *canaris* [big cookpots]" (120); "After lunch – catfish in stock with yams and taro root as side dishes – which Mo, served like a prince by Man Ya, swallowed without making a face" (111). Mirroring Félicie's curiosity and trust, the boy suspends fear and negative judgement in order to redraw the lines of community. The emphasis is on the fact that these foods are tied to the land and necessarily unknown to him. Crab, catfish, yams and taro root are typically Caribbean. The boy, notes Félicie, eagerly eats every unfamiliar thing that comes out of Man Ya's cookpots. Here Pineau does not use the French *marmites* for "cookpots" but rather the French Antillean dialect's *canaris*, taken from the Native American clay pots called *canalli*.[83] In this way, Man Ya's cooking reaches back to the Native Americans, forward to Félicie, and outward in rhizomic fashion to Mo and the many peoples of the world.

At the same time, these passages emphasize another component of effective coalition-building: radical hospitality. Man Ya serves Mo, a stranger in her home, "like a prince" (111) who is entirely welcome and worthy of respect. For Félicie, this combination of radical hospitality and intentional affirmation is the stuff dreams are made of. One evening in particular stands out to her: "A good cow-foot soup was waiting for us. I felt like I was living a dream. After dinner, we all went to lie down naturally in the big bed, on either side of Man Ya, with our heads buried in her smelly armpits" (112). Once again Félicie's grandmother has prepared a typical Guadeloupean dish, confident that Mo will embrace the unfamiliar. Once again her trust is rewarded with acceptance and appreciation. After the three share the meal, the children share a bed with Man Ya, snuggling up against her on either side like siblings, enjoying the warmth and protection of her arms as if they were both her own. In that posture of vulnerability and intimacy lies hope for a different kind of world.

FROM EXILE TO ERRANTRY

In *L'exil selon Julia* and *Un papillon dans la cité*, as Pineau engenders the French Antillean experience of exile and re-creolization in Paris, she also encapsulates a broader shift in the Caribbean relationship to diaspora during the second half of the twentieth century. In the first half of the century, the dominant forms of Caribbean deracination and cultural mixing remained those created by the importation of enslaved Africans and indentured East Indians into the region. However, for more than fifty years now, a second variety of Caribbean displacement and hybridity has joined and, in many respects, overtaken the first: the exportation of Caribbean labour and refugees to a handful of North American and European cities. No serious consideration of Caribbean womanhood can ignore the lived experience of millions of diasporic Caribbean women whose feminist resistance and response, like that of Pineau's youthful protagonists and grandmother characters, is homegrown in the City.[84] Pineau's culinary fiction inscribes the freedom struggle of these Western city-dwelling Caribbean women into the mosaic of Caribbean womanhood.

Likewise, in her twin works of culinary fiction, Pineau's depictions – of the bitter resentment of past generations of doubly excluded "Negropolitans" on the one hand (*L'Exil*) and the hope for creatively inclusive future generations of Caribbean women in the city on the other (*Papillon*) – illustrate the need for diasporic Caribbean women both to maintain a lifeline to Back Home and to carve out a place for themselves in multicultural Western urban spaces. Meanwhile, by linking food and fiction, Pineau urges a complementary use of old (retained African, Indian, Caribbean) and new (reappropriated Western, European French) means of preserving cultural memory and maintaining ties with the islands. Her close association of the culinary and the literary draws useful parallels between the circumstances that originally creolized Afro-Caribbean peoples in the islands and those that continue to re-creolize them in the city. In this way the author highlights the implicit slippage between voluntary and forced migration, challenging any vision of Western nations as ethnically egalitarian and post-colonial societies. As she depicts the everyday struggles of three generations of French Antillean women and girls in Paris, Pineau contributes to a more general Caribbean history, injecting both gender and humanity into the dominant narratives of migration and assimilation that have reduced the past sixty years of Caribbean diasporic experience in Europe and North America to mere economics.

Like all the authors in this study, Pineau engages with the question of the "authentic" in ethnic and cultural identity. However, because of her attachment to group identity and cultural continuity, she might be better described as transnational rather than post-national. Pineau redraws the contours of Caribbeanness, expanding it to include members of the diaspora, and reconfigures the republican universalist conception of Frenchness, reworking it into a pluralistic, multicultural potluck. In this way she highlights the diasporic capacity to live in two worlds at once, embracing multiple belongings.

In so doing she nevertheless articulates the ways in which "third island" French Antilleans are not only different from other ethnicities in France but also distinct from those Guadeloupeans who remain in the Caribbean.[85] In this she explores what H. Adlai Murdoch calls "the limitless promise of the *neither/nor*".[86]

Pineau's culinary fiction posits Caribbean identity as performative and independent of geography: one eats oneself Caribbean; one remembers oneself Caribbean; one writes oneself Caribbean. In this sense Pineau's protagonists are reflective of a wider cultural reality, for writing has become one of the key strategies adopted by Caribbean migrants in their attempt to construct a subjective space of self-expression.[87] By articulating her Caribbeanness in the context of the European territory of France, Pineau is not so unlike the *créolistes*, whose famous "We proclaim ourselves Creole" was first uttered not in Fort-de-France or Pointe-à-Pitre but in Seine-Saint-Denis,[88] even if the latter haven't quite lived up to their own geographically inclusive vision.[89] In fact, Pineau's food-focused writing illustrates that in some ways Caribbean peoples are even more Caribbean in diaspora.[90]

Exile According to Julia and *Un papillon dans la cité* also characterize Caribbean identity as relational. In the Parisian *banlieues*, under the hostility of the majority white gaze, *Exile*'s Gisèle learns solidarity with other black people in ways she might not have had she grown up in mostly black Guadeloupe.[91] In the context of the multicultural suburbs, where France's post-colonial heritage is most evident, *Papillon*'s Félicie positions herself within a plurality of post-colonial subjects in ways that would never have been possible had she stayed in the archipelago. These female protagonists embody Glissant's errantry, a process of displacement and exchange in which one finds oneself through contact with the Other.[92] At the same time, as Caribbean pluralisms are collapsed in the diaspora, authors such as Pineau stand to play a key role in reclaiming the heterogeneity of Caribbeans in the city, including the role of gender in shaping their experiences with racial discrimination, assimilation and intra- and inter-ethnic coalition-building.

Taken as a complementary pair, *Exile According to Julia* and *Un papillon dans la cité* epitomize Pineau's brand of homegrown Caribbean feminism: her double determination to affirm one's own origins and to reach out to others. In Pineau's potluck world vision, it is possible to pursue unexpected solidarities between formerly colonized groups. and even between the descendants of the colonizers and the colonized. Pineau, like the other women authors we will encounter in the chapters to come, intimates that women's individual self-realization and group liberation are interdependent processes, and even that the freedom struggles of the entire post-colonial world are inextricably linked to one another. For Pineau, "writing as a black Creole woman means feeling hope for a truly new world where peoples, languages, races, religions, mixed and interlocking cultures continually enrich and discover each other, respect and accept each other despite clear differences".[93] However, unlike the ferociously independent Condé (as we will see in chapter 5), Pineau suggests that people must above all enjoy cultural continuity in order to have something meaningful to bring to the table. In short, her homegrown Caribbean feminist vision is of a future in which Caribbean women mindfully nourish one another across both generations and oceans, and in which they find validation and solidarity abroad. As we will find in chapter 2, she is not the only one.

CHAPTER 2

EDWIDGE DANTICAT
THE HUNGER TO TELL

You are – we are all implicated in this.[1]

TWENTIETH-CENTURY HISPANIOLA WAS BLOODY, GOVERNED BY dictators and scarred by political violence on both sides of the Haiti–Dominican Republic border, violence that has left lasting scars on the people of Haiti. This violence must be understood within the larger context of US economic and political hegemony in the Caribbean, which created no fewer than eight dictatorships – ten if one counts two Somozas and two Duvaliers – in the first half of the century.[2] As US capital expanded into the Caribbean, it created unpaid debts and unstable economies that served as a pretext for military intervention in the region – the first wave of political violence. This economic and political instability created psychological conditions that spawned local support for brutal nationalistic dictatorships. All ten Caribbean dictatorships occurred under the same conditions: widespread poverty and hunger, dependence on the United States even for food, and mass emigration that propelled cheap labour out of the Caribbean and into the Global North. And all ten ruled by means of the same techniques: autocratic power, nationalistic tendencies and the indiscriminate use of terror to repress dissidents. Two of the most infamous Caribbean dictators of this era, whose regimes deeply impacted Haitians at home and in diaspora, were "Generalísimo" Rafael Trujillo in the Dominican Republic and François "Papa Doc" Duvalier in Haiti.[3]

The ghosts of Trujillo and Duvalier haunt Haitian author Edwidge Danticat's *oeuvre*. These regimes, next door to one another on the same

island, had much in common; both came to power after US economic interference and occupation: the United States occupied the Dominican Republic
from 1916 to 1924 and Haiti from 1915 to 1934. Both exploited deep-seated
racial prejudices and colour resentments that were rooted in the history of
racialized slavery in the Caribbean. Trujillo mobilized a Dominican identification with whiteness and Spanish heritage against black Haitian migrant
workers, and Duvalier weaponized black resentment against the mulatto
faction of the oligarchy in Haiti, which had collaborated with and benefited
from the US occupation. Both dictators rose from the ranks of the military
and civil service, and both used the rhetoric of taking back their countries for
the "authentic" people. In reality, though, both men plundered the islands
for personal gain and took over US capital's dirty work, including the Cold
War task of keeping Communism at bay. On Hispaniola, modernization
was limited to projects that benefited foreign capital, labour was kept cheap
by suppressing leftist organizations, and US capital in both countries was
protected by any means necessary – including extraordinary levels of political violence.

The violence was wrought under a muffling blanket of silence: all political
parties, newspapers, radio stations, trade unions and private associations
that did not agree with Trujillo ceased to exist,[4] and Duvalier arrested and
killed members of the press and broadcasters, burning and bombing their
offices and stations.[5] The United States maintained that silence, for decades
turning a blind eye to human rights abuses on both sides of the island. Both
regimes murdered and displaced thousands of Haitians, and their pain and
trauma were only intensified by the continuing silence surrounding their
experiences – a silence they preserved, in part, because they needed to eat.[6]

Edwidge Danticat's testimonial novels, *The Farming of Bones* (1998), *Breath,
Eyes, Memory* (1994) and *The Dew Breaker* (2004), break that silence. *The
Farming of Bones* tells the story of the 1937 Parsley Massacre, in which twelve
thousand Haitians were murdered upon Dominican dictator Rafael Trujillo's
order, from a female Haitian migrant worker's point of view. *Breath, Eyes,
Memory* and *The Dew Breaker*, meanwhile, depict generational trauma associated with the Duvalier dictatorships and their secret police, the Tonton
Macoutes, illustrating how victims can internalize harm and even become
perpetrators. In all these works, Danticat uses food to illustrate how the history

of dictatorship and political violence in the Caribbean affected women specifically.[7] In *The Farming of Bones, Breath, Eyes, Memory* and *The Dew Breaker*,
food imagery helps voice Haitian women's hurt and their healing.

THE HUNGER TO TELL

In *Silencing the Past: Power and the Production of History*, Haitian anthropologist Michel-Rolph Trouillot outlines the limitations inherent in both the
naive epistemology of positivism, which clings to the notion of an objective
set of facts and thus obscures the influence of power on historical narrative,
and the rabbit hole of constructivism, which views historical narrative as
merely one fiction among others.[8] History lies somewhere between the
two: "Human beings participate in history both as actors and as narrators",
he explains. "In vernacular use, history means both the facts of the matter
and a narrative of those facts, both 'what happened' and 'that which is said
to have happened'."[9] Indeed, he points out, history is produced as much by
popular culture as by academia; each of us, he says, is an amateur historian
participating in the production of history.[10] Trouillot focuses not on what history is but how history works – the differential exercise of power that makes
possible some narratives and silences others.[11] As he explains, silence and
history are intertwined: "Silences enter the process of historical production
at four crucial moments: the moment of fact creation (the making of *sources*);
the moment of fact assembly (the making of *archives*); the moment of fact
retrieval (the making of *narratives*); and the moment of retrospective significance (the making of *history* in the final instance)."[12] According to Trouillot,
each historical narrative is "a bundle of silences" whose deconstruction is
necessarily as unique as the narrative itself.

As Myriam Chancy points out, Haiti is the subject of many historical
silences, and Haitian women of even more; both anti-female oppression
and women's modes of resistance to this oppression are obscured or erased.
Indeed, she argues, Haitian women's history is told primarily through the
novel rather than through "non-fiction" such as official histories. Haitian
women novelists use the form to recover and preserve the role of Haitian
women in history – as both actors and as narrators, as both "participants and
witnesses".[13] Over the course of the twentieth century, she asserts, the fictional

has communicated a historical narrative that is elsewhere denied existence, and through the novel, Haitian women authors have forged a distinct space for Haitian women's voices within feminist discourse. These novels offer feminized and feminist readings of the history of Haiti that make visible the multiple axes of oppression faced by Haitian women under US imperialism. From these female-authored novels, where national identity is redefined in terms of the personal[14] and imagination is "a key to the real rather than its mere shadow",[15] there emerges a *culture lacune* – a sense of women's culture that defines itself through its silencing.[16] Chancy reads Edwidge Danticat's *Breath, Eyes, Memory* as one of the "revolutionary novels" by Haitian women; working against narrow definitions of resistance that perpetuate marginality rather than displacing it, she shows that engaging with the creation and perpetuation of silences is, in and of itself, a form of feminist response.

A number of other literary critics have examined the silencing of women in Danticat's major works on political violence and have shown how breaking the silence – articulating one's pain and trauma – helps to heal the teller of stories. Sharrón Sarthou has argued that in *Breath, Eyes, Memory*, Danticat shows how violence, fear and shame maintain silence about trauma;[17] only the hybridized transnational citizen can "see Haiti clearly" and "speak about Haiti freely", breaking that silence.[18] According to Judith Mishrahi-Barak, the source of suffering in *The Dew Breaker* is untold stories; she argues that silence is the counterpart and the catalyst of the orality that is central to understanding Caribbean women's experiences, pointing to the "hope in the uncovering of silence through oral confession in the written text".[19] "Silence, when inserted in the text," she argues, "heightens the possibility of speech."[20] Similarly, Maria Rice Bellamy associates silence in *The Dew Breaker* with the isolating and dislocating effects of unresolved trauma and speech with resolution, healing and restoration of community.[21]

Danticat's fiction illustrates the ways in which Haitian women are silenced by violence of all types – economic, physical and sexual. In an interview with Myriam Chancy, the author describes the forced silence that poor people like Amabelle, the protagonist of *The Farming of Bones*, must maintain in order to stay employed, to survive. "When people are poor," explains Danticat, "or when they serve other people, or when they can't read and write, they are often treated as if they are invisible, as if they have no interior life. . . .

People assume that she does not have an interior life, but she does; that she does not have laughter, love, sex, but she does."²² This economically imposed, hunger-driven "survival silence" also appears in *Breath, Eyes, Memory* and *The Dew Breaker*, in the nursing-home workers, janitors and waitresses who cannot afford to speak out about their traumatic past or their economically exploitative present. In short, Danticat's writing wrestles with the ways in which political violence and economic violence perpetuate each other, seeking to disentangle what that vicious cycle means for Caribbean women and to understand the long-term effects of silence on them at home and in diaspora.

WRITING AS TESTIMONY

Edwidge Danticat's novels seem to bear witness, in part, to her own experiences with trauma and silence. Danticat was born in 1969 to a working-class family in the Bel Air neighbourhood of Port-au-Prince, Haiti. In order to escape the repressive regimes of François and Jean-Claude Duvalier (1957–71 and 1971–86, respectively), her parents left Haiti for New York City in the early 1970s. Young Edwidge stayed on in Port-au-Prince for a number of years, living most of the year with her uncle Joseph, a Protestant minister, and his wife and spending the summer months with her *moun andeyò*²³ extended family in the mountains near Léogâne.²⁴ Even as a child in Haiti, Danticat heard the fear that permeated adult life, no matter how her family might have tried to hide it from her; she saw neighbours arrested and acquaintances disappeared, for the omnipresent political violence in Haiti could explode onto anyone, including women. In 1981 she went to live with her parents on Flatbush Avenue in Brooklyn, a move that would define her life and her work. The Haitian community she found there had its own causes for fear: irregular minimum-wage work; immigration raids; the constant pressure to provide for family, both in the United States and back in Haiti; and prejudice and persecution stemming from state and public reactions to the so-called "boat people" and the beginning of the AIDS crisis.

Danticat has spent her life working to break the silence impressed upon her in her youth. She has told her stories and shared her ideas in many popular venues, writing for publications such as *Seventeen, Essence* and the *New*

Yorker and appearing on National Public Radio and CNN. Indeed, journalists often treat Danticat as something of a default spokesperson for Haiti in the United States. She has been rewarded for her storytelling labours, winning the American Book Award (1999, for *The Farming of Bones*), a MacArthur "Genius Grant" (2009) and, most recently, the Neustadt International Prize for Literature (2018, for her entire *oeuvre*). She has produced children's books, travel writing, essays, editorials, films, translations, novels and even a few poems. Danticat is perhaps best known, however, for her fiction in a hybrid novel–short story collection form, including *Krik? Krak!* (1996), *The Dew Breaker* (2004), *Claire of the Sea Light* (2013) and *Everything Inside* (2019).

The terms critics use to describe Danticat's fiction suggest that it presents an individual, personal, still untold reality that, once uttered, has the potential to set in motion the wheels of justice. They note her "concern for historical and social *truth*" and her work's "quest for *truth*". They refer to her work's ability to "bear *witness*" for the voiceless as well as its "personalized, *testimonial* intimacy".[25] Danticat's *oeuvre* and activism are thus characterized by the imperative to break the silence, allowing individual testimony to be entered into the record. She explains, "On some level, we [writers] are filling in the gap, especially in some of the historical works, in historical novels, you feel like you're plugging in a hole. . . . The silences of history and even those ordinary moments during daily life, how people lived through that, interest me very much."[26] Danticat understands that poor people's near invisibility in life risks becoming complete oblivion in death. For them, fiction can intervene in particularly meaningful ways. "No one really dies as long as someone remembers," writes Danticat, "someone who will acknowledge that this person had in spite of everything been here."[27]

Danticat sees her own writing as growing out of two distinct but overlapping literary lineages. First she belongs to a line of Afro-Caribbean diasporic "kitchen poets": black immigrant women who use words as weapons to combat their triple invisibility.[28] Mirroring Pineau's attachment to the tales told by her grandmother Julia, Danticat names the "storytellers of my childhood" – "women like the ones Paule Marshall called kitchen poets" – as her best writing teachers. "They taught me that no story is mine alone," explains the author, "that a story lives and breathes and grows only when it is shared."[29] Second, Danticat sees herself as an eminently Haitian writer, part of a tradition of marvellous realism that captures the Haitian spirit and worldview by using indigenous forms of expression.[30] Just as Pineau writes herself back into the Guadeloupean Back Home, Danticat writes herself back into the Haitian homeland and its literary traditions – and, at the same time, redefines both to include the diaspora.[31] In her own gendered twist on Haitian marvellous realism, Danticat uses food as a culturally relevant self-determined code that allows her to engage with the concrete problems of everyday Haitian people, with the real and the socially relevant.[32] Writes Lyonel Trouillot, "There is another thing I read in Danticat's work; that is, the way she favors goodness. I know the word has a naïve, innocent connotation, but I can think of no other."[33] In this way Danticat is like her literary ancestor Jacques Stephen Alexis, for both pursue the nearly untranslatable *belle amour humaine* – literally "beautiful human love": a deep humanism and appreciation for the best of human qualities, an abiding solidarity with all people and peoples, and a profound optimism and belief in art's power to change the world for the better.[34]

In numerous essays and interviews, Danticat has emphasized the symbolic value of food, which serves to identify us – with family, with nation, with class. She insists, "We're nostalgic about food because it's really our most immediate, our most primary, most necessary connection to home, and every meal is a reminder that we're not home."[35] Like Pineau, Danticat recognizes that immigrants (including, and especially, economic and political refugees) seek out the foods they used to eat – the everyday staples of Back Home – in order to preserve cultural memory across time and space. The author describes the small victory of finding a good plantain in New York City: "Even though they are never quite as fibrous or as ripe as the ones I remember from my childhood in Haiti, I am always very grateful to find them because somehow it feels as if they've travelled on an enormous journey across time, space and borders to find me. . . . And they stick not only to your ribs and heart, but to your deepest memories as well."[36] Danticat also notes that in Haiti (as elsewhere), food both strengthens and communicates class identity. As a child, she recalls, she and her siblings were seen as "cornmeal eaters" by their more privileged cousins; they were taught to hide any signs of want, never showing up somewhere too hungry, for "you must not seem too famished, too desperate, too *empty*" when your hosts feed you.[37] Food is not simply material but also social, cultural and emotional: "It's not just nutrition," insists the author, "it's status; it's really a truth."[38]

In Danticat's essays, food's marvellous qualities encode Haitian folk culture, history and worldview(s). Salt wards off shock, strengthening one in the face of adversity;[39] it liberates zombies from their living death and is "the source of all forceful beginnings and the source of all freedom".[40] Haitian coffee is a "magic elixir, to help us remember and forget", a potion that can "instantly return us home".[41] Food is consolation, social and spiritual connection, life itself. Reflecting on her father's last days, the author recalls the profound moment when the dying man insisted that she share his bowl of rice. "For nearly a year," she observes, "my mother, my brothers, and I had constantly brought him food yet had rarely eaten with him. Somehow it hadn't occurred to us that he missed sharing a table or a dish, passing a spice or a spoon. But he did."[42] Eating alone is isolating, discouraging, necessarily unsatisfying; eating together is sacred fulfilment, something akin to communion.

Given these expressed beliefs about the importance of food, it is no surprise that food imagery permeates Danticat's fiction. In particular, from the earliest days of her writing career the author has used food to illustrate the consequences of political violence for women and girls. In her 1991 poem "Sawfish Soup", written when she was just twenty-two years old, a Tonton Macoute mistakes the narrator's father for someone else and shoots him dead in the street. The dead man's dinner stands untouched, a silent witness to the disruptive, paralysing power of Duvalier's ruthless regime. In the final lines of the poem, the narrator's mother emphasizes the senselessness of carrying on with the quotidian in the midst of such brutality:

> she said when someone is
> killed in the corner
> of a street of Haiti
> how can you discard his
> sawfish soup when
> you still don't have
> enough strength to go
> and stand over his
> corpse and steal him
> out of the street.

The bowl of soup is a stubborn reminder of the absent man, who will not be truly dead until he is forgotten. The soup thus resists History's amnesia as well as its statistics, its tendency to flatten and aggregate. There is individual humanity in this bowl of soup. Like Pineau (and Condé, as we will see in chapter 5), Danticat renounces the abstract, the ideological. Instead she focuses on the daily struggles of ordinary people to show the concrete connections between the personal and the political.[43] Through those connections, individual stories of violence and oppression become histories.[44]

In *The Farming of Bones* (1998), *Breath, Eyes, Memory* (1994) and *The Dew Breaker* (2004), food fills the silences around political violence; it is a parallel code that fleshes out the official history that subtends the novels. Sugar positions Haitian political and economic violence as cyclical, self-reinforcing and self-perpetuating, contextualizing that violence within Caribbean history and representing it as both endemic to the region and part of larger global structures of inequality. Sugar roots this violence in the plantation space, in slavery and in the inherent cruelty of global capitalism. Force-feeding is a recurrent metaphor, condensing women's fight to control their own lives, bodies and stories, exemplifying the ways in which women's voices are pushed down, stifled in their throats. Meanwhile, the shared meal is how women re-member community, resist atomization and catalyse healing.

THE PRICE OF SUGAR

In a 2014 editorial, Edwidge Danticat quotes one of *Candide*'s best-known scenes, in which Voltaire's eponymous protagonist meets an enslaved African whose right hand and left leg are missing. The man explains that he lost the hand to the sugar mill in an accident and that his leg was cut off for attempting to run away. This, he points out, is "the price at which you eat sugar in Europe". But, as Danticat points out, this scene of extreme exploitation is not unrelated to conditions for today's labourers: "We still eat sugar at a similar price. And not just in Europe, but all over the world."[45] Violent exploitation in the name of sugar still occurs, enabled by Dominican policies, and other countries look away. Under Dominican law, Haitian migrant workers cannot organize or defend themselves, for fear of deportation or judicial rulings such as the 2013 constitutional court decision that, for several months, rendered more than two hundred thousand Dominican-born people of Haitian descent stateless. Meanwhile, despite the reports of child labour, forced labour and inhumane living conditions, the United States remains the Dominican Republic's largest sugar partner.[46] This is the background to Danticat's repeated use of the sugarcane trope to represent violence against Caribbean women. Situated at the intersection of racial and class domination, of internal abuses and globalized systems of exploitation, of historical patterns and present-day concerns, of economic and political imperialism, sugar cane is a potent symbol of transgenerational trauma in the Caribbean.

Edwidge Danticat's 1998 work of historical fiction, *The Farming of Bones*, depicts the dysfunctional "family" of social classes and ethnic groups that live together in the 1930s Dominican Republic, just across the river from Haiti. The novel's climax is the so-called Parsley Massacre of 1937, during which fascist dictator General Rafael Trujillo's army murdered twelve thousand Haitians living on Dominican soil. The novel's protagonist, the Haitian migrant worker Amabelle, is a witness to these violent, traumatic events, her memory and narrative the only monument to the thousands who died leaving little or no trace. In *The Farming of Bones*, sugar, emblematic of extractive monocultural agriculture and globalized food production, epitomizes systems and cycles of interlocking economic and political violence born of colonialism, which were thriving in the 1930s and are still in full swing today.

The Farming of Bones opens with Amabelle describing her lover, the Haitian migrant worker Sebastien Onius, whose body is deeply marked by his work in sugar production. "The cane stalks have ripped apart most of the skin on his shiny black face, leaving him with crisscrossed trails of furrowed scars"; his arms "are steel, hardened by four years of sugarcane harvests"; "his palms have lost their life-lines to the machetes that cut the cane".[47] She senses the cane through his body: "his callused palms nip and chafe my skin" (2); his sweat "is as thick as sugarcane juice when he's worked too much" (3). At night "he was bothered by the heavy smell of cane that was always with him", and in the morning "he begrudged the sound of the cane being cut because it reminded him of the breaking of dry chicken bones" (174). The sugar cane overwhelms the senses, drowning out any external realities.

Later, a scene in the Haitian cane workers' encampment shows that

Sebastien's scars are the norm for those who endure the life of the cane. "Among the oldest women, one was missing an ear. Two had lost fingers. One had her right cheekbone cracked in half, the result of a runaway machete in the fields" (61). Abandoned by their former employers because they are "too sick, too weak, or too crippled" to work as domestic servants, cut cane or return home, the old women must depend on the (also desperately poor) cane workers to supplement the wild roots they dig up for sustenance (61). The cane workers' bodies emblematize the inhumanity and unsustainability of sugar production.

In this border town, everyone with eyes to see knows the price of sugar. Father Romain, the Haitian priest who ministers to the miserable migrant workers, wonders if the town's founders felt any sense of irony when they named it Alegría (joy). He muses, "Perhaps there had been joy for them in finding that sugar could be made from blood" (271). Kongo, an elder among the workers, knows that he and his companions are more zombies than human. "In sugar land," remarks the seasoned cane cutter, "a shack's for sleeping, not for living. Living is only work, the fields" (107). Sebastien's sister Mimi dreams of escape from this neo-slavery in which hunger has replaced the chains and whips of the past. "If they let us go," she says, "at least we'd have a few days of freedom before dying from hunger" (64). Sebastien longs to work in "anything but the cane" and considers his friend Joël, who died, "lucky to no longer be a part of the cane life, travay tè pou zo, the farming of bones" (55). The cane workers, who have left behind their homes in the Haitian countryside that offered subsistence through farming, are reduced to this *travay tè pou zo* – a phrase Danticat took from an interview with a migrant worker in the late 1990s. "He said it's like working for nothing," she reports, "digging your own grave, working the land to grow bones."[48] Like many of their enslaved African ancestors, Mimi and Sebastien prefer the thought of death to the idea of spending the rest of their time on earth as the working dead.[49]

Meanwhile, the Dominican planters, the *gente de primera*[50] who exploit the Haitian cane workers, inhabit a world that is differently (though equally) marked by sugar. Theirs is the sweet life of *cafecitos* poured into elegant, fragile cups quite literally served up on a silver platter (19) – thin china that might as well be filled with the blood of the cane workers on whom the *gente de primera* feed. The *cafecito* operates as a sign of respectability on the symbolic level as the Dominican planters imitate the consumption habits of the Spaniards with whom they identify. However, this typically very sweet *cafecito* is made up of two physically addictive substances, coffee and sugar.[51] The controlling planter class is itself enslaved – to its taste for luxury and *cafecitos*, and to the lust for endless accumulation that characterizes global capitalism as it has manifested itself in the Caribbean since slavery times.

Sugar's status as an enduring symbol of extreme economic exploitation is confirmed by a mysterious female figure, the "sugar woman", who visits Amabelle repeatedly in her dreams:

> I dream of the sugar woman. Again.
>
> As always, she is dressed in a long, three-tiered ruffled gown inflated like a balloon. Around her face, she wears a shiny silver muzzle, and on her neck there is a collar with a clasped lock dangling from it.
>
> The sugar woman grabs her skirt and skips back and forth around my room. She seems to be dancing a kalanda in a very fast spin, locks arms with the air, pretends to kiss someone much taller than herself. As she swings and shuffles, the chains on her ankles cymbal a rattled melody. She hops to the sound of the jingle of the chains, which with her twists grow louder and louder. (132)

Like Maryse Condé's culinary dreams in *Of Morsels and Marvels* (as we will see in chapter 5), Amabelle's dream can be deciphered only by using the codebook of history. The sugar woman dances the kalanda, embodying the memory of her African ancestors, but the dance is equally recognizable to Amabelle in the novel's present day; the kalanda thus evokes the reality of historical continuities, communicated through the ages even when they have been silenced in official accounts. The dream woman's dress places her in the distant colonial past and the muzzle signals her identity as a voiceless enslaved woman,[52] but the ghostly sugar woman refuses the silencing of both muzzle and death. She "rattles the chains of slavery"[53] louder and louder, and the sound resonates down through History to fill her descendant's unconscious.

When Amabelle asks the figure why she is there, she responds, "I am the sugar woman. You, my eternity" (133). The sugar woman – nameless, faceless, her identity collapsed into the sugar cane – is both a single forgotten woman (Amabelle's unknown ancestor) and all the silenced Haitian women who came before. Amabelle must carry her (and them) out of the cane and into eternity. History is remembered and conveyed not in a history book but through a story told in a dream. And just as Amabelle learns the sugar woman's history through her dream, the reader sees the history of Amabelle and the other Haitian migrant workers through Danticat's "dream" – her fiction. Explained Danticat in an interview, "The book to me is a memorial, and when people read it and are touched by it then their hearts become one more memorial to not only the past pain but also to the living pain we're in. And since there are no actual memorials to those who died in the 1937 massacre, we must have these living memorials in our hearts."[54] No one really dies until they are forgotten. Because Danticat's international readership has learned about Amabelle and the other migrant workers, they – *we* – have a duty to them and to History.

While *The Farming of Bones* focuses on physical violence as a tool of economic and political domination during the *Trujillato* (Trujillo era) in the Dominican Republic, *Breath, Eyes, Memory* moves across the border to Haiti in the 1960s, depicting the long-term effects of sexual violence used for political control under the dictatorship of François "Papa Doc" Duvalier. At the novel's opening, the protagonist of *Breath, Eyes, Memory*, Sophie Caco, lives with her maternal aunt Atie in Haiti; her mother, Martine, has gone ahead to New York City to escape the economic hardship and political violence that dominate daily life under "Papa Doc". When Sophie finally joins her mother in New York, she finds an overworked and exhausted Martine, a chronic insomniac and nervous wreck who relives the trauma of her rape nearly every night in her dreams.

Sophie discovers that she is the product of her mother's rape at the hands of a Tonton Macoute in the cane fields outside her village. Yet despite Martine's experience of sexual trauma, she herself sexually traumatizes Sophie as a means of control, "testing" her virginity regularly in a violation passed down through the maternal line – Martine's mother, Ifè, had done the same to her. Sophie's trauma at her mother's hands drives her to bulimia,[55] self-mutilation and sexual dysfunction, while Martine's past traumas drive her to paranoid delusions and eventually suicide. After the birth of her own daughter, Sophie, determined to end the cycle of familial suffering, returns to her grandmother's house in Haiti to confront her past. In *Breath, Eyes, Memory* the cycle of suffering caused by sexual violence is symbolized by the fields of sugar cane, the site of Martine's rape and the *raison d'être* behind the Duvalier regime's violent grip on the country. However, in keeping with Sophie's attempts to break that cycle in hopes of a better life for her daughter, the cane fields in the novel also come to figure revolt.

Sugar cane is the backdrop to virtually all the parts of *Breath, Eyes, Memory* that take place in Haiti. The cane is inescapable, spanning the full human life cycle. Martine and Atie "practically lived" in the cane fields as children, their father died there,[56] and it occupies every corner of the Haitian countryside: "all trains run between sugar mills and plantation towns" (77). And the cane is the site of an equally ubiquitous toxic masculinity and violence against women, which are rooted in Haitian folk culture and deployed as a gendered form of Duvalierian political intimidation and control. Every time Sophie walks near the cane fields, she can hear the (male) workers singing about dangerous women with marvellous qualities. The subject of these folk songs progresses from a terrifyingly untamed murderess to an easily broken *soucougnant* to an auto-domesticated mermaid, producing a narrative arc about how strong, magical women can be tamed and eventually controlled by men. The songs manifest Haitian culture's deeply rooted misogyny, which, like the sugar cane, is everywhere you look:

> We could hear the *konbit* song from the cane fields. The men were singing about a *platonnade*, a loose woman who made love to the men she met by a stream and then drowned them in the water. (118)

> I reached the cane fields. The men were singing about a woman who flew without her skin at night, and when she came back home, she found her skin peppered and could not put it back on. Her husband had done it to teach her a lesson. He ended up killing her. (150)

> In the cane fields, the men were singing about a mermaid who married a fisherman and became human. (229)

In Danticat's version of the first song, female sexual freedom, autonomy and strength are a triple threat. The dangerously independent "loose woman" plays the active role and the men she encounters are mere passive objects, victims of her desire and power. She chooses to make love to the men, not the other way around. And when she murders them, she does not use the weapons of the "weaker sex", such as poison or smothering in their sleep, nor does she trick or lead them to drown, making them victims of their own poor judgement. No, in this folk-song the mysteriously strong murderess actively drowns them; she alone bears the blame. In the author's version of the second song, another marvellously free woman appears. Presumably a dutiful wife during the day, this woman sheds her skin to fly free at night. She is a *soucougnant*, a sort of female vampire that is a well-known figure in Caribbean folklore. Once again the liberated woman is portrayed as a threat, and the man who restrains her (although it means her death) is the hero. In the final song, that freest of mystical female figures, the mermaid, willingly submits herself. It is only by renouncing her power and her independence that she becomes "human"; anything else in a woman is supernaturally disconcerting, threatening, even monstrous.

Each of the songs mirrors how homegrown forms of misogyny manifest themselves through the Caco women. Ifè has internalized the idea that female sexuality and independence are a danger to society. She treats her daughters like potential murderesses, testing them when they are young and judging their every move well into adulthood.[57] Martine, like the second woman, has been broken and is finally killed by a man's desire to dominate and humiliate her. She never recovers from the rape that took place deep in the cane fields where these songs are sung. The novel's central question is whether or not the third song will be about Sophie. Will she, like the mermaid, sacrifice her independence in order to be a good Haitian girl, her mother's daughter? Like Lakshmi Persaud's Sastra (see chapter 3) and Shani Mootoo's Viveka (see chapter 4), if Sophie insists on living her female sexuality on her own terms, she faces exclusion from her ethnic identity.

Alongside these images of rebellious women falls the shadow of another, more sinister folkloric figure: Tonton Macoute. In addition to the Caco women's sexually abusive virginity testing, Sophie suffers from another form of transgenerational sexual trauma, stemming from her mother's rape by a Tonton Macoute.[58] Tonton Macoute, literally "Uncle Gunnysack", is a folk-tale character who snatches children, carries them off in a sack and eats them alive. Beginning in the late 1950s, Haitians began using the term for

Duvalier's masked secret police.[59] When Martine tries to tell the story of her violation by the faceless monster, the details refuse to be said; she can only say that it happened in the cane. "A man grabbed me from the side of the road," she relates, "pulled me into a cane field, and put you in my body" (61). "He dragged her into the cane fields", says Sophie, "and pinned her down on the ground" (139). Sophie's therapist believes the cane to be an important component of her healing. When Sophie returns from her first trip to Haiti, during which she attempted to confront her grandmother Ifè about the virginity testing, the therapist wants to know if Sophie also confronted the other source of the Caco women's pain – her mother's rape. "In the thick of the cane field," asks the therapist, "did you go to the spot?" "I ran past it", admits Sophie (210). The silence remains, for Sophie is still too afraid to speak the gendered political violence of Duvalierian Haiti.

Worn down by years of insomnia and flashbacks, Martine at last succumbs completely to trauma-induced psychosis. Triggered by a second pregnancy that reminds her too much of the Tonton Macoute attack that led to her first pregnancy, her delusions drive her to suicide. When Sophie returns to Haiti for her mother's funeral, she realizes that she will not be able to bury the pain along with Martine's body; in order to heal, she will have to confront and work through her anger about the political violence that destroyed her mother and so many others. And for Sophie, that political violence – embodied by the faceless rapist, the Tonton Macoute – lives in the cane:

> I ran through the field, attacking the cane. I took off my shoes and began to beat a cane stalk. I pounded it until it began to lean over. I pushed over the cane stalk. It snapped back, striking my shoulder. I pulled at it, yanking it from the ground. My palm was bleeding.
>
> The cane cutters stared at me as though I was possessed. The funeral crowd was now standing between the stalks, watching me beat and pound the cane.
> (233)

In this scene (which is echoed in Shani Mootoo's *Valmiki's Daughter*, examined in chapter 4), the cane fields are a symbol both of cyclical oppression in the Caribbean and of freeing oneself. It is possible to end the cycle of abuse, to beat and break the cane as Sophie does here, or, as in *Valmiki's Daughter*, to burn it down to the ground. In Sophie's case the cane fights back, bruising her shoulder and cutting her hand, but she does not stop until she has pulled it up by its roots. As she does so, the cane cutters – that chorus of men who sing of dangerously independent women with marvellous qualities – look at Sophie as if she has some magic power of her own. The funeral crowd witnesses Sophie breaking her own and her family's silence (as do the readers of *Breath, Eyes, Memory*), and their witnessing validates the Caco women's experiences of political violence, transforming intimate individual events into History. It matters that they see – that *we* see – for the witnessing is part of the healing.

The other women of Sophie's family, Ifè and Atie, now break their own silence, refusing to continue their complicity in the family trauma. Holding back the priest who might try to silence Sophie's rage, Ifè raises her voice to acknowledge and encourage her granddaughter's freedom struggle: "From where she was standing, my grandmother shouted like the women from the marketplace, 'Ou libere?' Are you free? Tante Atie echoed her cry, her voice quivering with her sobs. 'Ou libere!'" By shouting out the Creole interrogative *"Ou libere?"* (traditionally called to a woman who has dropped a heavy load),[60] Ifè positions her granddaughter in a long line of Haitian women, reassuring her that once she has let go of her burden, she will still belong. Meanwhile, Atie's exclamatory *"Ou libere!"* confirms Sophie's freedom. It also suggests that Sophie's courage in speaking has freed the other women for whom she speaks – Atie herself, Ifè, the ghost of Martine, and the generations of women before them who had no voice of their own.[61]

FORCE-FEEDING

In a 2019 essay titled "This Is My Body: Of Food and Freedom", Edwidge Danticat highlights the ways in which political detainees, from HIV-positive Haitian "boat people" in the 1990s to political prisoners at Guantánamo in the early 2000s to immigrant detainees all over the United States as recently as 2019, have used refusal of food – the hunger strike – to "voice" their dissent. Using Guantánamo prisoner Lakhdar Boudediene's words, Danticat identifies the body itself as the final refuge of resistance:

> I stopped eating not because I wanted to die, but because I could not keep living without doing something to protest the injustice of my treatment. They

could lock me up for no reason and with no chance to argue my innocence. They could torture me, deprive me of sleep, put me in an isolation cell, control every single aspect of my life. But they couldn't make me swallow their food.[62]

In response to this self-abnegating form of protest, Danticat writes, the US government has embraced force-feeding as a means of suppression and political control, first at Guantánamo nearly a decade ago, and most recently in immigration detention centres across the United States, on the orders of a federal judge. For Danticat, force-feeding represents the most extreme form of silencing, an invasion of personal space and bodily integrity that compounds trauma through invalidation and erasure.

The Farming of Bones hinges around the so-called Parsley Massacre of 1937, during which Trujillo's army used the Spanish word for parsley, *perejil*, as a shibboleth to sort out the Haitian migrant workers, whose Creole tongues could not properly roll the Spanish *r* and whose throats could not produce the Spanish *jota*. Those who could not pronounce *perejil* were beaten and killed. The book opens with two inscriptions. First, the author includes the Bible verses Judges 12:4–6, in which forty-two thousand Ephraimites who cannot pronounce *shibboleth* correctly are seized and killed by the Gileadites at the Jordan River. This epigraph locates the 1937 tragedy at the Haitian-Dominican border within a broader history of exclusion and mass bloodshed between closely related tribes, characterizing political violence as part and parcel of the human condition. Second, the author inscribes a fictional dedication by Amabelle Désir, the novel's narrator, who dedicates her story to a Vodou *lwa*: "In confidence to you, Metrès Dlo, Mother of the Rivers."[63] This second reference emphasizes the specificity of the Haitian migrant workers' experience and worldview. "*Tout moun se moun*", declares the biblical allusion; "*men tout moun pa menm*" recalls the dedication to the *lwa*.[64] Taken together, the two epigraphs root *The Farming of Bones* in the tradition of Haitian marvellous realism, which seeks to reflect the universal through the specificity of Haiti.

Prior to the massacre, Amabelle, the young Haitian house-servant who is the novel's protagonist, comments on the physical, social and symbolic importance of parsley to the Haitian migrant worker community in the Dominican Republic:

We used pèsi, perejil, parsley, the damp summer morningness of it, the mingled sprigs, bristly and coarse, gentle and docile all at once, tasteless and bitter when chewed, a sweetened wind inside the mouth, the leaves a different taste than the stalk, all this we savored for our food, our teas, our baths, to cleanse our insides as well as our outsides of old aches and griefs, to shed a passing year's dust as a new one dawned, to wash a new infant's hair for the first time and – along with boiled orange leaves – a corpse's remains one final time. (62)

Amabelle's description of parsley, which represents the migrant workers' worldview, contrasts sharply with the novel's images of sugar cane, which emblematize the Dominican planter class's mindset. While sugar stands for parasitic global economic systems based on environmental degradation and dehumanizing oppression, parsley represents symbiotic subsistence practices in which the land and the human being can sustainably coexist. Amabelle's description begins with the Haitian Kreyòl *pèsi*, emphasizing the migrant workers' right to cultural self-determination, to the local and to the untranslatable. The phrase "damp summer morningness", meanwhile, defines time according to the earth's revolutions and rotation, underscoring that everything living obeys natural laws and revolves around the sun, not around the *zafra* (sugarcane harvest). Sugar, as we have seen, constitutes a greed-driven destructive cycle of violence, while parsley represents a sustainable natural cycle of birth and death. Whereas sugar rots the teeth and slowly poisons the body, parsley cleans the mouth and heals the insides. Labour in the sharp, brittle sugarcane maims and scars the body; parsley soothes and gently scrubs human skin from the cradle to the grave. A counterpoint to the Dominican planters' parasitic, profit-centred dominion of land and people, this portrait of Haitian folk foodways, another example of Danticat's marvellous realism, presents a humane, nature-inspired way of relating to living things and to community.

It is therefore doubly terrible that it is the near-sacred *pèsi* that separates the Haitians from the Dominicans. This ostensibly linguistic and cultural test, which supposedly separates Haitians from Dominicans, is in fact simply a cover for racism, xenophobia and the desire to violently enact power. In many cases the test is not even applied; the Dominicans simply attack all dark-skinned people who might be Haitian, force-feeding them *perejil*, choking them with it, giving them no chance to articulate the Spanish word that might save them. The dark-skinned Amabelle, who has lived among Dominicans since she was a small child and speaks native-like Spanish, is no more able to save herself than the recent arrivals:

> It was the kind of thing that if you were startled in the night, you might forget, but with all my senses calm, I could have said it. But I didn't get my chance. Our jaws were pried open and parsley stuffed into our mouths. My eyes watering, I chewed and swallowed as quickly as I could, but not nearly as fast as they were forcing the handfuls into my mouth. . . . I told myself that eating the parsley would keep me alive. (193–94)

As they force-feed Amabelle parsley, Trujillo's followers effectively silence her. The harsh invasion of Amabelle's body echoes rape, the form of political violence deployed against women that, as Danticat shows in *Breath, Eyes, Memory*, produces a profound and fearful silence that can be healed only by speaking one's story. However, speech is not available to Amabelle; she cannot speak the word that could save her. For her, a feminist response means chewing and swallowing – simply surviving. Where outright resistance is impossible, living to see another day will mean the chance to bear witness to what has happened to her and to others.

During their flight across the river to Haiti, Amabelle silences another Haitian woman, Odette, covering her mouth so that her half-drowning coughs do not give away the group's location to the murderous Dominican border patrol. But this silencing kills Odette. When the group of beleaguered Haitians drags her to shore, she spits up a chest full of water and then utters her last word:

> With her parting breath, she mouthed in Kreyòl "pèsi", not calmly and slowly as if she were asking for it at a roadside garden or open market, not questioning as if demanding of the face of Heaven the greater meaning of senseless acts, no effort to say "perejil" as if pleading for her life. . . . The Generalissimo's mind was surely as dark as death, but if he had heard Odette's "pèsi", it might have startled him, not the tears and supplications he would have expected, no shriek from unbound fear, but a provocation, a challenge, a dare. To the devil with your world, your grass, your wind, your water, your air, your words. You ask for perejil, I give you more. (203)

For the dying Odette, a feminist response means refusing to be silenced. The narrator draws out the full significance of Odette's choice by enumerating a number of non-viable linguistic functions: she is neither describing nor wondering nor begging nor crying out in terror. Instead, Odette is forcefully, deliberately asserting her ethnic identity and her dignity. Though the world and everything in it may belong to Trujillo, though he may even take her life, he will never take her identity as a Haitian woman. In this way Odette descends from the sugar woman, inheriting from her both her oppression and her resistance.

In *Breath, Eyes, Memory,* as in *The Farming of Bones,* force-feeding reflects the silencing of women's and girls' voices. Food and cooking bind Sophie to her grandmother, her aunt and then her mother, keeping her from individuating herself from them;[65] food stuffs her mouth full, preventing her from speaking of pain or giving voice to mutinous questions.[66] Even as a young girl in Haiti, Sophie eats to suppress emotion and avert difficult conversations. After learning that she is to join her biological mother, Martine, in New York – leaving behind Aunt Atie, who has been her surrogate mother most of her life – "good girl" Sophie dutifully downs her rice pudding to avoid discussing or even feeling her painful emotions: "I did not feel like eating, but if I did not eat, we would have had to sit and stare at one another, and sooner or later, one of us would have had to say something" (18). Later, on her last day with Atie, Sophie's aunt tutors her in the art of denying one's feelings:

> We sat across the table from one another and drank without saying anything. I tried to hide my tears behind the tea cup.
> "No crying," she said. "We are going to be strong as mountains."
> The tears had already fallen and hit my cheeks.
> "Mountains," she said, prodding my ribs with her elbow. (27)

In this case Sophie quite literally hides behind food, using it to veil the negative emotions she is forbidden to express. And Tante Atie approves of this, equating the normal range of emotions with weakness; she reinforces the fact that Sophie should not trust or acknowledge her own feelings, and that she should hold her tongue by any means necessary.

When she arrives in New York, Sophie is overwhelmed with feelings of loss, disruption and rejection. The first time she goes to a Haitian restaurant with her mother and her mother's new boyfriend, Marc, Sophie is careful to be agreeable, pleasant . . . *silent.*

> I shook my head yes, as though I was really very interested. I ate like I had been on a hunger strike, filling myself with the coconut milk they served us in real green coconuts. . . . I tried to stuff myself and keep quiet, pretending that I couldn't even see them. My mother now had two lives: Marc belonged to her present life, I was a living memory from the past. (56)

In this scene, it becomes clear that Sophie has now internalized the work of policing her thoughts, emotions and, above all, words, and that she has learned to use food both to silence herself and to mask the act of silencing, so that others need not feel the discomfort of acknowledging that emotions are being suppressed. Indeed, Sophie has by now nearly perfected the art of self-erasure. She sees that her real, current self will not fit into her mother's new life; labelling Marc "present life" and herself "living memory from the past", Sophie seems instinctively aware that her mother is unable to integrate the two. To force herself to fit into the small space Martine will allot to her, Sophie is willing to deny herself, to see herself solely in terms of her mother's experiences. She abdicates the right to her own experiences, emotional and otherwise.[67]

Sophie's reliance on food to suppress and silence her negative emotions intensifies after Martine traumatizes her by "testing" her virginity. When the young woman can no longer bear the sexual abuse, she puts an end to the weekly assaults by removing her own hymen with the pestle her mother uses to grind Haitian spices. Sophie has finally begun to assert her right to her own needs, emotions and bodily autonomy, to reclaim her selfhood rather than ceding it to her mother. She later tells her husband about the act. "Joseph could never understand why I had done something so horrible to myself", muses Sophie. "I could not explain to him that it was like breaking manacles, an act of freedom" (130). Although Sophie's self-mutilation might not have looked like a feminist response to her husband, it was in fact a subversive choice, an act of self-assertion – and one of the few at her disposal. As we will see time and again with the female characters examined in this volume, it is not *what* women do, but *why.*

Although Sophie's self-harm frees her physically from her mother's testing, it does not free her emotionally and spiritually from the trauma inflicted by the abuse, and she continues to use food to manage her emotions. After Sophie marries, she develops bulimia as a response to her unvoiced pain. When she tries to talk to her mother about her eating disorder, she encounters the same invalidation she experienced with Tante Atie as a child. For Martine, acknowledging Sophie's problems with food would also mean acknowledging Sophie's right to her own emotions, which she has repressed for so long. "Why would you do that?" her mother asks. "I have never heard of a Haitian woman getting anything like that. . . . You have become very American" (179). Female dissent is doubly forbidden in exile, where questioning home "tradition" – even including sexist, abusive practices – means you have forgotten where you came from. "What do you want for dinner?" Martine asks dismissively. "We'll have no more of that bulimia. I'll cure it with some good food" (182). Rather than hearing out her daughter, Martine piles food on top of the young woman's pain and her voice, shaming and stuffing her into silence.

Sophie's bulimia is a new iteration of the emotional repression and self-erasure she learned as a child, force-feeding herself to remain silent about the current consequences of the sexual trauma she experienced at the hands of her mother. She feels extreme distress during sexual contact with her husband, and she uses food to manage that distress. Rather than help her work through those feelings, her husband, Joseph – like Aunt Atie and Martine – approves of Sophie's attempts to suppress her emotions in aid of his comfort. After one of many one-sided lovemaking sessions, Sophie tries to bury her pain under heaps of food:

> "You were very good," he said.
> "I kept my eyes closed so the tears wouldn't slip out."
> I waited for him to fall asleep, then went to the kitchen. I ate every scrap of the dinner leftovers, then went to the bathroom, locked the door, and purged all the food out of my body. (200)

Even Sophie's loving and supportive husband praises her simulation of a "good girl" with healthy appetites for both food and sex – a simulation that depends on her silence.

Because the transgenerational trauma at the root of her suffering has yet to be truly addressed, the young woman continues using food to push down her pain. However, Sophie's purging is a new development in her journey with food and feelings. Like her previous sexual self-mutilation, her purging may be read as a form of feminist response in a situation where resistance is psychologically impossible, an initial step towards articulating the pain that imprisons her, and thus towards self-liberation, as she violently rejects the food that suppresses her voice. By purging, Sophie symbolically asserts the right to control over her own body, sexuality and narrative. However, as we have seen, true healing for Sophie will not come through food, nor through the rejection of food. It will come by articulating and confronting the harm that was done, by identifying its cyclical and self-perpetuating nature and by consciously and deliberately putting an end to it all before it can be passed on to her own daughter.

It seems that the use of food to manage shame and pain is not only the province of Haitian women or of victims of political sexual violence. The Dew Breaker, who traumatizes women like Martine and, by extension, others like Sophie, gorges himself in order to feel powerful and safe from the weakness and fear he felt as a younger man. This character is the central one in Danticat's 2004 *The Dew Breaker*, a hybrid novel/short story collection that (like *The Farming of Bones* and *Breath, Eyes, Memory*) examines the effect of Haitian political violence on everyday people, especially women, through a combination of history and fiction.

The work opens with the Dew Breaker's daughter, Ka Bienaimé, discovering that her father is not who she had thought he was. He had not been a political prisoner under "Papa Doc" Duvalier's infamously violent regime, as he had always said, but instead had been a prison guard, a Tonton Macoute. "We called them choukèt lawoze",[68] explains Beatrice, a former victim. "They'd break into your house. Mostly it was at night. But often they'd also come before dawn, as the dew was settling on the leaves, and they'd take you away."[69] Using multiple narrators, including the Dew Breaker's direct and indirect victims, his wife and daughter, and finally the Dew Breaker himself, the interwoven stories gradually paint a terrifying picture of life under François Duvalier's authoritarian regime. By alternating between present-day events and a series of flashbacks, the work also shows the aftermath of that violence within the Haitian diaspora in New York City and Miami.

We learn that the titular Dew Breaker, one of the notorious Tontons Macoutes, had become so precisely because he had once been their victim. Like the severely damaged Martine, who passed on to her daughter the sexual trauma inflicted on her by the state, her culture and her own family, the Dew Breaker is part of a seemingly endless cycle of abuse. His entire life was upended by Duvalier's soldiers, who confiscated his peasant family's land because they wanted to build summer homes there; subsequently his father lost his mind and his mother disappeared, leaving him utterly alone at nineteen years old. Therefore, when the Volunteers for National Security militia came rounding up people to make the president's rallies look more impressive, the young man's vulnerability wasn't difficult to exploit.

One day in 1967, as he watches a young boy sharing the small snack he has bought with the Dew Breaker's blood money, the corrupted man is reminded of himself at the time of his recruitment:

> And so he watched the boys suck the marrow out of the fried goat bones until the bones squeaked like whistles and clarinets and he thought of how hungry he'd been after the president's speech, when the crowd was left to find its own way home and when one of the many men in denim who were circling the palace that day had approached him and asked him whether he wanted to join the Miliciens, the Volunteers, what later would be called the Macoutes.[70] (195)

Watching the boy share the meagre spoils of his minor act of collaboration reminds the hardened criminal not only of his own vulnerability but also of his ability to compartmentalize his complicity in violence by sharing (when he feels like it) the spoils of his crimes. From his position of power on the inside, the Dew Breaker has been able to get his father's land back and even to protect his home village; as a Tonton Macoute, he has the power to channel resources and protection where he will, and that fact, he convinces himself, justifies his participation in violence and oppression. The Dew Breaker pities the boy and, by extension, experiences compassion for his own younger self: he sees himself as the erstwhile starved, lonely adolescent who allowed himself to be drawn into a life of state-sponsored crime – an innocent who sold his soul to be free of hunger and powerlessness.

However, the Dew Breaker is no longer hungry or powerless. Now he is powerful, and ever craving more power. Overfed by potential victims in hopes of suffocating his murderous rage, the Dew Breaker overeats in order to push down the feelings of impotence and humiliation that linger despite his present dominance:

> Restaurants fed him an enormous amount of food, which he ate eagerly several times a day because he enjoyed watching his body grow wider and meatier just as his sense of power did. . . . Bourgeois married women slept with him on the cash-filled mattress on his bedroom floor. . . . And the people who had looked down on him and his family in the past, well, now they came all the way from Léogâne to ask him for favors. (196)

Gorging himself is thus part of a larger power trip, a calculated revenge on the exploitative mulatto business-owning class. As he assimilates the source of their influence – control over food – into his own body, the Dew Breaker seeks to neutralize their economic power over him. By treating their wives, symbols of bourgeois respectability, as prostitutes through forced or coerced sex on a mattress full of money on the floor, he negates their symbolic dominance, reducing it to a question of transferrable capital that he can take by force. When these formerly dominant members of his community must come to him for help, the Dew Breaker revels in what he wants to see as a total and fully justified reversal of fortunes.[71] In his revenge he becomes what he most hated and feared. When he stuffs his belly and forces himself on women, he dehumanizes not only the bourgeoisie but also himself, reducing himself to a collection of insatiable appetites and desires.[72]

RE-MEMBERING COMMUNITY[73]

Danticat uses sugar to symbolize the plantation system's legacy of extractive monoculture, exploitative labour practices, violence and dehumanization; she also uses the trope of force-feeding to represent the forced silence surrounding those injustices and the repression of that trauma. However, she also offers a corrective: Haiti's other ancestral culinary inheritance, the shared meal, which grows out of the country's traditional sustainable small-scale subsistence agriculture, based on cooperative labour and mutual care. Danticat's female characters repair the damage wrought by sugar and the unequal power dynamics it entails via these collective meals, which re-member the community and its shared narrative of pain and overcoming. In this re-membering, there is communal healing.

In *The Farming of Bones*, a shared meal marks the beginning of Amabelle's long road to healing. Following the massacre, Amabelle flees with Yves, one of the cane workers, back to his ancestral village in rural Haiti. The village is poor, but it is a very different poverty from the grinding desperation of the cane workers' lives in the migrant camps. Danticat's contrasting portraits of village subsistence and cane-life misery illustrate the difference between what Vandana Shiva terms "perceived" poverty and "real material" poverty. Shiva notes that as agricultural workers participate in cash-crop production, they tend to move from perceived to real material poverty as economic growth for the benefit of a minority drains resources away from those who need them the most.[74] Danticat's depiction of Yves's village shows a sustainable rural Haitian way of life, an economy of sharing rather than charity, where villagers feed themselves and each other outside of global food systems.

Upon Yves and Amabelle's arrival, Yves's mother and extended family welcome the pair with open arms and set the welcome table for them:

> Yves' relations from the yard put together and cooked a large meal for him. They fried and stewed all his favorite foods: goat meat and eggplants, watercress in codfish sauce, corn mush, and black beans.
>
> Yves ate everything placed in front of him. Now and again his mother would interrupt his eating to tell a story about how much he had eaten as a boy, not only food and sweets, but also moist dirt from bean plant roots, which he liked to rub against his gums until they bled. (223)
>
> My own mouth was still too bruised for hard foods. A full plate of fried goat meat remained on my lap. Yves' mother walked over to me and asked, "Some soup for you? It won't be too hot or too thick."
>
> She took the full plate from my lap and came back with a small bowl of pumpkin soup. While the others watched, she fed me the soup with a tiny spoon as though I were a sick, bedridden child. (225)

This shared meal re-members Yves's kinship group, drawing the young man back into the fold and adopting the orphaned, severely injured Amabelle as one of their own. Yves's favourite foods tie the narrative to place and folk culture, centring rural Haitian experience and tastes. As the young man eats, his mother reminds him of literal and figurative roots, evoking childhood memories in which her son's body and the Haitian earth became one. Meanwhile, she feeds Amabelle like a child – like her very own child, come home again. Communal meal and community history are intertwined at this welcome table, where new bonds are honoured like old ones. At this meal, each person gets what he or she needs.

In *Breath, Eyes, Memory*, the shared meal is how Haitian women resist the multiple pressures that threaten to atomize their families and their communities: urbanization, migration to the Global North, and political violence.[75] The novel opens in Croiset-des-Rosets, near the capital, where Sophie lives with her aunt Atie in order to attend school. Most of their neighbours are transplants to the city, come to work in textile factories, leaving their ancestral subsistence agricultural way of life behind them in the provinces. Uprooted from their kinship groups and village communities, these migrants do their best to reproduce the *konbit* that cemented relationships back where they came from. Laden with sweet potato pudding (3), plantains and Negro yams, ginger tea and cassava bread (11), these men and women, including the elderly and the very young, come together to share in the bounty of the Haitian earth. As Tante Atie teaches Sophie about the origins of the *konbit*, the oral history of the custom, like the meal itself, binds generations together:

> The way these potlucks started was really a long time ago in the hills. Back then, a whole village would get together and clear a field for planting. The group would take turns clearing each person's land, until all the land in the village was cleared and planted. The women would cook large amounts of food while the men worked. Then at sunset, when the work was done, everyone would gather together and enjoy a feast of eating, dancing, and laughter. (11)

In this new iteration of an old custom, there are no fields to clear or plant, but groups of people who work together at the factory or whose ramshackle huts share a common courtyard organize themselves, reconstituting themselves into communities. In this way they dampen the atomizing effects of urbanization and the dehumanizing impact of manufacturing work. Realigning themselves with the measured time of the passing seasons, they break the spell of the factory's whistle. Despite the disruption of dislocation and relocation, the shared meal asserts cultural continuity and continued attachment to the land.[76]

The potluck also highlights the importance of gender roles in the *konbit* tradition. As we will see again in Lakshmi Persaud's food-focused writing (chapter 3) and Shani Mootoo's culinary fiction (chapter 4), the culinary requirements for "good" girls foreshadow the sexual expectations placed on them. The connection between good girls and cooking appears again when Sophie travels from New York back to her grandmother's village to confront Ifè about the virginity testing; she cooks a meal for Ifè and Atie to show them that she is still a good Haitian girl, that she has not forgotten where she comes from. Sophie easily executes the tasks of cooking, for the motions have been deeply ingrained in her since childhood: "I was surprised how fast it came back. . . . The fragrance of the spices guided my fingers the way no instructions or measurements could" (151). She cooks to reunify the three women across generational and geographic divides. And as she cooks, Sophie remembers that she, the estranged *dyaspora*, is not the first to object to the sexual and culinary demands placed on Haitian women from birth. In fact, her aunt before her had pushed back against the impossible standards for women:

> *Haitian men, they insist that their women are virgins and have their ten fingers.* According to Tante Atie, each finger had a purpose. It was the way she had been taught to prepare herself to become a woman. Mothering, Boiling, Loving, Baking, Nursing, Frying, Healing, Washing, Ironing, Scrubbing. It wasn't her fault, she said. Her ten fingers had been named for her even before she was born. Sometimes, she even wished she had six fingers on each hand so she could have two left for herself. (151)

Although the saying declares that Haitian men insist on female virginity and domestic servitude, in *Breath, Eyes, Memory* it is Haitian *women* who inculcate their daughters with patriarchal thinking and police their daughters' behaviour, both in the bedroom and in the kitchen. It was Ifè who named Atie's fingers before she was born. It was Ifè who taught Atie and Martine that if they did not know how to cook, clean, and care for children, they wouldn't be women at all.

Just as Pineau's Gisèle vows to write herself back into Guadeloupe in *L'exil selon Julia*, Danticat's Sophie aims to cook herself back into Haiti with this shared meal. The authenticity and quality of the Haitian meal Sophie prepares for Ifè and Atie testify to her continued ethnic and cultural belonging and to the filial obedience required by her identity as a Haitian woman. As Valérie Loichot puts it, "By cooking a Haitian meal in Haiti, she regrounds herself in the space and time of her childhood . . . to orders and rhythms of time connected to community and environment."[77] Sophie's aunt and grandmother approve wholeheartedly of the meal: "'Well done', Tante Atie said after her fourth serving of my rice and beans. My grandmother chewed slowly as she gave my daughter her bottle. 'If the wood is well carved', said my grandmother, 'it teaches us about the carpenter. Atie, you taught Sophie well'" (151). While Atie enthusiastically praises Sophie herself for her culinary success, Ifè gives credit elsewhere. Pulling the young woman into place within her maternal line, the old woman emphasizes that no woman belongs to herself alone – she is shaped by all those who came before her. Of course, if her aunt (and, by extension, the whole maternal line) deserves credit for the good things she taught Sophie, Atie must also take responsibility for the bad things. If Sophie is indeed a mere object, shaped (like Atie and Ifè before her) by the women who mothered her, then what else can we learn about the "carpenters" by looking at the "wood"? Aren't they to blame for her deep scars as well? This shared meal, a prelude to the verbal confrontation about the abusive "tradition" of virginity testing, is Sophie's way of reclaiming her maternal line, redefining it in her own terms and reshaping it to include healthy boundaries. In this way, moving forward, that line will nourish Sophie's baby girl without harming her.

Like Martine and Sophie, the Dew Breaker's victims are driven out of Haiti and into New York by the interlocking evils of political persecution and economic desperation. Yet this flight to safety has its price: the unmooring of the self from the land. The unnamed janitor of "Seven" works two seven-hour shifts a day for seven years in order to afford to bring his wife from Haiti. At last she comes to join him in the Brooklyn apartment he shares with two other Haitian immigrants, but she must first pass through the gauntlet of US Customs, where officials confiscate all the foods she has brought with her from home:

> The customs man was tearing her careful wrapping to shreds as he barked questions at her in mangled Creole.
> "Ki sa l ye?" He held a package in front of her before unveiling it.

What was it? She didn't know anymore. She could only guess by the shapes and sizes.

The customs man unwrapped all her gifts – the mangoes, sugarcane, avocados, the grapefruit-peel preserves, the peanut, cashew, and coconut confections, the coffee beans, which he threw into a green bin decorated with fruits and vegetables with red lines across them. (40)

The torn paper and the broken language, like the woman's fragmented memory, foreshadow the struggle that lies ahead of her – the long work of picking up the pieces of uprooted lives. As the customs officials strip away the tropical fruit and sugarcane, they forcibly separate the janitor's nameless wife from the Haitian earth. As they deprive her of the prepared sweets, they detach her from Haitian culture. And when they take her coffee beans, they rob her of a powerful folk remedy – a source of strength in hard times and a magic elixir that could transport her back home, at least in spirit.

Although she has lost all the anchoring foods she hoped to bring with her from Haiti, the janitor's wife remains determined to use the cookpot and the table to maintain a sense of Haitian community in Brooklyn. This comes as a welcome balm to her husband and his roommates, whose many years in exile and economic desperation have long since emptied their lives of any sense of connectedness or normalcy. She cooks the men a large meal, using what she can find in the kitchen, and insists that they all eat together, despite her husband's impending shift at work. The janitor notes the wondrous effect this has on the immigrant workers:

The men complimented her enthusiastically on her cooking, and he could tell that this meal made them feel as though they were part of a family, something they had not experienced for years. They seemed happy, eating for pleasure as well as sustenance, chewing more slowly than they ever had before. Usually they ate standing up, Chinese or Jamaican takeout from places down the street. Tonight there was little conversation, beyond praise for the food. The men offered to clean the pots and dishes once they were done, and he suspected that they wanted to lick them before washing them. (46)

In this passage, the author uses the exiled men's pleasureless subsistence on cheap restaurant fare to drive home what exile, privation and atomization look like – *taste* like – in the everyday. Refusing to bend to the merciless logic of the globalized market, which values efficiency above all else, the janitor's wife prioritizes the group's psychological and spiritual well-being. In turn, her cooking draws the individual roommates into a group that is more than the sum of its parts – a family. Thanks to her vision, as the men eat for pleasure they shed their identities as mere worker machines, automated and reduced to a bundle of physical needs. Through this shared meal they reclaim their dignity, their sense of community, their very humanity.[78]

Similarly, in "The Funeral Singer", Freda, another of the Dew Breaker's victims, finds solace in the company of two other immigrant Haitian women who attend night class with her. In a Haitian restaurant on the Upper West Side of Manhattan, Freda, Mariselle and Rézia remember Haiti and re-member community by eating and drinking together:

> The walls around us were covered with bright little paintings, portraits of young boys playing with tops and marbles and flying kites, old men casting nets in the ocean, women walking barefoot to the market with large baskets on their heads. . . . I was the one who started it one night over a bottle of urine-colored rum from Rézia's pantry. . . . "I used to play telephone with my mother. . . . I forgot all colors except blue when I went fishing with my father. . . . I was asked to sing at the national palace . . ." I thought exposing a few details of my life would inspire them to do the same and slowly we'd parcel out our sorrows, each walking out with fewer than we'd carried in. (170)

Idyllic images of an Eden-like Haiti, where innocent youngsters' lives are filled with simple joys, contrast sharply with the violence and trauma the three women experienced as children. The images of old men fishing suggest simplicity and natural abundance, giving no hint of the danger and uncertainty that Rézia's fisherman father faced at sea – and at the hands of the Tonton Macoutes, who knocked out all his teeth before he disappeared at sea. While the women in the paintings walk peacefully to market, weighed down only by the bounty of the Haitian earth, Freda, Mariselle and Rézia carry a heavy load of emotional baggage. Like the janitor's wife, the three women find themselves with shattered lives and fragmented memories. As they help each other piece back together their life stories, they begin to share the load ("parcel out our sorrows") and then to put down the burden – together. Eventually, over a meal they prepare as a group, the women are able to tell one another their respective histories in full, giving voice to their experiences of political violence: "Tonight we cook an entire meal together. Mariselle fries the plantains and ends up with a hot-oil burn on the knuckle of her middle finger. Rézia makes the meat, stewed goat. I cook the rice with pigeon peas. We talk about what brought us here" (172). Like Pineau's Julia, who cooks fish in bird-pepper sauce to return to Guadeloupe in spirit, the trio cooks Haitian in order to piece together their fragmented memories of assault, theft, murder and rape. The women's potluck-style dinner functions as an emotional *konbit*. Just as their ancestors found agricultural and culinary labour more manageable when shared, the three women find the work of constructing their trauma narrative easier when they support one another. *Yon sèl dwèt pa manje kalalou*, declares the Haitian proverb. "It takes more than one finger to eat kalalou", remarked Danticat in a 2007 interview, "because of the slippery nature of it. It's a statement of unity; the fingers have to work together to pick up the *kalalou*."[79]

The last time the women gather to eat and drink together, Mariselle suggests that they light a candle and pray to Saint Jude, the patron saint of lost causes. As Freda drinks the red wine, she has a strange, mystical experience. "It feels like I'm drinking blood," she says, "not the symbolic blood of the sacraments, but real blood, velvet blood, our own blood" (179). In this twist on transubstantiation, the wine does not become the blood of the crucified Christ but the blood of martyred Haitians, their own blood. This indicates that Freda already sees herself as a martyr, and on this night she tells the others that she plans to join a militia and return to Haiti to fight. Since all three women know that means certain death, Freda the funeral singer sings her own funeral song with her new friends:

> I clear my throat to show them that I can do it, am willing to do it, sing my own funeral song. Why not? And that's how I begin my final performance as a funeral singer, or any kind of singer at all. I sing "Brother Timonie". *Brother Timonie, Brother Timonie, we row on without you. But I know we'll meet again.* . . . And for the rest of the night we raise our glasses, broken and unbroken alike, to the terrible days behind us and the uncertain ones ahead. (181)

In this Haitian version of the Last Supper, Freda faces her own death unafraid, for she knows that, just as she pushes on without those she has lost, including the beloved father who taught her to sing "Brother Timonie", others will persist without her when she is gone. You can't kill an idea. The tree of liberty, as Freda well knows, will surely grow back from the roots.[80]

THE WELCOME TABLE

Recently Danticat contributed an essay to the *Welcome Table* edition of the faith-based *Plough Quarterly*.[81] She begins by drawing parallels among the experiences of several wrongly detained groups: the Haitian "boat people" detained in the 1990s, accused terrorists imprisoned at Guantánamo in the 2000s, and immigrants in detention centres all over the United States in 2019. Extending her comparison further across time and space, Danticat then reminds the reader that the Last Supper was a meal shared by a group of political dissidents whose leader was about to experience the ultimate form of political violence and silencing: execution. "The most legendary final meal is the Last Supper, which is the great-great-great-grandfather of all final meals." During this meal, Jesus and his disciples ate in defiance of political authority, their food and drink both symbolic of and synonymous with a collective narrative of solidarity as resistance that would live on long after Jesus's death. Meditating on the suffering of victims of political violence near and far, long past and present-day, Danticat ends her essay with a final question: "How many of us must recite these pleas, these prayers, these laments, and these dirges, before we are brought to the table in communion, and are allowed to sit and eat in peace?"[82] This question is at the heart of Danticat's food-focused fiction.

As Danticat engenders the Haitian experience of political violence in these three works, she also portrays a broader shift in imperialism's centre of gravity over the course of the twentieth century. Whereas in the four preceding centuries European colonialism was the dominant form of exploitation in the region, she shows that in the past century it is the United States' economic and political hegemony that has most affected Caribbean development and autonomy. US political policies have inspired, tolerated and even supported violent regimes, and, as Danticat's writing illustrates, Caribbean womanhood has been shaped and profoundly scarred by those experiences of dictatorship and political violence. Danticat's food-focused fiction shines a light on the survival strategies of Caribbean women threatened by state-sponsored physical and sexual intimidation. As her novels illustrate, living to tell the tale can be as feminist a response as fighting back.[83]

In all three of the works examined here, women's healing begins with going back to the cane, acknowledging both the historical processes and the economic systems that produced that violence. They move further in their journeys of healing by breaking their silence, defying the social, economic and political mechanisms that seek to keep Caribbean women quiet, prolonging their pain and impeding their healing. The final step in healing, Danticat posits, is the creation of a shared narrative, a process that is both represented and accompanied by the shared meal. In all of this, Danticat's fiction helps to create a more inclusive Caribbean history, adding gender specificity to existing historical narratives about the violence of the Haitian and Dominican states. These new narratives overturn simplistic historical accounts that collapse the complexities of global systems of power – and the complicity of a broad range of actors, both Haitian and non-Haitian – into the madness or megalomania of individual men.

As we have seen, Gisèle Pineau's culinary fiction contemplates the legacy of French colonialism in the Caribbean and beyond. In the chapters that follow, we will see that Lakshmi Persaud's and Shani Mootoo's food-focused writing engages with the residues of British colonialism in the archipelago. Danticat's novels, however, situate Haiti within a region and a hemisphere that has been characterized largely by US neocolonialism – both military intervention and economic interference – for more than a hundred years.

Danticat's work mirrors that of fellow Afro-Caribbean authors Condé and Pineau in many ways. *The Farming of Bones*, like Condé's *Victoire* (see chapter 5), portrays slavery-like labour conditions within the Caribbean, despite abolition, and both *Breath, Eyes, Memory* and *The Dew Breaker*, like Pineau's *Exile According to Julia*, depict the second-class citizenship and low labour status of Caribbean women in the Global North, despite official narratives of equality. But it is Danticat who draws the clearest lines of causality between the structure and functioning of a merciless global economy and violence against Caribbean women.

Danticat's culinary fiction positions Caribbean identity within the framework of the most extreme forms of capitalist exploitation, both within the region and in the wider hemisphere. These experiences of exploitation have profoundly shaped the Caribbean experience. As Michel-Rolph Trouillot reminds us, the French sugar islands were not simply societies that incidentally included enslaved people; they were enslavement-*based* societies. "Slavery defined their economic, social and cultural organization", he writes; "it was their raison d'être".[84] In much the same way, Danticat's novels illustrate the ways in which US exploitation of labour and natural resources was not just incidentally part of the twentieth-century Caribbean. Rather, that exploitation *defined* Caribbean economic, social and cultural organization, both within the archipelago and in its diaspora. For Danticat, then, as for Pineau, Caribbeanness is thus both performative and relational. To be Caribbean is to work, to live, to *exist* in unequal relation with the United States. In this, Haiti stands not as an exception, but rather as the most extreme form of the rule.

The Farming of Bones, *The Dew Breaker* and *Breath, Eyes, Memory* depict both survival and testimony as homegrown Caribbean feminist responses. For Danticat, coalition looks like the shared meal and shared narrative that, like Holy Communion, make memorials of human hearts. If Pineau's vision is of a potluck world, then Danticat's prayer is for a welcome table where all are nourished, where all are safe, where all have a voice, where *they* become *us*. For Danticat, the radical inclusion of the welcome table is sacred: a sense of food and cooking as a gateway to the divine that we will also see elaborated in the work of Lakshmi Persaud.

CHAPTER 3

LAKSHMI PERSAUD
FORBIDDEN FRUIT

It should have been of equal importance to all non-white races
in British colonial Trinidad; sadly, we were a people
already divided amongst ourselves.[1]

TWENTIETH-CENTURY TRINIDAD WAS MARKED BY THE rise of Indian consciousness.
Although in much of the region (including Pineau's Guadeloupe and
Danticat's Haiti), Afro-Caribbean people represent an overwhelming ethno-
racial majority, in Trinidad, as in a handful of other islands and nations in
the greater Caribbean, Indo-Caribbean people make up a plurality.[2] In fact,
by the turn of the twenty-first century there were more than a million people
of East Indian descent in Trinidad, Guyana and Suriname alone,[3] without
counting those places in the region, from Guadeloupe to Jamaica, where
they make up a significant minority. East Indians thus constitute not only
a substantial and influential segment of Trinidadian society but also an
essential component of Caribbeanness as a whole. Yet it has not been easy
for Indo-Caribbean people to carve out a cultural home for themselves in the
region. Césaire's Négritude – a call to rally around a common Afro-diasporic
heritage – has been hailed as a necessary building block, springboard and
catalyst for Caribbeanness and creoleness,[4] but Indian consciousness in the
Caribbean has not always been cast in the same positive light.

As Lakshmi Persaud's food-intensive novels show, in Trinidad (as elsewhere
in the Caribbean) intragroup differences, represented by divergent food
practices, have often been reduced to an opposition between creolized blacks,

whose modern, hybridized culture is proudly emblematic of the post-colonial nation,[5] and un-creolized East Indians whose traditional, purist attachment to the South Asian motherland precludes belonging to the new country.[6] This simplistic framing of the supposedly incompatible worldviews of two ethnic groups, which can be understood only within the context of an inherited divide-and-rule colonial mindset, has naturally had negative consequences for multicultural Caribbean societies. In *The Caribbean Postcolonial,* Shalini Puri contends that in the final decades of the twentieth century, a utopian artistic fascination with a supposedly unifying hybridity (whose culinary symbol, as Aisha Khan points out in *Callaloo Nation,* is the stew-like callaloo) did not facilitate a more harmonious multi-ethnic coexistence, nor did it address questions of social justice in the Caribbean. Instead, this monolithic, dehistoricized notion of hybridity contributed to racial polarization and even obscured gender and class inequalities.[7] While sweeping manifestos of Caribbean hybridity do the important work of imagining an ideal egalitarian society, she writes, their aesthetics are no substitute for a concrete politics of parity rooted in the specificities of the local.[8] Thus intragroup healing and tangible equality might begin with a fully contextualized, nuanced consideration not only of Indo-Caribbean people's historic relationship to Indianness and to creolization, but also of the material realities that contributed to that relationship.

Lakshmi Persaud's culinary fiction does just that. Her first food-focused novel, *Butterfly in the Wind* (1990), contextualizes the rise of Indian consciousness within the daily life of everyday people in the anglophone Caribbean, underscoring its usefulness in liberating the colonialized mind. Her second, *Sastra* (1993), places that double-edged consciousness at a crossroads between a potentially destructive religio-ethnic parochialism and the promise of a creative unity in diversity. Both works, set in mid-twentieth-century colonial Trinidad, follow young Indo-Caribbean girls from their insulated early childhood in tight-knit rural villages to their cosmopolitan young adulthood in double diaspora in the Global North. Whereas Gisèle Pineau uses food imagery to depict Afro-Caribbean women's experience(s) with authenticity and creoleness, Persaud's culinary fiction engenders the history of Indo-Caribbean people's relationship to both. While Danticat writes about the reality of political violence for women and girls in Haiti, Persaud writes about women's relationship to the ever-present latent *possibility* of political violence in Trinidad, fuelled by religious difference, economic inequality and racial antagonisms. In both of these food-focused novels, Persaud shines a light on Hindu Indo-Trinidadian women striving to act both as bulwarks against cultural erasure and as bridges across harmful religious, economic and ethnic divides.

POST-INDENTURESHIP HINDUISM

Lakshmi Persaud's *Butterfly in the Wind* and *Sastra* recount Hindu Indo-Trinidadian women's untold stories of the aftermath of indentureship. By the beginning of the twentieth century, most East Indians had moved off the sugar estates where they had done indentured labour and into villages as small-scale proprietary farmers.[9] They had set up small dairies and vegetable and rice farms around the urban settlements.[10] They had put down roots and changed Trinidadian agriculture, adding diversified local food production to the island's monocultural sugar production.[11] The descendants of those East Indian cane workers who had been at the bottom of an oppressive system of export-driven food production had, in many cases, successfully repositioned themselves as small-scale cattle or market-garden farmers.[12] By the 1940s and 1950s, Indo-Trinidadians (who remained mostly rural) had even begun to enter the tertiary sector in commerce, teaching and the liberal professions.[13] But indentureship had left lasting scars on East Indian communities. As Persaud's writing illustrates, those scars had particularly heavy consequences for women.

Indentureship disrupted traditional East Indian gender roles and marriage patterns. Post-indentureship Indo-Trinidadians were thus faced with a total breakdown of the family – the institution responsible for the systems regulating marriage, kinship practices and various rites of passage in the life cycle. The gradual re-establishment of East Indian traditional family values was very important, as Bridget Brereton explains, because the traditional family and village structure was an important source of psychological comfort.[14] Traditional Indian gender roles, writes Patricia Mohammed, had to be consciously reconstituted by the entire community. During the first half of the twentieth century, both men and women had to participate in rebuilding an East Indian patriarchy based on values that both genders considered important to the community.[15] East Indian women were caught in a double bind, as nonconformity to traditional Indian gender roles was seen as antithetical to the reconstruction of Indianness in the Caribbean.

For Hindu East Indians, indentureship was also experienced as an assault on their belief system. During indentureship, East Indians as a group did not necessarily share a common religion,[16] and the Hindu East Indians who came to Trinidad practised countless different variations of Hinduism. Once they were in the Caribbean, however, a new and more unified form of Hinduism gradually emerged. It was based on commonalities such as the recognition of a certain number of Sanskritic deities and a general acceptance of the ritual authority of the Brahman caste.[17] This "for export only" version of Hinduism operated under a heightened sense of authenticity and purity with regard to what constituted the "Indianness" of religious practice, especially dietary laws.

This particularly defensive version of Hinduism was made more so during indentureship by compression of the Hindu caste system into a single group, which produced one set of cultural expectations for the entire group.[18] Hinduism remained embedded in most East Indians' identity, and, despite the "official attitude of contempt"[19] towards the religion, few Hindus converted. In fact, they grew more intensely Hindu, for the group's shared beliefs offered psychological protection against the contempt of the colonial society.[20] Van der Veer and Vertovec argue that because Hindus in the Caribbean were disdained and deemed idolatrous heathens, they experienced a "greater call for self-rationalization and legitimation regarding the choice and performance of rites and other practices, and the sharpening of apologetics regarding beliefs and doctrines".[21] This entailed a ferocious adherence to dietary laws, accompanied by a fully articulated reasoning for doing so.[22]

The intertwining of religion and dietary laws in the Hindu Indian community renders food very fertile terrain for those who wish to write about the Indian diaspora around the world, including in the Caribbean. Historians, anthropologists and literary critics have tended to focus on the role of both Indian women at home and exiled diasporic Indian women in preserving their culture through spiritual vehicles, such as food that conforms to tradition and dietary laws: "The world was where the European power had challenged the non-European peoples and, by virtue of its superior material culture, had subjugated them. But it had failed to colonize the inner, essential, identity of the East that lay in its distinctive, and superior, spiritual culture. That is where the East was undominated, sovereign, master of its own fate."[23] Persaud's writing captures Indo-Trinidadians' need to believe that some unsullied part of the self and of the community survived the humiliation of the *kala pani*[24] and indentureship. And thanks to their close association with kitchen spaces, dietary laws and the culinary aspects of Hindu rituals, women have the power to preserve that "safe space" for themselves and for the whole community. In *Butterfly in the Wind*, as in *Sastra*, Persaud's female characters are both enamoured of that power and hindered by that responsibility.

WRITING THE INNER VOICE

Like the protagonists of *Butterfly in the Wind* and *Sastra*, Lakshmi Persaud was born in the late 1930s to a Hindu family in rural Trinidad. Her ancestors had come to the Caribbean from Uttar Pradesh, India, some generations before, in the 1890s. Persaud pursued her higher education in the British Isles, then taught grammar school in Guyana, Barbados and Trinidad. In 1974 she moved with her husband to the United Kingdom, where she took up writing as a second career. She has written five novels, the first of which were *Butterfly in the Wind* (1990) and *Sastra* (1993). In the three novels that followed, she continued to develop some of those books' core themes. *For the Love of My Name* (2001), a thinly disguised portrait of racial violence in Guyana, illustrates what can happen if one stokes the fires of racial tensions rather than addressing their roots. *Raise the Lanterns High* (2004), meanwhile, delves more deeply into the historical relationship between Hinduism and women's subjugation. Alternating between female-centred narratives in seventeenth-century India and present-day Trinidad, *Raise the Lanterns* ultimately places the responsibility for women's mistreatment on the interpreters of Hinduism's tenets, not on the faith itself. Most recently, *Daughters of Empire* (2012) scrutinizes Indo-Caribbean women's struggle to maintain Hindu Indo-Trinidadian cultural retention in double diaspora in the Global

North, following them as they rear children outside the Caribbean. In 2012, the fiftieth anniversary of independence for Trinidad and Tobago, Persaud was awarded a Lifetime Literary Award for her significant contribution to the development of her country's literature, and in 2013 the University of the West Indies awarded her an honorary degree.[25]

Mariam Pirbhai hails Lakshmi Persaud and Shani Mootoo (see chapter 4) as "pioneers of the Indo-Caribbean women's novel".[26] Persaud's *Butterfly in the Wind* was at the forefront of a wave of Indo-Caribbean women's writing, a new sub-genre of Trinidadian and Guyanese fiction that began to emerge in the 1990s. Similar to Gisèle Pineau, who worked as a psychiatric nurse for decades before becoming a writer, Persaud worked for years in grammar schools and identified strongly as a teacher. Also like Pineau, she came to writing as a form of therapy, in her case as a way of coming to terms with her traumatic memories of the psychic and corporal violence of the colonial school, then of understanding other aspects of her childhood in an agricultural village. Persaud cites Vidya (V.S.) Naipaul and Toni Morrison among her literary influences, the former because he was among the first to narrate the lives of Indo-Caribbean people, and the latter because she wrote her books the way she wanted to, without feeling the need to accommodate anyone else's perspectives. Self-identifying as a feminist writer, but on her own terms, Persaud explained in a 2011 interview, "If you define *feminism* as trying to point out difficulties inherent in being female that can be improved in all cultures, then I am a feminist."[27] She rejects not only colonial injustices but also home-community norms that place the burden of "authenticity" and group integrity on women and girls. The rebellious "inner voice" that Persaud was forced to silence as a child breaks through in her culinary fiction.[28]

Persaud wrote *Butterfly in the Wind* and *Sastra* in the 1990s, at a time when, as anthropologist Aisha Khan's interviews with Indo-Trinidadians reveal, a "back to India" movement was at work. Elite, middle-class and poor Indo-Trinidadians discovered that they could find common ground by turning to the greatness of their Indian past, made "not of 'shreds and patches' but of high culture and great tradition, the seeds of which had been sustained in the New World".[29] *Sastra*'s protagonist's final move to Canada reflects another historical trend of the late 1980s and early 1990s: a great exodus of

Trinidadians out of the country, mainly to North America.[30] Furthermore, Persaud's characters Kamla and Sastra correspond to Khan's general observation about the Indo-Trinidadians she interviewed in the mid-1990s. They exhibit, she claims, a "concurrence of cosmopolitanism with morality, dignity, and an unbroken connection with religious heritage – a modernity with limits".[31] They also reflect Persaud's own artistic standpoint, which might best be described as that of the new Indo-Caribbean woman, both firmly anchored in tradition and fully engaged with a diverse and rapidly changing world.

"KNOW WHEN TO PUT THE LID ON AND WHEN TO UNCOVER"[32]

Food permeates Persaud's entire *oeuvre* and illuminates two of her central preoccupations: first, how to improve Indo-Caribbean women's well-being and life possibilities without renouncing Hindu traditions and worldview, and second, how to achieve Hindu Indian cultural preservation without negating or alienating others, including Muslim Indo-Caribbean and Afro-Caribbean people. All five of her novels explore the complex task of defining ideal behaviours for Indo-Trinidadian women in the kitchen and in the bedroom, including the ascribed duty to reproduce so-called pure culture despite geographical and generational shifts.

In *Butterfly in the Wind* and *Sastra*, Hindu dietary laws and South Asian culinary traditions reinforce ties to a Hindu Indian past both real and imagined. However, they also erect barriers to full integration into the broader Trinidadian population. At the same time, some of the characters in the novels use food to break down those very walls. When Persaud's female characters engage in small acts of unorthodox culinary creativity or kitchen-based rebellion, they affirm not only a broader desire for increased female autonomy and more flexible gender roles, but also a hidden willingness to engage in creolization on their own terms. Grounding themselves in the Indianness of their rural communities and especially in the Hindu faith of their ancestors, yet wary of Indian consciousness as a final and exclusive goal, Persaud's devoutly Hindu and deeply humanist female role models use food to reach out to others without losing themselves.

Butterfly in the Wind is a largely autobiographical *Bildungsroman* whose protagonist is Kamla, a girl growing up in a rural Indo-Caribbean community in 1940s colonial Trinidad. At times Kamla's secure babyhood and pampered early childhood contrast sharply with the poverty and privation that exist alongside her own relatively privileged life in the village. Eventually she must leave her village in order to attend a colonial school in a larger town. As a result, the young girl finds herself caught between the competing cultural forces of the colonial school, her traditional Hindu village and the rapidly modernizing Caribbean society that surrounds them. Finally Kamla must leave Trinidad altogether to pursue her university studies in Ireland, but she vows never to forget where she comes from. For Kamla, growing into her Indo-Trinidadian womanhood means learning to appreciate the value and richness of her ancestral culture, acknowledging social and economic ills within her home community, and talking back to colonialism. Most of all, it means celebrating her mother as a Hindu female role model of compassion and openness who uses food to overcome socio-economic and religious difference.

Set a few years later, in 1950s Trinidad, *Sastra* is named for its protagonist, a Hindu woman who does not love her arranged fiancé Govind, a pleasant young medical student who could offer her security and contentment. She instead develops a passion for Rabindranath Pande, the brilliant, sensitive but critically ill village teacher whose family have converted to Christianity. Govind's mother, Shakuntala, is determined to have the lovely and accomplished young Sastra for her son. Parvatee, Sastra's mother, hopes to make a sensible match for her daughter without crushing the girl's own personhood. Ultimately, despite her heartbreak, Sastra does not dare defy her parents by marrying Rabindranath. Instead it is old Madam Tiwari, Govind's paternal grandmother, who calls off the wedding between Govind and Sastra, insisting that it is wrong to pressure the girl into a marriage against her inclinations.

Meanwhile, in a significant subplot, Rabindranath's live-in maid and cook, the Afro-Caribbean Milly, has been trained by the legendary chef and devout Hindu Draupadi. Like Kamla's mother, Draupadi models a Hindu womanly spirit of charity and unity, tapping into the divine power of food to bridge a daunting racial divide. Her pupil Milly fully masters Indian culinary traditions and Hindu dietary laws, blurring the culturally constructed lines between Indo- and Afro-Trinidadian communities and laying bare their racist roots. In the end, Sastra's search for love is nothing short of a quest to set aside parochialism and become a new kind of Indo-Trinidadian woman, one rooted in but not limited by tradition.

As we will see, in both *Butterfly* and *Sastra*, Persaud uses food to tell the story of mid-twentieth-century Indianness in Trinidad from a female perspective. In both novels women are cast as "custodians of culture" who use food as a tool of community defence and cultural preservation. In *Butterfly in the Wind*, food imagery also highlights the Indo-Trinidadian community's internal divisions, especially the strained relationship between the prosperous business-owning class and their less fortunate neighbours. Meanwhile, *Sastra* zooms out to examine, through the lens of food, racial tensions between the Indo-Trinidadian community as a whole and their Afro-Trinidadian compatriots. In both works, heroic homegrown feminists dare to be "first timers",[33] harnessing the sacred power of food to reimagine and reconfigure community.

CUSTODIANS OF CULTURE[34]

"They came to work in sugarcane fields and sugar factories", narrates Kamla in *Butterfly in the Wind*, describing her East Indian indentured ancestors. "They came to work under men who were once owners of slaves and for men who believed in their own inherent superiority before God and before man, but most of all before colonized men and women" (81). But those East Indians survived that brutal economic, political and cultural domination, and they put down roots in a new place. On their little plots of Caribbean land they strove for food security and food sovereignty by using South Asian agricultural and culinary know-how: Trinidadian mangos were harvested to make *achar* relish (82); cucumbers and beans were grown by using a traditional Indian trellis system called a *machan* (83); cooking was done over a *chulha*, a wood-burning earthen stove (83), feeding it with coconuts, corn husks or whatever was available during the Trinidadian season (84). And out of scattered fragments they successfully constructed, if not entirely the India of their memory, then at least the India of their imagination. In the isolated rural Indo-Trinidadian community where Kamla grew up, she notes, "At dusk it was easy to believe you were in India." Between "the aroma of *roties* on *chulhas*" and "the soft gentle sound of Hindi in the night", she claims, "even as late as the 1930s it was easy to believe" (81). As *Butterfly in the Wind* illustrates, for mid-twentieth-century Hindu Indo-Trinidadian communities, Indianness in the Caribbean pivoted around the interdependent relationship among Hinduism, food and femininity.

Yet, as Persaud was penning this mostly autobiographical novel,[35] it was not the 1930s. Time marches on, and what was more than half a century ago was no more. Looking back on her 1940s childhood, Persaud attempts to capture a pivotal moment for Indianness in the Caribbean. On the one hand, *Butterfly* is a story of profound loss: unbeknownst to her, the Indian way of life young Kamla has taken for granted since babyhood is passing away before her very eyes. On the other hand, this is a story of gain: as Kamla enters adolescence and young adulthood in the 1950s, she matures into a new, more conscious relationship with her Indian heritage, wilfully leveraging it as protective armour against British colonial power, especially the assimilationist agenda of the colonial school.[36]

Of the forty or so "untranslatable" Hindi terms Persaud italicizes in the text and includes in a glossary at the end of the novel, a full quarter pertain to Hindu religious personnel and paraphernalia and more than half refer to food or cooking, many of those in the context of religious practice. For example, when Kamla recalls a childhood visit to the Hindu temple with her mother, the girl's memories are flooded with images of the food stands that surround the temple, whose wares she can't fully describe using English alone. The tents are stacked with Indian sweets (*pehra, gulabjamun, jilebi, ladhu*) and savouries (*bara, pholourie, kachowrie, chatni*), all clearly beloved by the child and well familiar to her (41).

The food vendors capitalize on their customers' desire to preserve Indianness in diaspora, calling out to them through the shared languages of Hindi and food. Rama, Kamla's mother's usual vendor, underscores the centrality of culinary and religious traditions in bringing up new genera-tions of Indo-Caribbean children:

> Rama . . . greets my mother, saying in Hindi, "What will you have today, Maharajin?" "Just give me three of everything." . . . As he carefully places them in a two-pound paper bag he says again in Hindi, "Is that all you will have

today?" . . . He turns his attention to me and speaks in English, "So you come too to celebrate *Shivaratri,* the birth of Lord Shiva?" I nod. "It is a good thing, Maharajin, to bring the children. You have to introduce the young to their own tradition." He pauses and weighs the sweets. "You have to start young," he says again, "for by the time they reach fourteen-fifteen it is already too late." (42)

However, Rama's code-switching in order to both appeal to Kamla's mother and include little Kamla herself is a tacit acknowledgement that the Hindi language, even in its syncretized "plantation Hindi" form, is slipping away. At least Indian foodways – another vehicle for the oral transmission of culture, including religious beliefs – remain.[37] As Rama praises Kamla's mother for bringing the girl to temple to deepen her understanding of Hindu rituals and reinforce her attachment to Indian foods, he is also implicitly thanking her on behalf of the community, and of the child herself. Without a conscious proactive approach to cultural preservation, the East Indian community, an important source of psychological support, will fall apart. An Indian child will not learn to value minority-status Hinduism, her obscured history, her rural community, her *self* in the colonial school. In the humiliating assimilationist onslaught of colonial society, everyone knows Kamla will need all the help she can get.

Religious gatherings at home are described in a similar fashion, using numerous untranslatable terms for food. Kamla's narration stresses a ceremony's sensory appeal for the children, thanks to its culinary aspects:

> After the *arati,* the sharing of *panchamirit* followed, a sweet liquid of milk and honey and ghee and the aromatic magical Tulsi leaves. We would take this in the palm of our cupped hand. We could get only one tablespoon. It was never enough! Then would come what we had been waiting for: *prasad,* made by my mother. . . . We children did not understand much of the ceremony which was conducted in Sanskrit and explained to the gathering in Hindi. (127)

In contrast to the visit to the temple, which is framed as an exceptional event, this home-based worship is depicted as a common occurrence. The conditional tense conveys habitual action ("We would take this"; "Then would come"), as does the *never* of "It was never enough!" The centre of Kamla's rural Hinduism is not the temple but the home. Meanwhile, Kamla's account of these gatherings, like her memory of the temple, also emphasizes the inaccessibility of the linguistic aspects of sacred ritual. While the ancient Sanskrit is predictably indecipherable to all but the pundit, he, unlike Rama, doesn't seem to know or care that the youngest attendees cannot understand his religious lessons in Hindi. They are simply locked out. For the children, the high point of the ceremony, its most anticipated moment, is not the pundit's sermon but the sacred and delicious *prasad*, an offering to the gods. In Kamla's simple, rural Hinduism, her mother's kitchen is a treasured gateway to the divine.

While *Butterfly in the Wind* focuses on the positive, supportive role that women and the kitchen play in cultural preservation, and on the value of Indian consciousness in resisting colonialism, *Sastra* depicts some women as custodians of culture. These women's sanctimonious attitudes, perversions of Indian consciousness, not only limit Indo-Caribbean women's life possibilities but also unwittingly reproduce the colonizer's divide-and-rule tactics. The epitome of this dogmatism is Shakuntala. "Her religious values and her cultural values were one", explains the narrator. "Dharma was to her the path of righteousness, the way of life handed down, by teaching and example, from her parents and grandparents, to her and her son, Govind Tiwari" (39). For Shakuntala, right behaviour and social order are thus intimately tied to the (imagined) past and there is no room for the possibility of change – especially for women.

Shakuntala's reaction to an unorthodox wedding menu foreshadows her rigidly conservative approach to other Hindu traditions, including arranged marriage. She is shocked to find wedding cake at a Hindu wedding. Her friend Parvatee, Sastra's mother, is inclined to be more tolerant:

> "Tantie, try the wedding cake," she said. "Is this an orthodox Hindu wedding? This passed through my mind, I was very upset, Parvatee, but I didn't want to cause any dissention."
>
> "It is becoming fashionable to serve wedding cake, Shakuntala."
>
> "Parvatee, today – eggs; tomorrow what? Wine? Fried chicken? Who started all this at Hindu weddings? That's what I want to know!" (42)

Casting herself in the role of a "goodBrahminwoman"[38] whose moral judgement is above reproach, Shakuntala boasts about her own restraint in the face of such culinary insult. When Parvatee, who is less strident than her friend, tries to downplay the cake as an innocent trend, not intentional heresy, Shakuntala turns up the heat. The cake, she insists, is only the first step down a slippery slope to perdition – indeed, the road to total cultural annihilation.[39] And all of this, she points out, is somebody's fault, and that person should be called out. Sensing danger, Parvatee distances herself from the offending parties:

> "What must have happened, Shakuntala, is, you invite a few Christians to a Hindu wedding and they come expecting wine and cake," she lowered her voice and her eyes widened, "I hear they have wine in their church too, would you believe it?"
>
> "Why should they come expecting their culture at our weddings? You make a concession to Christians and before you know it they calling the tune. They are a very forward people, Parvatee." (42)

It is no accident that this exchange is about the food at a Hindu wedding – an arranged marriage that helps preserve Hindu culture unpolluted by outsiders marrying in for love. Changes in food (which is tightly bound up with religion) signal changes in other mores and values, especially sexual ones. Ultimately, dietary infractions figure sexual transgressions such as Western love marriages or racial miscegenation, acts that creolize the most private and protected aspect of Hindu Indo-Trinidadian life – the family. Shakuntala will have none of it: "Bit by bit. Bit by bit, Parvatee. Who knows? Next it will be English dancing, and then all dharma will fly through the window. Gone! And what will be left? A shell? – Ceremonies without meaning, without value, without dharma? . . . We have to protect our ways, all that is worthwhile, all that is good in this life, be on our guard" (43).

Ultimately Shakuntala's *we* (to be understood as "we women") highlights the mother's role as protector of the East Indian family. In short, it is the mother's job to resist assimilation in the private sphere. Anita Mannur writes that the task of the female Indian subject in diaspora is "to be vigilant about the faithful reproduction of Indianness", and "the domestic arena, so frequently associated with femininity, also becomes a space to reproduce culture and national identity".[40] If *Sastra*'s female characters display a certain "Hindu high-mindedness in relation to their cuisine", insists Brinda Mehta, that attitude stems from their conviction that cooking is culturally sacred.

Ironically, she points out, the women of *Sastra* are not preserving something real but, rather, creating a nostalgic fantasy.[41] They are, as Mannur puts it, "fabricating authenticity".[42]

"The Village Women", the seventh chapter of *Sastra*, also illustrates women's role in cultural preservation. In this section, multiple generations of women gather to cook communally for the following day's *katha*, a social gathering that will be punctuated by the telling of ancient religious stories that contain a moral lesson of some kind. The *katha* will be followed by a commentary on how those values, constant from the dawn of Hindu history, can be interpreted by the modern Hindu practitioner and applied to the improvement of everyday life. The *katha* is, in essence, a ritual whose purpose is to strengthen ties within the present-day Hindu community while reminding that group of the moral legitimacy of its shared past.

Women's cooperative cooking plays a vital role in this ritual of religious and cultural continuity. Provisions are gathered, the host's house is cleaned and the village women bring utensils from their own homes, from "favourite knives" to "large pots, basins, rolling pins and wooden trays" (59). Their collective culinary skill and authority transform the domestic space into a heavenly realm: "In this larger circle the women's fingers moved nimbly on, taking pieces of fresh dough, smooth and elastic, filling them with dhal – ground dhal with onions and garlic, dhal with turmeric and jeera – until, burnished bright and orange-yellow, it floods the house with its essence, overflows into the yard, evoking a near spiritual warmth, entrancing the imagination, lifting it higher than soaring kites" (60). The women's repeated movements evoke not tedium but a trance-like ecstasy.[43] Cooking is not labour but art, worship, spiritual transcendence. And the village women have this power quite literally at their fingertips.

This pivotal scene vividly illustrates the process of socialization and religious indoctrination that transforms ordinary women into custodians of culture. This portrait of community women preparing for the *katha* directly links food and femininity to the sacred beliefs of Hinduism. In this way the reader learns how thoroughly the female protagonist Sastra has been trained *by other women* to adhere to traditional Hindu dietary laws and gender role expectations: "So closely bound together these women were, and Sastra was with them, for how else are womanly attitudes, ways, notions and skills passed on? Parvatee was only too well aware of this; her daughter would not be found wanting when called upon to perform these womanly duties: duties of honourable wife, dedicated mother and trustworthy friend" (60). Sastra's existence is thus deeply embedded in Hindu tradition and communal life. The young woman depends on other women to prepare her for adult female responsibilities. Parvatee, Sastra's mother, allows and encourages a whole village of female co-mothers to teach her daughter how a Hindu woman is expected to fulfil various relationally defined roles. Parvatee is well aware that one is not born a goodBrahminwoman; a girl child is shaped into one by many womanly hands.

Underneath the rhythmic, entrancing repetition, however, lies the tiniest of chinks in the culture's armour: "But it is their fingers which attract: stretching, opening, filling, closing. The mystery is locked within the dough. But unlike bees buzzing into the sweet floral vortex of nectar, these fingers are not programmed by a common genetic code, but by the powerful order of tradition. But like the bees in never stopping to ask wherefore or why, the women's fingers moved nimbly on" (60). Since Sastra's fingers are programmed not by nature but rather by tradition, they, along with her heart and her will, might be programmed altogether differently. Sastra is like the bees only as long as she fails to ask wherefore or why. The mystery and the tradition draw their power from unquestioning submission. Without it, they are more fragile than they appear.

TO DIE FOR A FEW COCONUTS

In addition to its meditations on the relationships among food, cultural continuity and social cohesion, *Butterfly in the Wind* uses food to vividly illustrate the inequalities that divide Indo-Caribbean communities. Like Shani Mootoo (as we will see in chapter 4), Persaud critiques ambitious well-to-do Indo-Caribbean people, depicting them as not only sometimes out of touch with the daily struggles of their impoverished neighbours, but also wilfully blind to their own role and stake in sustaining social inequalities.[44] Kamla's childhood memories are peppered with food imagery that highlights the gap between the village haves and have-nots, the ways in which well-off people wash their hands of poor people's suffering, and the simmering resentments that the poor harbour against the business-owning class. This series of memories culminates in a revelatory family story (also revolving around food) that explains once and for all why the upwardly mobile close their fingers so tightly around what they have.

As the adult narrator Kamla looks back on her younger self, she sees a spoiled child. Little Kamla's father owns both the general store and a rum shop, so the girl never wants for anything. She sometimes turns up her nose at her parents' dinner table, which is always overflowing with homegrown fruits and vegetables prepared by Daya, the family's hired cook. Visits to Port of Spain with her mother, which include both a trip to the movie theatre and a shopping spree, invariably end in gluttony: "an enormous glass of ice cream sundae followed by delicious flaky Danish pastry filled with warm cherry jelly" (15). But the family's relative wealth is most glaringly obvious at Christmastime:

> There were bottles of cashew nuts and large peanuts; freshly baked white bread and sweet bread made with fruit and nuts and ginger. There were home-made ginger ale and cherry brandy and, on the table beside a most elegant, patterned glass cakestand (supporting a perfect cake to be cut), red wine in a frosted decanter. Daya had left long ago but the tender roasted turkey, with its fresh herb and liver stuffing which she had cooked, would be there, covered securely from the cat. We were expected to help ourselves to it and the home-made bread. (94)

In this food-focused scene, one of the very few in the novel in which Indian food does not take centre stage, Kamla's family enjoys a British-style holiday meal. The elegant table setting distinguishes Christmas Eve from ordinary days and, more important, distinguishes Kamla's family from ordinary families. The young girl eats to her heart's content, relishing mouth-watering foodstuffs gathered from the four corners of the Empire, from Indian cashews to Irish ginger ale to turkey from the Americas. Best of all, like the Empire itself, Kamla's family benefits from cheap labour. Their cook, Daya, has prepared the feast, and they have only to enjoy it.

Replete with the evening's copious meal, Kamla feels utterly content. "It was easy to believe I was at peace with myself," she recalls, "after I had showered and supped and sat on sweet-smelling cushion covers, with a piece of lemon cake in my hand" (95). Indeed, hers was a picture-perfect evening, like "those newly passe-partout-framed pictures taken from a calendar, of Norwegian or Canadian mountains and forests and lakes and streams, which my sister had hung on the walls". But Kamla's home is not in an idyllic setting in an imagined Global North, but in a (mostly poor) rural village in the very real Global South. And although her family has begun its social and economic ascent and enjoys overflowing abundance, for many of their impoverished customers, as she puts it, "there was another side to Christmas" (95).

One Christmas Eve, a desperate woman arrives at Kamla's father's shop. The woman she works for has let her off late, and she needed her pay to buy the doll she promised her daughter for Christmas. Unfortunately, the shop's only remaining doll has a broken leg, and Kamla can see that the woman can't afford it anyway. Kamla's little brother, who empathizes with the women's obvious distress, gives her his old toy, a wind-up train engine that no longer runs. Following his son's example, the shop owner lets the woman take the broken doll for free, assuring her that it is against the law for him to sell a broken item. Even for Kamla's generally unsympathetic father, it is hard to watch the exhausted woman pack up the broken toys to take home to her daughter, who has been waiting for her all day. "You are not having a very good Christmas are you?" he says, more of a statement than a question. "Well," she says, "what to do? You have to trust in God." Moved by the woman's faith in the face of such penury, Kamla's father throws in a handful of balloons, a 1945 calendar and a bottle of cherry brandy.

But Christmas is defined by its very exceptionality. Kamla's parents' quotidian is ruled not by open-handed generosity but by hard-nosed ambition. And the rum that has built Kamla's comfortable life wreaks pure havoc on the poor. The family's washerwoman, Renee, for example, who irons for them all day every Friday in the blistering heat, medicates her exhaustion and despair with alcohol and cigarettes. Renee feels judged and judges herself for being weak: "Kamla dear. You can know you are doing something wrong and yet not have the strength to fight it" (33). Unlike the rest of "respectable" society, the little girl does not condemn her friend Renee for her reliance on alcohol, an anaesthetic for the painful realities of her life; if she were Renee's judge, declares Kamla, she would announce "Case dismissed!" (34). But society does not judge Kamla's father for his part in Renee's undoing, even when he breaks the law. In fact, by bribing the police, Kamla's father keeps his rum shop open seven days a week, although it is illegal to sell alcohol on Sundays. "Case dismissed", remarks Kamla, "were two words I had heard my father use frequently" (34).

Like Renee, Daya, the family cook, has a very hard life. Her workday begins long before she arrives at Kamla's house:

> "You know, Kam, she said, "I got up since five o'clock with the alarm. Didi doesn't know that. . . . I have to knead the flour and make six good-size roti. And when I finish that, I have to make a big pot of *baigan* and *aloo* and saltfish."
>
> "He does eat a lot," I said.
>
> "Yes Kam. He does have to work real hard. Task work in the cane field is hard you know."
>
> "He does eat six roti one time?"
>
> "He does eat two for breakfast and does carry two for lunch. And in the evening when he comes home, I does still be here and he does be hungry."
> (35–36)

Kamla's mother, who scolds Daya harshly if she is a minute late, should – must – know that Daya has a household of her own to run and mouths of her own to feed. After all, all the village women do. But she doesn't want to know, any more than Kamla's father wants to know that Daya's husband "drinks all the money" in his rum shop (37). Far removed from the ritual sweets of the Hindu temple and home religious gatherings, and further still from the Christmas feast's glass cake stand and frosted decanter, roti with saltfish is the Trinidadian working man's food, emblematic of the popular masses (as we will see again in chapter 5). Daya's husband's working man's appetite, another class marker, highlights the strenuous, physically demanding nature of his labour. Meanwhile, Daya's double shift in the kitchen – at home and at work – is another glimpse into how women experience the class differences that divide Kamla's village. Caught between her obligations to home and husband and her low-status domestic-sector employment, gender roles and expectations cost women like Daya twice as much.

If Kamla's parents are deliberately clueless as to their role in reproducing social ills and economic inequalities, the same can't be said of the poor girls who go to school with Kamla. They are seething with envy, their animosity ever ready to explode into violence. While Kamla's daily pocket money is enough to buy her both a morning snack and an afternoon treat, many of her schoolmates never have any money at all. While most of those impoverished girls seem to accept their lot, a few of the toughest form a gang and take by force what they cannot afford to buy:

> One day I was standing in the school yard and had just peeled off with my teeth a portion of the skin from a box and spice mango. I had taken one bite into that yellow sweetness – sheer nectar, the thick yellow juice spilling over my hands onto my wrist. Suddenly, as from nowhere, I was surrounded by Inez, the gang leader and two other bullies, Monica and Millicent. They surrounded me, pushing their chests closer to me. Inez said, "Give me that mango," moving her waist and hips. (67)

The ripe mango thus appears in Persaud's work just as it does in Gisèle Pineau's and Shani Mootoo's (see chapter 4). For all three authors, mango juice running down one's arms is a quintessentially Caribbean childhood memory, an innocent pleasure. For little Kamla, however, the mango is more than that. It is also a symbol of her island's limited resources and of scarcity-inspired infighting and resentments. Often, her elder self recounts, the boldest of the poor girls would pressure their luckier schoolmates – "Give me a bite!" or "Give me! Give me!"– and, "By the time you had shared it around, you had precious little or nothing left" (67). But this time, Kamla has decided to take a stand and hold on to what is hers. "It's mine", she tells the gang of girls, much to their surprise – and, frankly, to her own: "Then they stared at me, unbelieving, as torturers must do, at the obstinacy of a victim before the kill. They pressed in closer, their faces large and callous. Inez pushed me backwards and, as I tried to regain my balance, Millicent struck the mango from my clasp. It fell and rolled on the fine sand and then came to rest looking like a sand ball" (68). This scene, one of three in a row in which very poor children physically lash out at Kamla and extort her, out of jealousy and class resentment, highlights the ill will that the poor harbour towards those who are a little better off than themselves. At the same time it illustrates the frustrations and anxieties of those who have a little something. The poor children's violent tactics only simplify things for Kamla: she is the victim and they are the wrongdoers. Moreover, in many ways quite representative of her slightly more privileged class, Kamla fears that if she is forced to share indiscriminately with the masses, in the end there will be nothing left for her. The result of this destructive class warfare – a new iteration of colonial divide-and-rule tactics – is that the mango is ruined, of no use to anybody.

In a pivotal conversation with her grandmother, Kamla comes to understand why her parents and other upwardly mobile people like them cling so tightly to what they have: fear of slippage. As they climb the social and economic ladder, the dire poverty that ruled their grandparents' and even their parents' lives nips fiercely at their heels. Kamla's grandmother tearfully recounts her ten-year-old brother-in-law Mitra's death, his rail-thin body "as light as a fallen bird", thrown from a coconut tree by a strong wind. "What could he eat? There was never enough. Cheese, butter, eggs, meat: they were scarce. He didn't have anything to fall back on" (115). Then Kamla's mother impresses upon the children the real cause of Mitra's death – hunger. "'To die for a few coconuts; that's what being poor means.' My mother's words hurled themselves upon me like a mighty wave and their impact stayed with me. To die for a few coconuts that is what poverty means: a denial, a smothering of all the possibilities of a growing life, all for a few coconuts on a tree" (116). With this impactful family story comes the realization that for all her ice cream sundaes and roast turkeys, lemon cakes and juicy mangos, Kamla's comfortable good fortune hangs by a thread. In a society – a world – where such a short time ago their own blood kin died of hunger, swept off the earth by a single strong wind, how can the newly emerged Indo-Caribbean business class feel safe enough to risk solidarity with the lower classes? As we will see, when that class differential is compounded by religion and especially race, the question becomes all the more complex.

SIAMESE TWINS

Kamla of *Butterfly in the Wind* remembers Indian independence in 1947 as a triumphant moment, a cause for celebration and hope. "It should have been of equal importance to all non-white races in British colonial Trinidad", narrates the adult Kamla. "[But] sadly, we were a people already divided amongst ourselves" (178). Looking back on the event's psychic importance to her own Hindu community, she wishes that all Indo- and Afro-Trinidadians had seen it as a symbol of their shared struggle against European hegemony. In that way, she imagines, they could have celebrated victory together.[45] Unfortunately, as Kamla laments, Trinidadians were a divided people in many respects, especially along racial lines. This racial divide, which is merely alluded to in *Butterfly*, is a core theme in *Sastra*, and it plays out most strikingly on the palate.

Patricia Mohammed concedes that racial separateness in Trinidad is due partly to its geographic isolation; rural East Indian communities such as Kamla's village in *Butterfly* sprang up around plantations in parts of the islands that blacks had mostly left behind when they relocated to cities. However, insists Mohammed, Indo-Caribbean people's isolation from Afro-Caribbean influences is also a function of racial politics, a deliberate attempt to separate themselves from blackness:

> Although Indo- and Afro-Trinidadians have far more in common with each other than they have with any native of India or Africa and the constantly emerging space of Creoleness in the region is as much Indian as it is European or African at this time, there is an Asian resistance to becoming subsumed into a politics of blackness. . . . To associate with blackness is to side with the losing rather than the winning team.[46] . . . To ally with whiteness is to go against the grain of the history of labour.[47]

Indo-Caribbean people thus avoided what they saw as an essentially black/white power struggle by falling back on the script of their ancient spiritual culture and colluding with their own casting as Other. As a result, they have often been excluded from the creole nationalist project. Although Afro-Caribbean ethnic pride and ancestral memory were viewed as essential to and enriching of the nation, points out Mohammed, similar attempts by Indo-Caribbean people were interpreted primarily as disloyal to the nation. Add to this the manipulation of both ethno-racial communities by political parties deeply invested in keeping their Afro- and Indo-Caribbean constituencies antithetical – "the post-independence competition for scarce, state-dispensed resources" and "separate-but-equal representation of constituent groups", observes Aisha Khan – and mistrust between Afro- and Indo-Caribbean peoples becomes not only understandable but nearly inevitable.[48]

In *Sastra,* explains Brinda Mehta, food chauvinism parallels cultural chauvinism, and cultural preservation becomes an excuse for racism.[49] Persaud's second novel, she argues, illustrates how women were designated responsibility for the whole group's cultural closed-mindedness, their culinary parochialism reflective of a larger racial parochialism.[50] Trained by the inflexible custodians of culture who balked at unorthodox food at a Hindu wedding, young Sastra hesitates at the idea of eating food prepared by the Pande's Afro-Barbadian maid, even though she has been trained by Draupadi, one of the community's finest chefs:

> Upstairs in the sanctuary of her room, she wondered how someone like Draupadi, from the heart of Hindu Chaguanas, a vegetarian by principle, a devout Hindu by disposition, could have made that Hanuman leap across cultural chasms to reach out to a complete stranger. For this was what had been required of Draupadi when she was told by Surinder Pande, only on her arrival, that it was his housekeeper, a young, creole, unmarried woman – making up his bed, cooking for him – whom he wished her to teach. (57)

Before spending time with Milly, surmises Sastra, Draupadi would have mixed very little with Afro-Caribbean people. Triply "pure" – in culture, for she is from Chaguanas, a hub of Indo-Caribbean culture; in body, for she eats no flesh; and in spirit, for she is a devout Hindu – Draupadi would have taken an enormous chance with Milly, placing her trust in someone who was not just a stranger to her personally but whose whole race was a stranger to her own. Drawing upon her own Hindu worldview, Sastra draws parallels between Draupadi's story and that of Sita – often held up as the ideal Hindu woman – as told in the sacred Ramayana. However, as Sastra describes Draupadi's daring, she casts not her but Milly in the role of Sita, who is waiting to be saved, and Draupadi instead as Hanuman, who made a great leap to help Lord Rama find his wife. Meanwhile, the "cultural chasm" beneath denotes not only the great distance to be traversed but also the risk that Draupadi takes upon herself in accepting the task.

For a devout Hindu woman such as Draupadi, meat is forbidden, a "demonic food" associated with heathens and the culturally inferior.[51] Afro-Caribbean foodways remain both foreign to Hindu women and repugnant, a formidable barrier to assimilation into the larger Trinidadian nation as defined by Afro-Trinidadian folk culture.

Draupadi would only have met black people on the streets and in the market place and passed shops where the hot piercing vapours of brine from the open barrels of meat they purchased – pigs' feet and pigs' tails in brine – would have brought her much discomfort. She would have observed, too, black pudding and souse sold on the roadside and concluded that she had little in common with their ways. She would never have been in one of their homes; but neither have I, Sastra thought. (57)

Sastra's musings highlight some very real obstacles to full cohabitation. Although Hindu Indo-Trinidadians share space with Afro-Trinidadians, the two groups have widely divergent food cultures. Hindus adhere to vegetarianism and similar food-prohibition practices, such that meat-eating is stigmatized; Afro-Trinidadians are descended from African peoples who exhibit "meat hunger": for them, a meal that lacks meat is a social failure and not much of a meal at all.[52] This opposition renders a culinary melting pot an exceedingly unlikely outcome.

In *Sastra* Persaud critiques the ways in which Hindu women's distaste for Afro-Caribbean foodways all too easily translates into a rejection of Afro-Caribbean people. Milly, for example, "is reduced to a state of untouchability reminiscent of caste disparities justified by Hinduism".[53]

Wealthy Indians employed Negroes, but not as cooks. To vegetarians like Draupadi and old Madam Tiwari, chicken, goat and lamb were the carcasses of once living things; to have meat was to have death on one's plate, a savagery they would not touch. To kill, cook and eat the sacred cow, as well as an animal that wallowed in mud and made grunting sounds was sacrilegious and obscene, especially when freshly picked green, leafy spinach, bygan choka, dhal and paratha were so delicious and nutritious. So, to have the hand that put those meats in its mouth touching one's pillow, one's cup, was deeply repugnant to these brahmin ladies, and this Sastra understood. (58)

As this passage illustrates, even if Hindu Indo-Caribbean people wanted to fully assimilate into a new food culture and leave their dietary restrictions behind, that might prove to be a daunting if not impossible task. "Once established, prohibitions are difficult to overcome because they are associated with disgust and revulsion", writes Caribbean historian B.W. Higman, "and eating such disgusting food is likely to be a highly emotional experience, associated with nausea and even vomiting."[54] However, it isn't just about the food.

When Sastra's family and friends gather for a meal at Shakuntala's house, the handful of guests is abuzz with the news of an Indian-owned business suspected to have been burned down by some Afro-Caribbean borrowers, in retaliation for charging an exorbitant interest rate on loans. Scared and shocked by what appears to be a racially motivated incident, Madam Tiwari insists, "We are a hardworking people. Who else would stay all day, up to their waist in mud and water and plant rice? Planting rice is a back breaking job. Garden work too too hard" (74). Indo-Trinidadians have been patient and willing to work to earn their place, implies the old woman. They have even sunk their very bodies into the Trinidadian earth. What more must they do to belong to the place? Her daughter-in-law Shakuntala is indignant that key Indo-Trinidadian contributions to society seem to be taken for granted. "Go to Tunapuna market," she tells the others, "any market for that matter, on a Saturday morning, on a Sunday morning, and what you see – we feeding them, and you think we getting thanks?" (75). Shakuntala's exceedingly broad *we* lumps in the women themselves, the moneylender and the whole privileged little dinner group with the most oppressed of Indo-Trinidadian agricultural workers. By asserting a monolithic Indo-Trinidadian identity, Shakuntala, like her mother-in-law, erases any element of labour or class struggle that may be embedded in what they read as a purely racially motivated incident. The economic violence of usury gets lost in the shuffle.

Sastra's brother-in-law, Dr Capil, believes the problem unsolvable. "They not like us", he insists; "they so different, man". At first, tender-hearted, fair-minded Sastra tries to resist. "At one level," she concurs, "the differences are wide. At another level they are non-existent." But then a lifetime of food-based programming kicks in:

> She lowered her voice. "Have you ever seen how Govind's ajee lifts a dressed chicken?"
> "With the outermost tips of the forefinger and thumb," Sati said.
> "Imagine her having to touch pork and beef. The Indian Mutiny speaks." (81)

Spurred on by their food-inspired indignance, the group slides down a rabbit hole of racism. Carnival, declares the group, is nothing but "gay abandon, a pounding rhythm, a pulsating beat, a stirring up sensuality". Pipes up Sati, Sastra's sister, "Don't forget the unstable family, the abandoned women, the disappearing, absent fathers and that brine of pickled meats" (81). To them, repugnant Afro-Trinidadian foodways are a warning, a sign of chaotic communities ruled by uncontrolled sexual impulses. Above all, they are no place for an East Indian woman.

But Rabindranath Pande, the brilliant young schoolteacher who works with both Indo- and Afro-Caribbean children every day, sees things differently. "We are both loving, warm-hearted people", he points out. "We can harness ourselves together to the same cart – the building of our small island", he suggests, and "I think that what we have in common is more important than our differences" (82). When his reminders of Afro-Trinidadians' celebrated achievements, contributions and past enslavement are met with a defensive portrait of Indo-Trinidadians' unrecognized work ethic, self-reliance and present-day (that is, mid-twentieth century) state of dire poverty, the exasperated Rabindranath goes further still. "We are inseparably bound together," he declares, "like Siamese twins and neither of us have the good sense to know it" (85). As we will see, *Butterfly in the Wind*'s mother character and *Sastra*'s Draupadi manifest a similar desire to build coalition among a people divided against itself.

MANY A DIVINE THOUGHT IN THE KITCHEN

Ethnologist Arjun Appadurai claims that Hindu South Asians are perhaps more invested in imbuing food with moral and cosmological meaning than any other culture in the world. For them, he explains, the kitchen is the most sacred area of the house. "In a very real sense," writes Appadurai, "in Hindu thought, food, in its physical and moral forms, *is* the cosmos. It is thought to be the fundamental link between men and gods."[55] In many ways Persaud's entire *oeuvre* is a prolonged meditation on the divine nature of food – its sacred power to uplift, heal, comfort and connect. In both *Butterfly in the Wind* and *Sastra*, her heroines, fictional female Hindu role models, harness food's spiritual essence as a tool of inclusion, reimagining community through the shared meal.

In *Butterfly in the Wind*, Lakshmi Persaud sifts through her childhood memories of her parents, fictionalizing them (and her childhood self) not only to make them into a cohesive novel but also, like Maryse Condé, to "forge an identity" (see chapter 5) for the adult author herself. At times, as we have seen, she depicts the parents (and the child) as wilfully blind to the suffering of their less fortunate neighbours, as when her father profits from the rum that decimates poor families, when her mother shows little concern for the double bind her female domestic workers face, or when little Kamla finds it's easy to believe herself at peace amid the abundance of her Christmas feast. In this way Persaud asserts her own adult sense of ethics by pushing back, refusing to accept in fictional retrospect what she may in reality have swallowed whole at the time. At other times she recalls (or invents, or both) prouder moments when her parents, especially her mother, showed an admirable sense of human solidarity. On those occasions, guided and inspired by the sacred qualities of the food itself, her mother sets a sublime example.

One way in which Kamla's mother regularly reaches across socio-economic class divides is through the religious gatherings she hosts in her home. In these divine moments, food and Hindu femininity redraw the lines of community: "My mother, when she was young and had lots of energy, would invite all our neighbours, as well as anyone who was around my father's rum shop and any of the wandering poor who slept in the open at nights. I have seen her stop men, ragged and foul smelling, as they walked slowly past our shop, and invite them in to have some *katha* food" (123). In ever widening circles of radically inclusive hospitality, Kamla's mother's communal meal includes first her prosperous business-owning-class neighbours, then the working-class poor with whom they normally have a strained relationship, and finally the homeless underclass, with whom they have next to no relationship at all. Like Edwidge Danticat's welcome table, Kamla's mother's home has room for them all. Meanwhile, the food itself equalizes the crowd, resolving the power differential inherent in acts of charity:

> Food that has been blessed by God should not be refused by man. Everyone knew this, so when my mother invited the wandering poor and the stationary poor, they knew they were obliged to accept the invitation. To refuse was to court the disapproval of the gods; and so the poor could warm their stomachs with good wholesome food and please both God and their hostess at the same time. After they had eaten and washed their hands she would offer some a

length of white cotton suitable for a dhoti and others a silver coin. As they left
they thanked God and blessed her. (123)

The well-to-do let go of their pretentions; the exploited set aside their
resentments; the marginalized shed their shame. Together they witness
the outside world's logic turned on its head. Rather than having no right to
access bounty, the impoverished have no right to refuse it. Instead of the rich
having the means to deprive the poor, it is the poor who have the ability to
deny the rich the ability to please God. Unlike the schoolyard, where there
was only enough mango for one, at this sacred shared meal there is more
than enough for all. In fact, recalls Kamla with admiration, "If at the end
of the day there was still some food left over, the remainder would be taken
to a river and placed on its bed so that the fishes too could rejoice" (127).

Just as Kamla's mother harnesses the spiritual power of food to bring
various socio-economic classes together in Hindu worship, she also uses
food to bridge the religious divide between Hindus and Muslims in the
village. Although many thought of the Indo-Trinidadians of Tunapuna as
a homogeneous group, explains the narrator, they were in fact a "mosaic
of peoples" whose differences are summed up in dietary laws. There were
"Moslems who would not eat pork but would eat beef and who distrusted
Hindus, and we Hindus who ate neither and distrusted the Moslems" (90).
Muslims were not invited to Hindu *katha*s and *puja*s, and Hindus were not
invited to mosques. As a result, concludes the narrator, "Side by side we
walked the dirt roads not knowing anything about the deeper feelings of
the other" (90).

Dissatisfied with the current state of affairs, Kamla's mother takes it
upon herself to befriend Mrs Hassan, her Muslim neighbour. However,
every time she invites Mrs Hassan for a shared meal, Mrs Hassan shrugs
off the invitation. Suspecting dietary law is at the root of these refusals,
Kamla's mother finally confronts the woman she would like to befriend.
"If you don't tell me what it is," says Kamla's mother, "I will never know,
because I'm not a mind reader" (90). The chicken, admits Mrs Hassan at
last, has to be killed in the way the Koran instructs, or she can't eat it. "I say
prayers too", Kamla's mother reassures her Muslim neighbour. "I always
say prayers before I kill the hens and I always give them a drink of water"

(91). But, since Mrs Hassan insists that it isn't the same, Kamla's mother proposes a creative solution to their shared dilemma:

> "Now this Sunday I will send Kamla for you, and you will come and kill the chickens. I could ask Hamid next door to do it but you might still have doubts in your mind, so the best thing is, for you to come and do it." That Sunday Mrs Hassan came over and killed four chickens "her way". My mother asked me not to "hang about her" as she might require privacy. And so it was that from then on we had a happy and more relaxed Mrs Hassan who occasionally accepted our invitation, and from time to time sent us a bowl of vermicelli boiled in milk and sugar and spices. (91)

In this passage, the shared meal is a blueprint for a shared society. Coexistence, like the women's chicken dinner, begins with clear communication – the willingness to make oneself vulnerable, to be honest and to listen. One must be willing to look for common ground (mutual respect for the chicken's life and for its suffering) and to make room for difference (for Muslims, Muslim prayers are not entirely interchangeable with Hindu prayers). Multiculturalism depends not upon equality but upon equity. Those who feel respected and safe, like Mrs Hassan, are able to stop living their lives on the defensive, to step up and take their place at the table. And those who accommodate others, such as Kamla's mother, reap sweet rewards.[56]

In *Sastra,* Hindu Indo-Trinidadian Draupadi and Christian Afro-Barbadian Milly share kitchen space and culinary know-how. Milly has been hired by Surinder Pande, the local schoolteacher, to replace the Pandes' previous, insensitive cook. That cook, as the village women note with a frown, looked Indian but had "lost all her Indianness" and "didn't keep any of her good culture" (122). When Milly first comes to work for Pande, he gives her a taste of *gulab jamun,*[57] exhorting her to open herself to all the wide world has to offer. "Milly," he urges the young woman, "let all cultures be your inheritance; be like a bird not a tree. A culture is like a forest, it stands in a certain place for a certain time. Those that are bound by their culture are like trees, but why not be a bird, Milly, and dwell in all forests" (123). In so doing, Pande, in direct opposition to the village women, explicitly associates food – Indian food – with openness towards other communities, something that Milly herself comes to embody as she learns to "cook Indian".

As she gradually masters Indian culinary traditions, Milly's character stirs up all kinds of questions regarding who owns culture and who has the right to inherit it. Her sensitive, skilful execution of the most difficult and delicate of Indian dishes – with hands that are "unclean" by Hindu standards – demands a rethinking of filiation-based identity. Like Shani Mootoo's "kitchen Indian" characters (Indian "in plate only", as we will see in chapter 4), Lakshmi Persaud's Milly blurs the boundaries between neat cultural categories, unmasking the performative nature of Indianness. Is it possible that Milly is able to recreate the physical aspects of Hindu culinary tradition without any understanding of their ritual meaning and value? Or – more unthinkable still – can it be that she, an outsider, has actually managed to learn both? If so, Milly's very willingness to learn threatens Shakuntala and the village women's monopoly on culinary authority and moral legitimacy.

Fortunately, Draupadi, Milly's teacher, reputed among the village women to be "the best of all our cooks" (53), is a master Hindu chef, a spiritual guide and, as is alluded to by her very name, a homegrown Caribbean feminist. *Sastra*'s Draupadi is named for the Mahabharata's Draupadi, one of five iconic heroines of the Hindu epics whom Hindu wives remember each morning in prayer. While Sita, the most famous of the five, sets the gold standard for wifely and womanly virtue, thanks to her long-suffering submissiveness, Draupadi sets another kind of example. In contrast with the passive Sita, who insists on waiting for her husband to rescue her, the polyandrous Draupadi saves herself and her five husbands from impending slavery by using her bravery and her wits.[58] Persaud's Draupadi thus alludes to an alternative legitimate model for ideal Hindu womanhood, one that could open new possibilities for the future without cutting ties to the ancient past.

Draupadi's spiritual evolution dwarfs Shakuntala's, reducing the latter's religious zealotry to pettiness and bigotry. Rather than imposing her own holier-than-thou notions on food, as Shakuntala might do, Draupadi listens for what the food itself – a link between men and the gods – has to say. As Milly recalls, her mentor used to say, "A kitchen is where many a divine thought first reveals itself, Milly; it was when the creator was in his kitchen, listening to the throb of creamy kheer, that the idea of the universe came to him" (98). Milly suspects that when Draupadi agreed to teach an outsider the intimate details of her sacred craft, it must have had something to do with the Indian spices, which the Afro-Caribbean Milly rattles off with impeccable accuracy. "I think having come all the way here with her spices – adrak, ilaychi, laung, dalchini, jaiphal, jeera, methi, javitri, saunf, kesar, masala, turmeric, chili, mustard seed, bottled mango and imli," recalls Draupadi's former pupil, "she decided to go through with it" (98).

Indeed, Draupadi's decision did have something to do with her spices, for they spoke to her in a dream, as she recounts in a letter to her long-time friend Madam Tiwari, Shakuntala's open-minded mother-in-law:

> A damp cold wind surrounds my spice basket, shaking it, tumbling it over, scattering spices on the floor. Two paper bags are intact but when I opened them, one has gone mouldy and the other has weevils. Another wind comes through the shutters with the face of the man with tail and horns; he laughs and laughs, whirling and jumping, running backwards and forwards into corners and cupboards. I manage somehow to save a little of the spice by collecting what has spilt on the table, but it is no use, Bahin; the spices had become charcoal in my hands. (165)

The spices are a potent symbol of cultural continuity and intactness. In the *kala pani* and beyond, as Brinda Mehta puts it, "pouches of spices became pockets of memory that preserved the now-tenuous links with the motherland".[59] The cold wind, meanwhile, symbolizes the inhospitable environment of the new Caribbean land, where the destabilizing forces of colonization and creolization threaten the integrity of the home culture. Desperate to hold on to their sense of self, East Indians insulated their culture so thoroughly that it had no room to breathe, to evolve, to *live*. Ruled by their fear of change, East Indians practised defensiveness to the point of rot, decay, mummification. But Draupadi, inspired by her spices, chooses life:

> I had a choice of becoming a spice that was fragrant, rich, exciting, a warm spice that had not lost its essence or aroma for this young black student, or of becoming dust, charcoal, of no use to her . . . the very spices that I had all my life treated with great care, these minuscule grains and buds, were now showing me such a large, magnificent way. I never would have thought, Bahin, that I, Draupadi, would one day be so obligated to my spices. I was truly humbled, as a child before the sparks of light in the night sky. (166)

The spices are therefore more than just a bridge to a past India; they are also the road to a future Trinidad. Unlike meat's divisiveness, remarks Mehta, spices represent common culinary ground: "Spices advocate the urgency of a creative 'massalafication' or creolization of cultures as a prerequisite for achieving dynamic cultural plurality in the Caribbean."[60] Thus, like Maryse Condé's culinary dreams (as we will see in chapter 5), Draupadi's nocturnal vision encodes a message about the artist's role in the human liberation project. If Draupadi as a culinary artist limits herself to memorializing the past, she will miss her opportunity to reimagine the limits of community through food.[61] In order to do that, realizes the master chef, she will have to reject high-handed religious posturing and embrace genuine spiritual awe.

The sacred power of the spices notwithstanding, if Draupadi eventually finds the courage to blur the boundaries of Indianness, it is also because her own father was a "first timer" – a homegrown feminist in his own right who pushed back against community limitations on his girl-child. As she thinks through her dilemma, Draupadi's self-talk about the futility of teaching Milly ("a complete stranger – a black creole lady, who could leave any time") to cook triggers childhood memories of the men in her community who were disgusted to learn that Draupadi's father was teaching a girl-child Sanskrit. "To a girl child?" they said. "What will she do with Sanskrit? To what purpose? A waste! A waste of your time, Punditji" (164). But in an act of everyday heroism, her father stood up for his child:

> My father replied so simply: "Why, she would enjoy reading the sacred texts just as we do. Reasons should be required only when denying someone a splendid thing, not when offering." It was his warm, gentle tone, Bahin, I would never forget this, God bless him. "If my daughter is not taught, if she does not know how to read the sacred texts, they don't exist for her, and though she is younger, she would be living in a darker age than you and I. Why deny her? Why deny?" (164)

Draupadi, once nearly robbed of the wisdom of ancient Hindu religious texts because of her sex, finds herself moved at the thought of depriving Milly of the wonders of Indian cuisine because of her race. Like Pineau, Persaud frames culinary knowledge as akin to literacy, in that it is key to understanding the past, to understanding each other and, most important, to living one's richest, fullest life.

Draupadi's true genius is encapsulated in her culinary "commandments", which hinge on the primordial importance of balance. Like the sacred texts her father taught her to cherish, these commandments work both as a conservative tool for the preservation of Hindu tradition – "Be alert that other properties do not enter uninvited, lest unaware of their presence you are caught off guard, unprepared for the havoc they cause" – and as a progressive force for unity in diversity – "Treat every vegetable with courtesy, retain its colour, texture and unique taste. Why should a marrow taste like a pumpkin?" – and necessary change – "Know when to put the lid on, to enable breaking down of toughness, and when to uncover, to allow powerful forces to leave, lest everything becomes mush" (56). Meanwhile, Milly's wisdom lies in her own moderation and patience, which she too expresses through culinary similes: "There was now a continuous clamour for instant change as if it could be had as easily as instant coffee. Life, she knew, like good recipes, did not work that way" (179). In the end, Draupadi and Milly's shared kitchen figures the open, creative, rich society that new generations of Indo- and Afro-Caribbean women, with hard work, could build together, if only they let the spices show them the way.

FORBIDDEN FRUIT

Persaud's culinary fiction highlights the unique challenges facing Indo-Trinidadian women, including the increased stakes of creolization, which for them is forbidden fruit.[62] Gabrielle Hosein has observed a marked "differential creolization" among young men and women in Trinidad. Because creolization is associated with masculinity, reputation, and Afro-Trinidadian and working-class Indo-Caribbean sexual freedom, Indo-Trinidadian males gain masculine status by becoming creolized. Creolized Indo-Caribbean girls, on the other hand, risk loss of their "Indianness", "femininity" and "difference" – all markers of Indo-Trinidadian female honour – without gaining in prestige.[63] Indo-Trinidadian girls therefore typically avoid creolization (especially its association with Afro-Trinidadians), instead pursuing women's empowerment through "modernization", that is, identification with (often white) North American women, who are seen as "up to date with everything, cool and liberal".[64] Hosein highlights the role of US cultural imperialism, including the globalization of US racial hierarchies, popular culture and capitalism, in Indo-Trinidadian girls' turn towards North America for female role models. Furthermore, she sees this tendency as an obstacle to coalitional homegrown Caribbean feminism(s): "Both girls' gender differential experience of creolization and their turn to modernization suggest a need for continuing inter-ethnic, inter-religious and feminist work to create autochthonous intersections, identities and discourses which can reject the stereotypes and disavowals resulting from historical ethnic and gender tensions in the society, while enabling the solace and salience of community to endure."[65] In light of this social reality, the creoleness Persaud's female characters embrace on their own terms in *Butterfly in the Wind* and *Sastra* can be read as a commitment not only to multicultural nation-building but also to homegrown Caribbean feminism(s). Therefore, despite the apparent lack of militancy in her work, Persaud – whose creative writing helped articulate Indo-Caribbean feminist thought while the scholarship was still in its embryonic stage[66] – nevertheless belongs to a radical tradition.

As Persaud introduces gender specificity into mid-twentieth-century Hindu Indianness in Trinidad, she also depicts the tensions inherent in post-colonial nation-building in multicultural Caribbean societies. Whereas dominant narratives tend to portray most Caribbean nations as homogeneously African-derived and creolized, Persaud shows that Indianness, including a uniquely Indo-Caribbean relationship to creolization, is also an integral part of post-colonial Caribbeanness. Her fiction features key Indo-Caribbean contributions to Caribbean societies, including their agricultural labour, their participation in commerce and their service as teachers and doctors. Her novels also capture some of the problems that dog Indo-Caribbean communities, from poverty and class inequalities to racism and excessive insularity. As Persaud's writing illustrates, Indo-Caribbean women are especially burdened with perpetuating that insularity. As a result, her novels suggest, those women are uniquely positioned to challenge it.

In both of the novels examined here, long-term solutions begin with admitting there is a problem. In *Butterfly in the Wind* and *Sastra*, the author unmasks the deep resentments that divide Trinidadian social classes and racial groups respectively. In each case Persaud alludes to the inevitable consequences of these differences if they go on unresolved: there is an ever-latent violence in Caribbean societies, ready to erupt and hurt everyone. But she proposes an antidote to that looming threat: an equitable multicultural society, represented by the shared ritual meal and shared kitchen space. In all of this, Persaud's fiction helps to create a more inclusive Caribbean history, bringing a female perspective to internal divisions, tensions and competition. Her narratives repeatedly challenge reductive historical accounts that oversimplify post-colonial Caribbean nations, reducing them to colonizer/colonized or black/white binaries.

Like Pineau and Danticat, Persaud writes about the power dynamics between women in her culinary fiction. From Aurélie force-feeding French culture to Félicie in *Un papillon dans la cité* to Martine stuffing into silence Sophie's voice in *Breath, Eyes, Memory* to the village women policing one another's kitchens (and lives) in *Sastra*, many of the female characters we have seen so far invalidate, control and betray one another, all in the name of "authenticity" and of meeting community expectations for acceptable forms of Caribbean girlhood and womanhood. For each of these authors, the freedom to be themselves entails managing multiple circles of belonging. For Pineau, those include being Guadeloupean, black, French and post-colonial; for Danticat it means remaining deeply attached to the traditions of her Haitian homeland while engaging with them on her own terms. In similar fashion, Persaud reclaims her Hindu Indo-Trinidadian identity, reinterpreting it to leave room for female empowerment and coalitional Caribbean feminisms that cut across class, religion and race.

Persaud's culinary fiction positions Caribbean identity within a framework of deeply divided societies. In a region already characterized by scarcity, the constant channelling of resources, from oil to cheap labour, into the Global North stokes fierce competition at home. Meanwhile, generational poverty and socio-economic disparities continue to be tolerated in societies predicated on dehumanizing labour practices, such that precarity and class resentments are a fact of life. Moreover, in an archipelago where racial antagonisms were originally instigated to dismantle any hope of collective resistance to colonial power[67] – and continue to be manipulated to further the interests of political parties[68] – instead of working together to solve collective problems and build a common future, people only too easily turn on one another. In Caribbean societies, divisions along racial and colour lines are not encountered randomly; rather, they are a fundamental characteristic of the region. To be Caribbean is to live with racial antagonisms that muddy internal abuses, from dehumanizing labour practices to sexism, and run counter to an effective collective defence against external forms of exploitation. In this, Trinidad is no special case, but rather a relatively obvious iteration of an ingrained endemic pattern.

For Lakshmi Persaud, coalition resembles those sacred Hindu gatherings of her youth, where the divine power of food drew people in, welcomed them exactly as they were and sent them away fulfilled. It also looks like a shared kitchen where everyone has access to the wonders of humanity's common heritage. Pineau's vision of a potluck world and Danticat's prayer for a welcome table find their echo in Persaud's meditation on the kitchen as a site of divine connection. For Persaud, the kitchen is where totally unexpected alliances are formed, a creative reimagining of community that we will also see in Shani Mootoo's culinary fiction.

CHAPTER 4

SHANI MOOTOO
KITCHEN INDIANS

And den dey look at yuh disdainful disdainful –
like yuh disloyal, like yuh is a traitor.[1]

IN 1962, WHEN TRINIDAD AND TOBAGO became politically independent from
Britain, they did not quickly become culturally, socially or psychically
independent. According to Norman Given, the Trinidad and Tobago
Independence Act that ratified the islands' independence was really an
"Independence Pact" that was less about full independence than about
preserving the cultural and political status quo.[2] The new Commonwealth
nations retained the colonial state's laws, institutions and core symbols,
including property rights, a two-party system and the Queen herself.
This political and symbolic continuity effectively devalued the meaning
of independence and prevented full psychological self-emancipation of the
colonized people,[3] particularly the native elites. Those elites had absorbed
and internalized colonial norms, and under independence they re-enacted
and enforced those norms, for they saw them as the path to consolidating
economic and political power (as they had done for the colonizers). Among
the Indo-Trinidadian elites, community attachment to Indian foodways, once
an impactful form of class resistance among their indentured ancestors,
was emptied of its radical roots in labour liberation. As Girvan argues, "The
implanting of colonial ways of thinking into native elites was one of the
outstanding successes of British policy in the Caribbean."[4] Writes George
Lamming of his own twentieth-century generation, "It was not a physical

cruelty that we knew. The Caribbean endured a different kind of subjugation: it was a *terror of the mind,* a daily exercise in self-mutilation. . . . This was the breeding ground for every uncertain self."[5]

Without a true psychic rupture from the colonial past, Trinidadians, like other Commonwealth Caribbean peoples, lack what Lamming calls "the sovereignty of the imagination" – the ability to imagine and thus fully define their own individual and cultural identities. In other words, they remain *post*-colonial rather than *de*colonial. In the post-colonial state, oppressive structures of inequality are not overturned; instead, existing structural positions are simply occupied by new groups as elites take over the roles previously held by the colonizers. Post-colonial states define their identity in terms of how they differ from the former colonial power – thus continuing to define themselves in relation to that power, even if it is a negative relationship – and their internal power dynamics continue to depend on colonial-style divide and rule. In contrast, in a decolonial state the colonial structures of inequality are dismantled, state identity is unyoked from that of the former colonizer, and new solidarities upend internal power dynamics. As we will see, Shani Mootoo imagines the move from post-colonial to decolonial in culinary terms. Her food-focused writing intimates that the shared table, historically an important site of resistance to colonial assimilation and exploitative labour practices, might be wrested away from the post-colonial elites that have lost sight of its radical potential. Instead, Trinidad's (economic, racial and sexual) underclasses might take back commensality as a symbol of what could and should be their shared freedom struggle.

This chapter explores the engagement of Shani Mootoo's fiction with the residues of colonialism, which continue to affect the Indo-Trinidadian community's attitudes towards class, gender, sexuality and their Hindu and Indian roots. Mootoo's *Out on Main Street and Other Stories* (1993) and *Valmiki's Daughter* (2008) depict mid- to late-twentieth-century and twenty-first-century upper middle-class South Asian diasporic communities, both in Trinidad and in double diaspora in Canada. In these works – a collection of short stories and a novel – Mootoo uses vivid food imagery from India, Europe and Trinidad to depict the Indo-Trinidadian relationship to the enduring cultural and psychological aspects of the "independence pact", including and especially homophobia.

Like the food-focused writing of the other writers featured in this volume, Mootoo's culinary fiction brings gender specificity to the historical processes surrounding the Caribbean freedom struggle. Laying bare both the legacy of colonialism and the internal divisions that have in some ways taken its place – including the policing of sexuality and gender expression, especially by other women – Mootoo's fiction presents a sophisticated study of interlocking forms of oppression in the Caribbean context. And, as we will see, her work also points to how Trinidad might begin to decolonize itself, in part by addressing its British colonial legacy of homophobia. *Out on Main Street* and *Valmiki's Daughter*, like the other works examined in this book, seek to create a new, more inclusive Caribbean history, in this case, one that includes and interrogates the role of homophobia in post-colonial Caribbean nation-building.

THE INDEPENDENCE PACT

Trinidad's independence from Britain was granted by the Trinidad and Tobago Independence Act, which was designed to guarantee political and cultural continuity for post-colonial states and therefore encoded the legacies of colonialism. One of the British statutes retained under the Independence Act was section 377 of the British penal code, which criminalized homosexual conduct. As we will see, Trinidadian culture has generally absorbed British homophobia, and there has never been a strong domestic constituency in favour of repealing this inherited legislation. In fact, in 1986 Trinidad and Tobago repealed the original British laws only to replace them in 2000 with their own Sexual Offences Act, which outlawed homosexuality, asserting that heterosexual vaginal intercourse is the only "natural" option for sexual expression, and imposed a unique ban on homosexual immigration. These two laws effectively prohibited or criminalized homosexuality, which was seen as a danger to the nation.[6]

Although anti-homosexual attitudes seem to be deeply ingrained in post-colonial Trinidadian culture, recent scholarship argues that this was not always the case. Contemporary post-colonial discourses that portray homosexuality as a Western import of corrupted morality, framing anti-homosexuality as pro-nationalist, in fact obscure the often more flexible, variable and non-prescriptive nature of precolonial sexuality around the former British Empire[7] and ignore the utility of homophobia as a political tool.[8] In Trinidad, homosexuality functions as a convenient common enemy, the subject of general moral agreement, especially when framed as a "foreign and possibly Western moral contaminant against which a newly independent nation had to guard".[9] Citing moral consensus as a precondition of post-colonial state sovereignty,[10] Wahab highlights the usefulness of homophobia in building accord between the oppressive "respectable" reproductive heterosexuality of middle-class elites and the resistant "reputational" profligate heterosexuality of the poor masses.[11] Symbolically positioned outside the framework of both respectability and reputation, same-sex practices and self-orientations are framed as being at odds with both the dominant values of hetero-reproductive sexuality and the countervalues of hetero-profligate sexuality.[12] And as Mahalia Jackman argues, these internalized colonial mores benefit those in power. The original inherited colonially imposed homophobia has been reappropriated and repurposed by post-colonial elites who benefit from all forms of consensus (such as racism or anti-homosexuality) that mask class divisions and economic inequalities.

In April 2018 the High Court of Justice in Trinidad and Tobago ruled unconstitutional the country's laws criminalizing same-sex intimacy between consensual adults. However, as of 2018 it still remained rare for people to live as openly gay or lesbian in Trinidad, and homosexuals continued to face persecution, harassment and sexual violence.[13] While Jackman found in 2017 that neither cohort replacement nor increasing education levels promises a substantial decline in homophobia, she did find that increased public interactions with lesbians and gay men could reduce anti-gay bias, and that their greater visibility could foster more positive attitudes towards homosexuals in Trinidad.[14]

THE INDIAN STARBOY

The overlap between homophobia, colonialism and the development of fully decolonized Caribbean identities is a key theme in Shani Mootoo's works. As we will see, her protagonists (nearly always women, nearly always gay) explore the intersections of their various identities – as Trinidadians, as

Indians, as Hindus, as lesbians, as gender-bending, as diasporic residents of other countries – through the medium of food.

In her 2013 essay "On Being an Indian Starboy", Mootoo writes about the difficulty of growing up in a homophobic Caribbean society. As a child she could identify with neither men nor women as those identities were defined within her Indo-Trinidadian community. She found an alternative in the Bollywood movies her family watched together, in which the young male lead actors performed a kind of masculinity that was well outside rigid Trinidadian notions of how heterosexual men behaved. Those actors became for Mootoo a model for nonbinary gender expression, and she began to identify herself with the young, androgynous movie stars, a gender performance that she thinks of as "Indian starboy". These early experiences revealed to her the performative nature of both gender and Indianness, allowing her to perceive the arbitrary nature of Trinidadian cultural exclusion of her own complex gender and sexual identity. The principal aim of Mootoo's body of fictional writing, then, is to deconstruct the supposedly immutable categories of class, sex, race and ethnicity, a project that can be traced back to this original encounter with the "Indian starboy".[15]

Many of her themes are based on Mootoo's own identities and experiences, including her Indo-Trinidadianness as the child of Indian parents raised in Trinidad; her Hinduism, which she describes as "bred in the marrow of this family I come from"; and her experience of double diaspora when she moved from the Trinidad of her childhood to Canada. Her characters seem to share the isolation, secrecy and exclusion she experienced as a young lesbian in Trinidad, and the "transitioning into a queerness of no return" she discovered when she emigrated to Canada.[16] Many of them also articulate the conflict that Mootoo experienced between Indo-Trinidadian expectations about gender performance (particularly the performance of a particular kind of good Indian womanhood) and her own "female masculinity".[17] According to Mootoo, she seeks through her fiction a place in which her multiple identities can co-exist, for "permission to exist as a woman, a woman of colour, as a lesbian, within – not on the out-side of the everyday world of society".[18]

Mootoo's deeply personal writing is filled with food imagery, for it is on the table that she depicts and negotiates the conflicts between her heritage and her identity. She writes often about Indian and Indian-derived dishes in a prolonged meditation on the nature of Indianness in the Caribbean and its diaspora, particularly its intersections with gender roles and its imperfect overlap with Hinduism. Mootoo also uses culinary symbolism and metaphors to show the legacies of colonialism within the Caribbean and the Caribbean diaspora. She writes of cocoa and sugar to highlight the enduring structures and lingering effects of indentureship and the plantation economy; her treatment of British table manners and French *haute cuisine* engages with modern Eurocentrism; and her descriptions of Trinidadian street fare and everyday family meals provide insight into the island's cultural hybridity and its class and racial divides. In her fiction, Mootoo uses food imagery to depict and unpack the complicated relationship between race, ethnicity, gender and sexuality in a post-colonial Caribbean society and its diaspora.

KITCHEN INDIANS

All these themes of intersectional identity are visible in Mootoo's first published literary work, the 1993 collection of nine short stories titled *Out on Main Street*, whose title points to both a public claiming of one's sexual and gender identity ("out") and to the stories' diasporic North American setting ("Main Street"). All but one of the stories feature female protagonists of South Asian descent. The stories have an intimate, personal feel thanks to their narration style, which is usually first-person but in some cases third-person with internal focalization. They are set largely in quiet, private domestic locations where the narrators are able to comfortably be themselves. However, some scenes are set in public, and in those scenes (which are often food-focused) Mootoo's narrators bump up against others' expectations for them – expectations around gender performance, sexuality, language and Indianness. Some of the stories are set in rural Trinidad, but most are set in urban Canada. Many of them depict lesbian desire, both clandestine and overt, as well as male jealousy, infidelity and sexual frustration.

The stories at the core of the collection, including the title story, "Out on Main Street", engender the experience of "kitchen Indians" (45) – Indians in plate only. Mootoo's female characters are out of touch with their Indianness or they grapple with what Indianness is in the Indo-Trinidadian double diaspora. In *Out on Main Street* they, like many of those we have examined in previous chapters, long to be themselves and to connect to their roots on their own terms.

OUT ON MAIN STREET

The tension between Indianness, diasporic identity and gender/sexuality is clear in the collection's title story, "Out on Main Street". The main characters – Indo-Trinidadians who are described as a couple of "watered-down Indians" rather than "good grade A Indians" (45) – visit an Indian sweet shop in modern-day urban Canada and experience intense alienation from other, more "authentic" Indians. If authentic Indian food is a marker of (and a way to connect to) authentic "Indianness", the narrator's upbringing in Trinidad has marked her as foreign – as a tourist in her own ancestral culture. In the opening lines of the story, the narrator and her girlfriend, Janet, who are both of Indian descent, seem not to belong among either the native Indians they mingle with or the native Canadians in their new city. They seem to be tourists in both groups: "We does go to Main Street to see pretty pretty sari and bangle," she declares, "and to eat we belly full a burfi and gulub jamoon" (45). Perhaps the narrator does not even know what "authentic Indianness" might be. For example, the Indian food that she used to eat every day lacked authentic Indian spices such as cardamom, which were not readily available in the Caribbean. Yet she views the Indo-Trinidadian *meethai* and *sweetrice* she ate back home as "overly authentic, like de day Naana and Naani step off de boat in Port of Spain harbour over a hundred and sixty years ago" (45–46).

The story is written in Trinidadian dialect in the first person – an authorial choice that underscores the language difference between the narrator and the other Indians she encounters. Although she looks Indian with her brown skin and dark hair, it is made clear that she is not a "real" Indian, either to herself or to other, more "authentic" Indians; the visible race that is marked on her skin does not make her authentically Indian. This is shown by the differences in language that keep the narrator from even communicating effectively with other Indians. We are told that she dreads speaking to people who look like her, because they respond to her questions (in Trinidadian

English) in Hindi, Punjabi, Urdu or Gujarati, which are all incomprehensible to her. Not only can she not understand the answers, she cannot even recognize what language they are speaking: "How I suppose to know de difference even!" she objects. And, sensitive to her linguistic inadequacy, the narrator feels keenly her exclusion from the group *Indians*: "And den dey look at yuh disdainful disdainful – like yuh disloyal, like yuh is a traitor" (48).

Therefore, before she enters the sweet shop where she will encounter both native Indians and Indo-Canadians, the narrator carefully searches her memory for accurate Indian culinary vocabulary, for she doesn't want to "make a fool a mih Brown self by asking what dis one name? and what dat one name?" (49). *Sweetrice*, she reminds herself, is called *kheer* here. Overwhelmed by a case full of confections – most of which she cannot even recognize, much less name – she attempts to order her favourite sweet, which is known as *meethai* back home in the Caribbean. But the Indo-Canadian clerk who is serving her does not understand: *meethai*, he tells her, is the general word for sweets, not the name of any particular candy. He explains that the fried dough she wants is called *koorma*, and the sugar cake she wants is called a *chum-chum*. The clerk smiles during the interaction, and just as the narrator had imagined the "disdainful" looks from the native Indians, she sees the clerk as "half-pitying, half-laughing at dis Indian-in-skin-colour-only" (51).[19]

Not only language isolates the narrator from Indian culture and Indian food; she seems to feel that her gender also separates her from her heritage, and that the two are entwined. Because she refused the typical "womanly" gender roles and activities of her Indian family members, she never learned to make authentic Indian food. Because she cannot make Indian food (as women should be able to do), she had to come to Main Street to eat it, and because she came to Main Street, she has to face these humiliating and isolating encounters with other Indians. "If only it wasn't for burfi and gulub jamoon!" she thinks. "If only I had a learned how to cook dem kind a thing before I leave home and come up here to live!" (49). In other words, the narrator seems to think that if she had taken up her assigned gender role, she might also have measured up to ethnic expectations: if she were a better woman, she would be a better Indian.

But, as the narrator discovers, while Indianness and gender are intertwined, it is not in the way she thinks (and not in the way that Persaud's Sastra experiences that intersection). She discovers that both gender and Indianness are *performative*. In the sweet shop she performs femininity, based on the campy femininity performed by gay men – "I jiggle and wiggle in mih best imitation a some a dem gay fellas dat I see downtown Vancouver, de ones who more femme dan even Janet" (50) – and her efforts to use the correct names for the sweets to hide her "non-authenticity" are a performance of Indianness. In both cases there is a shame- and anxiety-filled gap between the presumed intersectional identity written on the narrator's brown, physically female body and her ability to act out the elements of that supposed identity, but, like her beloved Indian starboy, she performs both Indianness and gender. Like the culinary fiction examined in previous chapters, "Out on Main Street" exposes the performative nature of these imagined categories, creating the potential for ways of relating to other Indians and other women that do not depend on authenticity or identity with others in the group. It imagines a new mode of kinship and offers the hidden promise of moving beyond performance and on to liberated personhood – to decolonization.

THE INDIAN CRO-MAGNON

Another story in the *Out on Main Street* collection, "Sushila's Bhakti", addresses similar issues: the Indo-Trinidadian desire to connect with one's Indian/Hindu roots and the role played by gender in women's access to those roots. This story hinges around a single painting session carried out by an Indo-Trinidadian artist who feels that she is "floating rootlessly in the Canadian landscape", neither Trinidadian nor Indian, "certainly not white and hardly Canadian either" (60). She sets out to perform a *bhakti* – an age-old form of devotional worship through visual art that uses symbolically charged elements – to revive her distant Indian past and take control of her present. She aims to skip over the modern Indians and Indo-Trinidadians who are split by language, culture, geography and food practices, instead seeking to access a common ancestor shared by both groups – the Cro-Magnon of the title.

As she seeks "the origin of Indian-ness" (64), Sushila finds herself sifting through layers of colonially inflicted confusion and loss in an effort to touch a kind of pure Indianness, an authentic Indian identity. But, ironically, the artist has learned the elements of her *bhakti* – the limited vocabulary and her fundamental understanding of the South Asian spiritual practice – not from her Indo-Trinidadian family but from the one beginners' class of meditation yoga she took a few years earlier at a community centre in Canada. For her, this Indian tradition has already been filtered through diasporic culture.

Yet it seems to work. To begin the ceremony, the artist calls upon God, beauty, truth and the Self: "She raised her hands, palms opened upward, gesturing to the canvas-stretcher covered with burlap from a basmati rice bag and said, 'This is my *bhakti*'" (59). Her rice-bag canvas is stamped "Dehradoon No. 1, Basmatee Rice", imported directly from India. For paints she uses *mendhi* (henna), best known for its use in body art for Hindu weddings and other festivals, and metanil yellow, a dye commonly used as food colouring in India but banned for that use in Canada because of its toxicity. These materials are all connected to female gender roles in India: *mendhi* is most commonly associated with women's body art, and metanil and rice are connected to the woman-centred and caste-defined realm of food preparation. Sushila is thus performing a version of Indian womanhood. Her use of specific media that come directly from India and were unknown to her in her Trinidadian past indicates where and with whom she thinks authentic Indianness lies. As the artist's rootless present converges with her ancestral past, she is overcome with divine ecstasy. In the earthen quality of the *mendhi* paste she "had glimpsed the core of her identity" (62) and "was deliriously transported in her imagination to the soils of her foreparents" (64).

But Sushila's mind does not remain in precolonial India, in the distant past of the Cro-Magnon Indian; it also moves to colonial Trinidad. Her movements during the ritual remind her of her grandmother's work in the kitchen:

> Sushila made a well in the centre of the mendhi lying in a mound of the stretched
> rice bag, and in an act of bhakti she filled the well with water. She launched her
> hands into it the way she remembered her grandmother back home in Trinidad
> beginning to knead flour and water for roti. Sushila juggled the experience of
> this new sensation and of imitating her Brahmin grandmother (not the action
> only, but the ritual devotion to family, the preparing of sustenance for their body

and soul – fulfilling, according to her father, the duty of woman and mother – that transported her beyond her grandmother to her earliest ancestors). (61–62)

In Sushila's mind, *bhakti* is connected to food preparation; this indicates the importance of food to the Hindu religion, and the importance of women in transmitting the Indian culinary and religious heritage. Her grandmother is the embodiment of virtuous Brahmin womanhood; she seeks to guard the traditional Indian idea of caste, which is an expression of spiritual and cultural value, and to keep it from being conflated with British ideas of socio-economic class. She works to transmit her native Indian culture to her family, making a point of teaching her grandchildren the Hindi alphabet and reading to them from the Bhagavad Gita. She seeks to separate her Indian heritage and identification from the legacies of British colonialism that suffuse modern Indo-Trinidadian identities.

As the *bhakti* – this "act of forgetting and remembering and inventing" (66) – connects the artist with her grandmother, Sushila appears to be poised to follow the rigid Indian gender roles that she sees as guiding her grandmother, who aspires to be a "goodBrahminwoman" – a portmanteau word that binds together gender, caste and religious identity. Each is inseparable from the others, for one's womanhood cannot be separated from one's caste identity, and one cannot be good without fulfilling one's caste-based gender identity. She seems to be ready to follow a path laid out for her at birth: the artist's very name, Sushila, means "good conduct" or "well-behaved girl".

Yet Sushila's grandmother had not been a hidebound traditionalist who refused to update Indian customs for her new home. The grandmother was both authentically Indian (she had emigrated from India to Trinidad in her youth) and Indo-Trinidadian. She embraced the rich cultural and spiritual hybridity available to her as a resident of that melting pot. She was tolerant of other religions; when a pleasant stranger stopped by the house and gave her a book of Christian prayers, the old woman accepted it and taught the children to pray at night, "Now I lay me down to sleep . . ." (59). Likewise, the artist's grandmother incorporated elements of Muslim practice, refusing to eat either beef or pork "because she couldn't remember which one it is that she, as a goodBrahminwoman, wasn't supposed to eat" (66). This is in fact eminently and truly Indian behaviour, for it is authentically Hindu:

Hinduism does not believe in an exclusive path or in one way for all. As the mirror image of her grandmother, then, Sushila (like Persaud's wise Draupadi) is able to connect to the new possibilities of an intersectional identity that can incorporate both her Hindu roots and her Indo-Trinidadian diasporic identity.

Crucially, although the artist connects in her *bhakti* with traditional Indian values and gender roles, she also connects with her own personal experiences of growing up in Trinidad, combining those two sets of values and expectations. She forges an intersectional identity for herself rather than passively inheriting and following Indian tradition. This is apparent in Sushila's modification of the ceremony. Her use of culinary materials for the ceremony demonstrates her symbolic participation in Indian and Hindu expectations of women, a theme that is carried through by the marks on her hands. By the end of the ceremony, when she finishes the painting, her hands are symbolically marked, in an echo of the traditional *mendhi* paste designs on the arms and hands of Hindu brides and other celebrants. The delicate, intricate *mendhi* designs are traditionally painted on the bride's hands by someone else; however, here the artist marks herself, with broad, messy, spreading stains: "Sushila's hands were bright orange. There wasn't a hint of white or pink in her fingernails. The dye had trickled down her arm, marking a crooked trail to her elbow" (66). Her body, like her identity, is no passive canvas; rather, her painted arms are the tools of an active creator. The protagonist has co-opted the implements of tradition to serve as instruments of self-realization.

As Sushila completes her own hybrid version of this purifying act of faithfulness, filtered through modern Canadian ideas about Indian spirituality and woven together with her own Indo-Trinidadian culture, she sheds her rigid ideas about the "authentic" faith of her ancestors, of a mythical Indian past:

> She was beginning to recognize in the painting, in herself, an identity being excavated. She played and fretted and worked and invented until she came to a junction where she could take a turn that skirted needing to be pinned down as Hindu, or as "Indian", or as Trinidadian (in themselves difficult identities to pin down) in favour of attempting to write a story of her own, using her own tools. (66)

In this sanctifying act of creation, she frees herself to reinvent each of these categories of womanhood and to make them her own.

HOW TO EAT A MANGO

"The Upside-downness of the World as It Unfolds" is the last story in Mootoo's *Out on Main Street* collection. The first-person narrative is divided into three parts, tracing the arc of the protagonist narrator's relationship to Indianness from her childhood in Trinidad to her adulthood in Canada.

Part 1 is set in Trinidad and recounts how the ten-year-old protagonist and her sister were taught to assimilate – to become colonized – through formal education. Although the girls' *ahji*, their Indo-Trinidadian grand-mother, resists the family's assimilation with all her might, wearing saris, performing poojas and playing Indian and Hindu religious music in the home (111), neither the girls nor their parents take the old woman's lessons and warnings seriously, instead seeking to educate the girls into the domi-nant culture. This indoctrination is represented in the story by the mango: the protagonist's different relationships to mangoes mark her journey from an innocent child who comfortably inhabits her complex identity to a con-flicted adult, ashamed of her intersectional identity and her inability to fully conform to colonial norms because of those identities.

The story begins with an idyllic scene from the narrator's childhood in which she and her young sister entirely give themselves over to the pleasures of ripe mangoes:

> A glass of cow's milk and a plate of currant rolls ("dead fly cemetery" they are called, flaky pastry triangles studded with hundreds of dark reddish brown shrivelled currants) and the unpeeled cheeks of ripe Julie mangoes sit on a kitchen table. Two girls, my sister Sharda and I, nine and ten years old, ignore the dead fly cemetery and grab the mangoes first, each cheek held up to the mouth, teeth sunk into the golden flesh, yellow creamy juice slipping down the corner of a mouth and running in a crooked egg-yellow rivulet down the finger, down the palm, down the arm to drip off the elbow. (106–7)

Before they are taught to be ashamed of their hybrid identities, the girls pass over the "dead fly cemeteries" – traditional Scottish pastries made with cooler-climate red currants – for tropical Julie mangoes, arguably Trinidad's favourite fruit. The dry ("flaky"), sharply geometric ("triangular") manmade currant rolls, symbols of colonial culture, are decidedly unappealing compared to the hidden ("unpeeled") vitality ("cheeks", "ripe") of the mango, which is emblematic of the Caribbean. As the girls unapologetically eat the mangoes Trinidadian-style, they enjoy them with all the senses of their unaffected youth. The fruit's vibrant colour and abundant juice reflect the young girls' own vitality and youthful vigour, while the "shrivelled" currants foreshadow the withered severity of Mrs Ramsey, the British tutor who "civilizes" them away from their mango-filled Eden.

Mrs Ramsey's home is littered with relics of the colonial past, from the shrubs scattered "missionary style all over the lawn" to the curios commemorating the coronation of Queen Elizabeth in 1952 and the two-hundred-year-old colonial-style mahogany dining table and chairs (108). These are important reminders of the enduring colonial relationship. Although Mrs Ramsey technically works for the girls' parents, the order of things remains intact, with the colonizers on top and the colonized in subjugation. And as Mrs Ramsey teaches the protagonist and her sister grammar and vocabulary, she also teaches them Eurocentrism and self-hatred. In the vocabulary lessons, the woman force-feeds them European culture and a colonialist worldview along with their new language. "New words were fitted into our mouths", recalls the narrator, "and we were taught how to use them" (109). In one particularly humiliating lesson, the girls must memorize definitions and usage for the word *pagan*: "1. One who is not a Christian, Moslem, or Jew, heathen. 2. One who has no religion. 3. A non-Christian. Sentence: The pagans of Indian ancestry pray to images of a dancing Shiva, a blue Krishna, or the cow" (109). This definition frames the protagonist's ancestral past as definitionally marginalized, as not fitting into the Eurocentric model that defines spirituality in Abrahamic or even exclusively Christian terms. As the practice sentence makes very clear, as long as the girls are loyal to their Hindu community, they will never gain access to the global centres of power and prestige.

Mrs Ramsey is not content just to teach the girls English grammar and vocabulary. She also teaches them how to behave according to British standards of etiquette. As the protagonist remembers, the elderly tutor teaches her students

[h]ow, with knife and fork, to eat roti and curried châtaigne, which her Afro-Indo-Trinidadian half-day maid cooked. Soup and cereal, to tip or not to tip, when and how. And how to eat a mango correctly. Never ripping with hands and teeth, or slurping off the edge of a cheek; always cutting with a knife and fork. Slice off cheeks, grid the inside with knife, then slide knife under the sections and release with fork. (109)

The roti and curried châtaigne are typical Trinidadian dishes, no doubt utterly unknown to Mrs Ramsey before her arrival in the tropics. These dishes are native to the Afro- and Indo-Trinidadian communities who invented them and prepare and eat them every day. Nonetheless, the tutor declares herself an expert on how to eat these dishes, whose preparation is drawn from the maid's know-how and not her own. It is for colonized peoples to grow and prepare food; it is for colonizing peoples to consume that food in style.

The culmination of Mrs Ramsey's audacity is, of course, her lessons on how to eat a mango. As the girls learn that their way is all wrong, they also learn that they and their family are all wrong as well. Colonialism, as represented by Mrs Ramsay's teachings, divides the girls from their parents:

One night Mrs. Ramsey tried to slice up and grid my family. My parents, my sister and I were invited for supper; Mrs. Ramsey served plump, perfumed and runny mangoes for dessert. My parents ate their cheeks the way mangoes have always been enjoyed in Trinidad, cupped in one hand and sucked and slurped, the meat dragged off the skin with happy grinning teeth. Mrs. Ramsey sat straight-backed as she gridded her mango cheeks and proceeded with knife and fork to deal with one manageable square at a time. Without a word to each other, Sharda and I weighed the wisdom of choosing one mango-eating method over the other and decided to decline dessert. (109)

In this scene, the disruptive violence of colonialism is brought to the fore, as is the decidedly intentional nature of that assault. In this culinary metaphor for divide and rule, Mrs Ramsey's colonial design acts like a knife, attempting to sever the fibrous ties between the girls and their parents, isolating them from one another, cutting them into "manageable" chunks. The girls will never again be able to watch their parents' everyday gestures without judgement. Though their parents' obvious pleasure and their own sense of nostalgia tempts the girls to revert to their former ways, fear of Mrs

Ramsey's self-declared cultural authority holds them back. Yet the girls cannot bring themselves to betray their parents by eating the Trinidadian mangoes European-style. In the end they are paralysed and atomized, completely estranged from the favourite food of their childhood. It is this shame and cultural alienation that the protagonist will carry with her well into adulthood and right across the hemisphere.

In part 2 of the story, the narrator is in Canada, where she meets a pair of white lesbian women, Meghan and Virginia, who have a keen interest in and considerable familiarity with many aspects of Indian culture. This proves painful and humiliating for the protagonist, who has been largely alienated from her ancestral way of life. Her new friends' fascination with all things Indian stands in stark contrast to the cultural erasure she experienced as a child: "White friends, unlike my White childhood tutor, no longer want to whiten me but rather they want to be brown and sugary like me, so much so that two of them in particular have embarked on a mission to rub back in the brown that Mrs. Ramsey tried so hard to bleach out" (112). The women's way of simply taking on wholesale elements of Indian culture that please them substitutes cultural appropriation for colonization. They adopt and deploy without penalty the very behaviours native to the colonized culture that are framed as immoral or uncivilized when performed by the colonized.

This cultural appropriation is represented by images that connect the narrator to food, which the white women seem to swallow whole, denying her personhood and making her and her culture part of themselves. In *The Farming of Bones*, Edwidge Danticat describes skin as looking like "Brazil nut shells" and "cherimoya milk" (11) in order to unyoke the physical appearance of colour from the socially constructed and sometimes imagined colour inherent in the concept of race; Mootoo's comparisons of appearance to food accomplish something else entirely. By associating "brown" with "sugary", the narrator evokes the exoticized, commodified, appetizing woman of colour: brown sugar, as it were, a delicious treat for white people to enjoy.

The narrator's new friends define her Indianness for her, urging her to drink chai or lassi when she prefers a cappuccino (113) and exhorting her to eat at Indian restaurants her stomach cannot tolerate (114). They model for her what they think is authentic Indian behaviour, replicating the characteristic head bobble and even imitating an Indian accent. "Sliding her neck, Meghan would say in an accent thick and syrupy as a jilebi, 'All we want is peace and happiness in this world. I am wishing you these this very morning!'" (115). By connecting the head shake, the feigned accent and *jilebi*, a well-known Indian dessert, the narrator again depicts Indianness as something palatable to be consumed by others at will.

Indeed, sometimes it seems as if the white women are more Indian than the narrator. Meghan knows a good deal of Hindi and conspicuously drops common interjections and even whole sentences into conversations (117). The narrator, on the other hand, like Kamla of Persaud's *Butterfly in the Wind*, has only a meagre Hindi vocabulary, made up primarily of culinary terms: "The only Indian words I know are those on the menus in Indian restaurants and in my very own *Indian Cookery by Mrs. Balbir Singh. . . .* Mrs. Singh taught me words like vindaloo, mulligatawny, bhuna, matar, pullao and gosht, and of course, roti in some of its varieties: chapati, puri, naan, and so on" (117). Having failed to learn Hindi from her grandmother as a child, instead learning English grammar from Mrs Ramsay, the narrator's relationship with her ancestors' mother tongue is culinary only, little more than a tourist's rapport. Her grandmother, she notes, couldn't possibly have imagined that one day a white woman would speak better Hindi than her granddaughter, and would have been "baffled by the upside-downness of the world as it unfolds" (117).

In part 3, the protagonist visits a Hindu temple with her new Indophile friends. In the story's climax, her grief at having lost so much of her culture to colonization comes to a head when Meghan and Victoria invite her to go with them to a nearby Hare Krishna ashram. When they arrive to pick her up, wearing full saris, the narrator's suppressed resentment rises to the surface. "What business do you have showing me what I have lost?" she fumes to herself. "Go check out your own ancestry!" (119). Things only get worse once they arrive at the ashram, where all the women, white and brown, are outfitted in full Indian garb, whereas the brown men wear "quiet, polite Western suits" (120). Indian culture is thus under a dual assault: from both the brown men's attrition and the white women's encroachment. In this moment the protagonist finally fully appreciates her grandmother's former dismay: "Dressed as I was, the only female Browny in Western wear, I understood, as if it were a revelation, Ahji's panic and distress at the unravelling of her culture right before her eyes" (120). Although the playfully generic "Browny" offers some comic relief, it can hardly balance out the tragic intensity of *panic* and *distress*. The narrator's "revelation" is a kind of divine vision that allows her to understand her grandmother's earlier prophetic ability.

Throughout the story, the narrator is torn between knowing that her friends are genuinely benevolent and feeling shame and irritation because of their behaviour. Victoria, whose very name conjures up images of the former Empress of India, and especially Meghan, whose obtuseness is unmatched, both seem to believe that the ashram and those who frequent it stand outside the colonial past and the unequal present. But the behaviour in the religious space demonstrates how colonial racial and religious dynamics persist. His Holiness, a white man dressed in Hare Krishna orange, sits on a throne surrounded by his white devotees. The white men sit closest to him, with the white women at the back and the women of colour the farthest back of all. In the temple, these women of colour are "put in their place" both literally and figuratively. They are also called away from the service, unable to finish their worship, in order to prepare food for the others:

> The Brown women fell into their places at the very back, against the wall. Midway through the sermon a young man came to fetch women, who were needed in the kitchen to serve the food. He crossed over and meandered among the congregation of White women who were nearest to him, heading for the Brown ones. They dutifully rose and followed him into the kitchen missing the ending of the sermon. (121)

Meghan perceives those inequalities, but only through the lens of gender, not of class or race: "Meghan followed my eyes as I watched the Brown women walking single-file to the kitchen", recounts the narrator. "In her favourite accent, full of empathy, she said, 'Pretty sexist, eh! That's a problem for us too'" (121). Meaghan's white privilege blinds her to the glaringly intersectional character of the Indian women's exclusion from public Hindu religious life in a post-colonial world, where racism and patriarchy are inextricably bound together. In "The Upside-downness of the World as It Unfolds" there is no space outside of history, no space that can fully oppose or resist the inequality of the world.

This is not to say that Mootoo's story is generally pessimistic. On the contrary, it offers hope. It shows that real progress can be made in the future if we honestly engage with both the past and the present. As she observes the social dynamics at play between the browns and the whites, the protagonist discovers that Indianness is not just a culture to be consumed, but also a history to be assumed and a reality to be lived. From Mrs Ramsey's frank colonialism to Meghan and Virginia's well-meaning cluelessness, Mootoo finely renders the complexity of the power dynamics between women. Like the other authors in this study, she here implicitly calls for awareness of intersectionality and multiple ways of relating between women as the first step towards solidarity and coalitional feminism(s).

SUGAR INDIANS AND CACAO INDIANS

Shani Mootoo's third novel, *Valmiki's Daughter* (2009), engenders the struggle to decolonize the mind not in the Canadian diaspora but within Trinidad itself. The book conducts an intergenerational interrogation of the relationships among class, race, gender and sexuality among the Indo-Caribbean elites of contemporary Trinidad – connections that are often demonstrated by food imagery.

Valmiki's Daughter focuses on two elite Trinidadian families, both descended from indentured East Indians. The ancestors of Dr Krishnu and his family once endured the brutal life of cane workers, but the family is now well respected and they are wealthy members of the professional class. The ancestors of Ram Prakash and his clan had worked the cocoa plantations, and his forefather Deudnath had eventually bought the very plantation he had worked as an indentured man; today the Prakash family strives for respectability among the business elite, especially the Europeans with whom they do business. The novel begins and ends in the present day, as Dr Valmiki Krishnu, a gay man who has been in the closet his entire life, agonizes over his secretly lesbian daughter Viveka's impending marriage to a man. The middle of the novel is divided into four parts set over the course of the preceding several months, which explain how Valmiki and his daughter arrived at this situation.

Each of the four parts is set in a single place: part I in the seaside city of San

Fernando, part 2 in the nearby gated community of Luminada Heights, part 3 in the inland mountain plantation of Chayu, and part 4 in San Fernando again. Each section begins with a second-person narrative titled "Your Journey" that offers an ethnographic, somewhat didactic overview of the setting, describing its sights, sounds, smells and sensations as they would appear to a newcomer or tourist. The rest of the chapter in each part is in third person with variable internal focalization, going below the surface to explore hidden, highly gendered personal experiences and perspectives. The focal characters of each chapter rotate, and the chapters' analeptic passages further contextualize the characters' individual lives within the community's historical trajectory.

In part 1, "San Fernando", the narrator introduces the reader to a multiracial, highly unequal society born of a colonial past. Trinidadian street vendors and their wares, the reader learns, are an integral part of the noisescape and scentscape of the city, and the vendors' carts and stalls serve as de facto social hubs. By putting these merchants and their wares front and centre, Mootoo establishes the context as specifically Trinidadian, with its own distinct foodways and worldview. The narrator begins by vaunting street-vendor culture as one would to a tourist, asserting that if the reader went to San Fernando, "The aroma of roasting peanuts, of corn boiling in garlic-infused water, of over-used vegetable oils in which split-pea fritters with cumin seeds have been fried, of the cheery, spicy foreignness of the apples and grapes being sold in the open-air counter on the corner would activate your tastebuds."[20] She notes that between the unshelled peanuts, hot dogs and hamburgers, "The scent of food rising up from all corners of the city is a blessing" (19).

However, teenaged Vashti, the younger of the Krishnu daughters, must eat the Trinidadian street food surreptitiously. As the girl waits in line outside her single-sex school to buy doubles for lunch, she rubs elbows with people who are not like herself: the lower classes, other ethnicities, boys. None of this, explains the narrator, would please the elitist Valmiki and his wife, Devika:

> Her parents, Dr. and Mrs. Krishnu, who consider themselves to be of high-calibre Indian ancestry, prefer not to know that their two daughters buy and eat street food. They know it is fashionable. The food section of the daily paper

often praises the inventiveness and culturally hybrid taste of Trinidadian street food – the doubles, aloo pies, tamarind balls, pone, sugar cake – hailing it to be among the tastiest in the world. But still Dr. and Mrs. Krishnu can't bring themselves to eat food prepared by people whose sanitary habits are unknown, food served in the germ-filled and fly-infested outdoors. (20–21)

This episode, the first significant food-based scene of the book, condenses many of the novel's major themes: the intersection of class, ethnicity and (imagined) intergenerational history – the Krishnus' "high-calibre Indian ancestry"; the possibility that one could take pride in the joyfully, richly hybrid Trinidadian identity; and Indo-Trinidadians' resistance to assimilating into the racially and culturally mixed nation they inhabit. These expectations and limitations weigh especially heavily on the Krishnus' daughters, for in Indian and Indo-Trinidadian culture, girls are much more subject to demands that they adhere rigidly to class-based and cultural norms of behaviour – including heterosexuality.

In this introductory scene Vashti commits a minor alimentary infraction at the food truck, secretly buying a double for lunch. There she encounters Merle Bedi, a former classmate of her sister's, who was thrown out of her house when it became known that she is homosexual. Vashti, terrified of public guilt by association with this rumoured "buller" (23), is torn between compassion for the bedraggled, barefoot, homeless Merle and the culturally instilled bigotry that justifies the young lesbian's condition. The bewildered teen tries at first to give her sister's friend the double she has just purchased, then rushes inside to escape her own discomfort and, more important, the public eye. Vashti's transgression and her encounter with Merle echo Viveka's similar (but more consequential) transgressions: her queer desire and queer sexual expression, public knowledge of which would endanger her ethnic belonging and class status. Both girls respond to unreasonable limitations with secrecy and evasion to avoid consequences from their community, who see class status, Indianness, womanhood and heterosexuality as mutually determined categories. A threat to one type of identity is necessarily a threat to all.

The social status with which the Krishnus are so concerned comes from Valmiki Krishnu's high-status work as a doctor and his family's current wealth, not from their actual origins, for the family is descended from indentured East Indian sugarcane workers. The cane workers – "sugar Indians" – had a remarkably low status even among manual workers, just above that of the enslaved Africans they replaced in the fields, and lower than that of the "cocoa Indians", from whom the Krishnus' friends the Prakash family are descended. Sugar Indians worked under more brutal conditions, and because the cocoa market collapsed long before the sugar market, they shed their indentured status much later. Although the Krishnus' highly successful family members were "among the fortunate few who had managed to get out early", there remains a hidden symbolic gulf between them and the Prakash family. When Viveka's friend Nayan Prakash speaks about his cocoa Indian grandfather, Viveka feels "the sting of that difference" between their forebears (216), despite the Krishnus' present-day social superiority.

Although the Krishnus imagine themselves fully Indian, they are in fact Indo-Trinidadian, as illustrated by the Trinidadian food they eat. For example, although the parents tell their daughters not to eat street food, Valmiki and his daughters regularly have doubles, Trinidad's most famous street food, for lunch (41, 96, 145). In one of Viveka's most vivid childhood memories, the whole family enjoys boiled corn, another of the island's favourite street dishes, together in the car (164). At the Krishnu home there is daily fresh coconut bake for breakfast (156), leftover paratha roti in the fridge (145) and black cake (140) at afternoon tea, all of which mark the family as distinctly Trinidadian, in daily practice if not in spirit.

Despite their daily cultural and culinary participation in Trinidadian culture, the Indo-Trinidadian elites romanticize themselves as "authentic" Indians, closely attached to faraway cousins in Mother India. But Nayan Prakash discovers to his dismay that the feeling is not mutual. In fact, Indian immigrants in North America and Europe view Indo-Trinidadians as "watered-down Indians" rather than "good grade A Indians" (45), as the narrator of "Out on Main Street" puts it. Laments Nayan:

> In their eyes, too, we – the sugar-cane and cacao Indians, those of us from Trinidad, Guyana, Fiji – we don't exist. . . . Even they, who share our ancestors – dismiss us. As if we are poor, poor, poor copies of an original that no longer exists. . . . So many years after leaving India, after losing the language, after watering down the culture, the religion, we're groping, still shy of becoming

Trinidadian. . . . We are not properly Indian, and don't know how to be Trinidadian. We are nothing. (307)

Nayan asserts that Indo-Trinidadians insist on being something they can never be (Indian) instead of trying to be something they should be (Trinidadian). In so doing, he claims, they become nothing at all. It seems that Indo-Trinidadian elites cling to imagined Indianness as a bulwark against assimilation – into Europeanism on one side and black Trinidadian culture on the other.

COLONIAL APPETITES

Mootoo, like Persaud, sees the living legacy of colonialism in Trinidad in the island's social inequality, anti-blackness, Eurocentrism and nostalgic attachment to the "authentic" – all conditions that women are expected to maintain. Mirroring *Sastra*'s Shakuntala, Devika Krishnu guards the family's class status by throwing lavish parties to impress other members of the Indo-Trinidadian elite. However, when Nayan Prakash brings home a French wife, Devika instinctively understands that the lavish spending of money – "several choices of meat" and "after dinner drinks", "flowers and candleholders" and "vases for every table" (118) – cannot take the place of cultural capital:

> No, no, definitely no pork or beef, and the Chinese food would have to be done without a hint of pork, as there would be Hindus and Muslims at the party. Fish, chicken, duck – all three. Shrimp is fine, but you know how quickly it can turn in the heat. Nothing but the best, everything done with, with, with a European flair, if you know what I mean. Authentic Indian, authentic Chinese, whichever, but arranged and served with European – well, not just any European – more like *French* class and flair. (146)

In her decisions about food – her desire to serve "authentic" (read "pure") precolonial Asian cuisines – Devika rejects the hybridity and syncretism of Caribbeanness, which is closely associated with Afro-Caribbean people. Her attachment to the purity of "ancient" precolonial cultures plays into colonial logic, for Eurocentricity defines itself as the "pure" absence of blackness. As Devika dreams of French "class and flair", she amalgamates ethnicity, race, class and status, equating Frenchness (and the whiteness it entails) with economic dominance and superior social standing – a perfect storm of Eurocentrism rooted in the colonial past.

At the same time, Devika's attachment to ancient precolonial cultures is simultaneously a form of resistance to Eurocentrism, for those are cuisines and cultures that have not yet been tainted by colonialism. Devika thus has a dialectical relationship with Europeanness, which is further illustrated by her differing attitudes towards Indian women and European women. In contrast to her admiration for Anick's French "flair", Devika looks down on Viveka's friend Helen for being too European, too assimilated:

> Helen is not even Indian. At least, not *properly* Indian. Her father is white. . . .
> On top of that, Helen's mother is a brassy Port of Spain Indian. Those Indians
> from the north like to think they are too different. . . . Those town Indians
> have no respect for their origins, they forget their place, they ooh and they
> aaah over curry as if they never had curry before, and they give their children
> names like Helen. (48)

Here Devika objects to miscegenation and to assimilation, ostensibly because she cares about preserving Indianness in the diaspora. But in fact her objections to Helen's mother seem rooted in class threat and rejection of the gender norms of Indian culture. Indian women who marry white men instead of dutifully marrying an Indian, who view Indian food as a tourist would instead of fulfilling their moral obligation to reproduce Indian foodways, who name their daughter Helen – after a European ideal of rebellious, seductive femininity – instead of a good Indian name that encodes submissive femininity – these Indian women "forget their place", becoming "brassy", vulgar, shrill, impudent, shameless. In the face of this rebellious Indo-Trinidadian womanhood – intersectional rather than "pure", oblivious to shame as a tool of control – the internal logic of upper-class Indo-Caribbean hetero-femininity simply falls apart. Indo-Caribbean mothers should not, simply *must* not let that happen.

Valmiki, Devika's husband, keeps up class expectations in public but in private enjoys nearly unlimited freedom, both culinary and sexual. Valmiki is gay and has been in the closet since before he married Devika, his partner in maintaining their public respectable, high-status life. But he is also involved in a long-standing affair with a lower-status Afro-Trinidadian man. He goes on hunting trips with his lover, Saul, and Saul's working-class Afro-Caribbean friends. During meals at Saul's house, Valmiki relishes the opportunity to drop all pretence, escaping the confines of class, race and sexuality:

> There would suddenly be a platter heaped with lengths of limp sugary plantain that glistened in a slick of the oil in which they had been deep fried until they looked, but were not, burnt. . . . The other men ate with their hands, but they always gave Valmiki a thin, light spoon that bent with the slightest pressure, or a fork, each of its tines making off in a different direction, and a knife. But he would use his hands, and then he would lick his fingers, one at a time, each one deep in his mouth, down to the knuckle almost, pulled out slow, his teeth gripping and scraping off the very last tastes, with an indiscreet pop. (58–59)

The plantain, a Caribbean favourite, stands in sharp contrast to the cuisines Devika values, all of which come from abroad. Deep-fried until very dark, piled onto a platter and covered with oil, the plantains are a simple, spontaneous working-class food, in opposition to the elegance of Devika's studied, formal society dinners.

This Trinidadian food is connected to other forms of desire. Valmiki refuses the utensils his hunting companions offer him and deliberately eats with his hands. The erotic, almost obscene description of his behaviour at the table, the way he "would lick his fingers, one at a time, each one deep in his mouth" and pulled them out "slow . . . with an indiscreet pop" seems to mimic the performance of oral sex on a man. This pivotal scene is simultaneously a rebellious show of class and ethnic solidarity with the workingmen and a kind of frank, in-your-face homosexuality, both of which are utterly at odds with prevailing Trinidadian societal norms. This juxtaposition perfectly encapsulates Mootoo's reimagining of coalitional possibilities between sexual minorities and economic and racial underclasses, based on a mutual rejection of the hierarchical scramble to meet standards of respectability that were never meant to include them in the first place.

Part 2 opens with a drive from San Fernando to Luminada Heights, a journey that the narrator tells us "is a social lesson in and of itself" (187). Below that affluent neighbourhood lie poor neighbourhoods with "outdoor latrines and shower stalls", where "squatters live in huts and shacks with no running water or electricity" (188). To arrive at the Heights, one must ignore the poverty-stricken people along the way: "the barefoot wiry man in . . . torn trousers meandering dangerously in a drugged stupor" and the "bent, bodi-thin woman sweeping the step of her one-room shack" (188). Once out of these desperately poor areas, the upward climb offers a "chronology of affluence", first meandering past the homes of schoolteachers and store clerks, then winding through neighbourhoods full of self-employed electricians and painters, then passing the houses of engineers and stockbrokers. At the peak of the hill, the highest, most desirable terrain, an elite community of Indo-Trinidadian doctors and lawyers look down on their less fortunate neighbours, both literally and figuratively.

Built on a former pasture that was abandoned and sold by its French owners when Trinidad's independence from Britain became imminent, Luminada Heights is a hotbed of attachment to both the ancestral Mother India and the colonial "motherland", Europe. Like the very earth beneath their homes, the community's attitudes and value judgements are tied up in the history of colonialism on the island. When newlywed Nayan Prakash brings his beautiful French wife to live there, it becomes clear that the Trinidadian elites who live on the Heights remain bound up in a need for approval from Europe – they are post-colonial rather than decolonial.

Nearly everyone seems to agree that Nayan's new bride represents the height of taste. In Luminada Heights, Europeanness – and specifically Frenchness – is seen as definitionally beautiful and charming, as having unquestionable universal appeal. Ram, Nayan's father, cannot deny the cultural capital she has brought as a dowry into the marriage:

> He was not unaware of the prestige Anick's Frenchness, her beauty and charm, brought to his family. . . . People built parties around Anick. . . . They had food catered, and their home rearranged, and pieces of furniture and accessories bought with her eyes and approval in mind. . . . His son might have been worth three hundred dollars an hour in cash; but even Nayan knew that this worth had been increased by Anick's presence in his life in ways that numbers and dollars could not measure. (233–34)

The young woman herself regularly draws upon the cultural currency her Frenchness affords her, confident that others will – *must* – recognize her inherent cultural superiority, especially with regard to food. When Nayan attempts to assert his opinions about Anick's brother-in-law's cooking, she immediately objects: "What do you mean *pretty good*? Of course he know to cook. He learn to cook in France, after all. We French, we know about food" (206).

Anick's snobbery about food is not a personal oddity or learned from her family culture; it stems from a global cultural order in which French cultural imperialism is internalized and sustained by others on the cultural peripheries, as Nayan observes:

> He had felt in France that while a notable few were born into fortune, the French, by dint of being just that – French – regardless of their class came into the world with a sense of style as part of their heritage. He didn't know if this was true, but they certainly made you feel they were the owners of all things cultural. And, of course, they were only encouraged in this when they were copied by others everywhere. High-society Trinidadians often left the island to purchase this international style. (242)

While it may have lost its monopoly on political power, Europe has maintained its grip on cultural influence throughout the rest of the world. Nayan pinpoints the complicity of post-colonial elites in perpetuating European cultural domination a full half-century after political independence.

Nayan himself, however, remains mired in post-colonial attitudes, although he resists and competes with Europeanness even as he fetishizes it. This resistant relationship – the basing of identity on differentiation from the other rather than imitation – is still a relationship. His enmeshment with Europeanness is visible in his heated desire for revenge on the Europeans, which he seeks to carry out by marrying one of their women and vanquishing them in business: "He would show white France, and the immigrant populations there. He would show Canadians. He would show other Trinidadians. He would show Anick" (241). For Nayan, bedding, then marrying Anick was sweet revenge on every European person who had ever doubted his value because of his dark skin. As he recalls their courtship, he remembers the satisfaction he felt at his sexual conquest: "They were in France, and France in all its Frenchness, all its self-assuredness, went on around them, and no Frenchman was in bed with her, the most beautiful woman he had ever seen, but he, from Trinidad, was" (227).

Likewise, Nayan's ambition to create a line of chocolates that will appeal to even the most discerning of European palates is another act of retribution, an attempt to redress the humiliation he felt when he first witnessed how Anick's family related to fine chocolate: "He, the son of a cacao estate owner and all-things-chocolate maker, wasn't familiar with such dark chocolate . . . the Thieberts and their friends, to a background of classical music, were breaking off tiny bits of the dark chocolate, putting them on the tips of their tongues and masticating very animatedly, grunting in their analyses, judicious with their displays of pleasure, all as if they were critics evaluating wines" (222). Here Nayan recalls the inadequacy he felt when faced with discriminating European tastes. Although he owns a cacao estate bought from the French, he simply produces the chocolate (just as Mrs Ramsay's maid produced the food). European tastes and modes of consumption remain the rule.

In some ways Nayan's desire for revenge against European cultural hegemony reprises the actions of his ancestor Deudnath, who turned the tables on the French by buying the cocoa plantation on which he had been an indentured worker: "The lore of the Prakash family was that Deudnath bought Chayu – the entire forty-five-acre estate – with cash, his savings from employment there, handed over to the French owner in the very cacao sacks in which he had been saving the money" (216). Nayan finds the tale of his ancestor's exploit deeply satisfying, concrete proof of an emergent new world order in which the sugar and cacao Indians of the Caribbean will finally get their due. For him, the story is "evidence in truth of the decline of Empire and the rise of the Indian" (216). Once he conquers the French chocolate market, he tells himself, that victory, begun generations ago, will finally be complete.

QUEERING THE PLANTATION

Part 3 travels to the very cacao plantation, Chayu, that Deudnath bought. In the opening of this part of the book, the narrator leads the reader out of the affluent coastal community of Luminada Heights and heads due east, down past the misery of the cane fields and on into the centre of the island. There, in the low mountains of the Central Range, past the simple country houses and the little plots of citrus, banana and peewah (268), lies Chayu. An imposing presence in the region, the Prakash family's cacao estate is well-known by the simple rural folk who live in its shadow. "Just off the main road, still going east," directs the narrator, "you turn left at the first main road, and ask anyone – and they will jab their forefinger decidedly in the direction of Chayu" (269).

Nayan and Anick take up residence in the original French plantation house at Chayu. Within the space of the plantation – emblematic of the colonial past and all its inheritances – they grapple with the colonial past, each in their own way. It is also at Chayu that Anick and Viveka's mutual attraction finally ignites into a full-fledged romantic and sexual affair, a queering of the plantation that is both literal and symbolic.

Anick is drawn to Chayu out of a desire to recapture the glory of French dominance. She is enamoured of "[t]he romance of living deep in the central hills with tropical forest all around, in an original French plantation house" (275) and hires experts to "restore Chayu to its colonial origins" (276). She is particularly thrilled to find a nearly effaced inscription, "Le Ciel de Chaillou", carved into a gable:

> The original French owners of the estate obviously knew the history of chocolate in France and had named it in honour of David Chaillou – "Chaillou's Heaven". It was a pleasant irony to Anick that she had ended up living in this particular estate, this particular house. The discovery of the name of the house was, to her mind, like unearthing an umbilical cord to France. It gave her a humorous sense of "right of presence". (279)

Anick's callous reaction to this proof of the plantation's colonial origins – the words *pleasant* and *humorous* are particularly striking – is a cogent reminder of the way that European cultural and economic dominance can quite easily be detached from its context and emptied of meaning. Anick's charming new home at Chayu, like the France she came from, was not built upon French people's discriminating taste or great culinary tradition, but rather on the colonial power's willingness to dehumanize, enslave and indenture others in the pursuit of profit. But for the culturally privileged Anick, the romanticized plantation symbolizes only natural beauty, human ingenuity and material abundance. Clearly she understands neither how hard East Indians had to fight to establish their own "right of presence" in the Caribbean nor the vital role the land played in that fight.[21]

His French wife's glossing-over of colonial history is not lost on Indo-Trinidadian Nayan. While Anick's relationship to the plantation (and indeed to history itself) is one of denial, his is the opposite, bordering on obsession. He rebuts her attempt to lay cultural claim to the plantation by firmly refusing the French version of its name: "But the connection, and her talk of it in this manner, irritated Nayan. He had an ornate brass plaque made, on which was inscribed the single word *Chayu*. This is how the house had come to be known, with a name that sounded Indian enough, and so, according to Nayan, it would remain" (279). The shift from the French *Chaillou* to the Indian-sounding *Chayu* asserts the connection between East Indians and the Caribbean lands where they had worked and lived for generations. The plaque thus commemorates the triumphant ascendency of those Indians who had risen from one-time indentureship to become Indo-Trinidadian elites – a sweet and fitting reversal.

However, as we have noted, Nayan's very obsession with destroying the colonial relationship is a form of post-colonialism, and the plaque reminds us that neither Trinidad nor Nayan has reached a state of true decolonization. He is hyper-aware of his own racial and cultural marginalization but quite indifferent to the class-, gender- and sexuality-based ways in which he marginalizes others. The orthographic change from *Chaillou* to the nearly identically pronounced *Chayu* indicates that Nayan is himself reproducing the very colonial hierarchies he despises: he exploits the Indo- and Afro-Trinidadian labourers who work the plantation and has little regard for his poorer neighbours. At Chayu, both Ram and Nayan focus on policing the cacao estate and the local population. The neighbouring poor, they insist, must ask permission before gathering wild honey on the estate (289). The maid must be scolded and intimidated into submission (291). Nayan retains the colonizer/colonized binary, simply replacing the European colonizers on top with Indo-Trinidadian elites such as himself.[22]

Strikingly, Anick's behaviour contrasts sharply with her husband's. Although she often acts with the blind racial and cultural privilege of the European colonizer (as in her attitude towards the plantation itself), in a show of class-conscious solidarity with the working man that is also quite

French, she treats Chayu's employees and neighbours with non-hierarchical respect, making genuine efforts to connect with them: "Anick now made an even greater effort to speak and understand English. . . . The result of her making extra efforts and learning the names of neighbours, visiting people, and allowing herself to be visited in turn, was that she was looked out for *by* the villagers as much as she came to look out *for* them" (281). Perhaps Anick's empathy for the lower classes comes from one of the more marginalized elements of her identity, for Anick is bisexual. Her parents, she reveals, were never supportive of her same-sex relationships, and the racial and cultural privilege that protects her in some ways does not allow her to be fully free, fully herself. "French does not mean enlightenment", she explains. "It does not mean freedom" (346). Anick's parents, it turns out, are far more accepting of interracial relationships than of homosexual ones. Nevertheless, to the Frenchwoman's great peril, at Chayu she and Viveka begin a romantic and sexual affair.

Viveka and Anick's clandestine courtship is at first conducted at the level of food, that sensuous pleasure that has already been connected with homosexuality in the book (Vashti's encounter with Merle at the food truck; Valmiki's plantains). Anick begins to seduce Viveka by offering her an hors-d'oeuvre: "She brought the cap up to Viveka's mouth and looked directly at Viveka's lips, parting her own. Viveka felt the mushroom cap brush her lips and she opened her mouth. She offered the tip of her tongue to take the morsel. Anick rested her forefinger and thumb on Viveka's lower lip. The two women looked directly at each other now. Anick bit her bottom lip. Viveka's mouth was full" (295). The slow, circular progression from one sensual body part to another ("mouth . . . [eyes] . . . lips . . . lips . . . mouth . . . tip of her tongue . . . forefinger and thumb . . . lip . . . [eyes] . . . lip . . . mouth") with its emphasis on the mouth, the hands and the eyes, creates a woman-centred homoerotic narrative of seduction and desire. The repetition of *lip(s)*, especially when combined with the verb forms *parting, brush* and *bit*, accentuates the word's potential for *double entendre* and its intimate connection with female sexuality. It is important that their affair begins within the space of the plantation, for their enactment of tabooed homosexual love – a taboo that originated with the British Empire and was retained (and internalized) under the Independence Pact – undercuts the colonial binary that the plantation represents.

At first this queering of the plantation[23] seems to hold the promise of psychic liberation. As she makes love to Anick, Viveka breaks free of a lifetime of imposed ideology about the nature of her own womanhood. Letting go of the gender identity assigned to her by her race, ethnicity, class and colonial history, she catches a glimpse of what it might feel like to be fully herself: "this was the strongest sensation of that sort Viveka had ever had – of not being what she looked like, female. And yet, she knew now more than ever that her feelings and her way with Anick were hers and hers alone. Not a boy's. Not a man's. Whatever she was, these feelings were hers" (322–23). Mootoo's Viveka is not "what she looked like"; neither the Other's gaze nor the Other's notions of the parameters of femininity determine her essence. Instead, "her feelings" – her own emotions and worldview – and "her way" – her actions and choices – constitute who and what she is, and for this first time they are expressed in her behaviour. As Viveka learns to trust her own experience and personal embodiment of gender and sexuality over the heteronormative ideology of strictly binary gender, she lays the groundwork for breaking free of the Independence Pact once and for all.

But Viveka understands that the plantation logic of categorization, hierarchy, domination and exclusion cannot be dismantled by one person's clear vision, and she considers retaining her new freedom by leaving Trinidad. Anick too dreams of leaving the plantation, urging Viveka to flee with her to Canada, "to Toronto or Montreal or Vancouver – where there were thriving communities of people like the two of them. There, she said, they could disappear if they wanted to, and reinvent themselves" (335). Despite the ethnic and racial forms of discrimination that Viveka the Indo-Trinidadian will no doubt face there, for Viveka the lesbian, Canada represents freedom. In Canada she will be free from the Independence Pact and free to forge her own identity. But Viveka is realistic. Although she and Anick may experience psychic liberation in North America, they will not be liberated from the material realities of the world in which they live: "Neither of them would be able to find anyone in their regular circles who would help them. . . . It would cause a public scandal, and there would be the very real threat of physical harm being done to both of them" (346). Viveka teeters on the brink of a life like her father's, of repressing her desires or remaining in the closet, unable to publicly be her full self.

The deciding moment arrives when Nayan's parents throw a large anniversary party for their son and his wife at Chayu, where Nayan triumphantly announces that he and Anick are expecting their first child. Both of the Krishnu parents seem to know about Viveka and Anick's relationship, but they respond in very different ways. Devika seeks to force Viveka to keep her feelings secret. She orders Viveka not to threaten the long-standing relationship between the two families, saying "You *better* watch yourself" (350). Valmiki, on the other hand, decides to defy his wife, come out from under the veil of secrecy behind which his real emotional and sexual life takes place, and support his daughter, urging her to embrace her identity and her freedom. "This place is too small for you", Dr Krishnu tells her. "Take a deep breath, and leave this behind. There is so much more waiting for you elsewhere. So much, you can't imagine" (354).

Viveka considers taking Valmiki's advice, for she does not wish to live her life chafing under the bonds of legal and cultural disapproval: "She could not live clandestinely. She would not. . . . There simply had to be a place where she would fit in, and she would find that place" (359). But to do so, she will have to leave Trinidad behind: "She had to leave. That was clear . . . in her heart she knew that there was nowhere on her small island far away and safe enough. After all, it was not only her security but that of her family, her mother and her father and Vashti, that would be affected" (360). For Viveka, the only way to escape the plantation's merciless logic is to run. Canada again figures as a place of freedom from the Independence Pact's anti-homosexuality.

A THIRD WAY

Thus far the novel has offered only two options for Viveka: to remain in Trinidad and (like her father) deny or hide an enormous part of her identity, or flee alone to Canada, cutting family and community ties and becoming part of the crowd of diasporic Indo-Trinidadian Canadians we saw represented in *Out on Main Street*. But in part 4, "Valmiki's Daughter", the novel offers a third option, a devious, insightful feminist response that refuses to submit, even where outright resistance is impossible.[24] This is the kind of homegrown feminism that takes into account all the nuances of self-actualization in one's real, complicated life.

Part 4 leaves the isolated plantation and returns to society, to San Fernando, where the whole story began and where family ties and ethnic responsibilities lie more heavily, pull more tightly. It seems that the interlude at Chayu has been just that – an interlude – and back down in the real world, nothing has really changed. "In any case," remarks the narrator, "as the saying goes, wherever you go, there you are. There you are" (363). This speaks to how the internalization of oppressive norms into the self, into its deepest values and perspectives, works to perpetuate them. The oppressed carry with them the source of their coercion wherever they go, for it is within the self.

To her mother's delight and her father's mixed feelings (both grief and relief), young Viveka has decided not to flee alone to Canada to honour her gay identity at the expense of the other elements of her intersectional identity: family, religion, ethnicity, race. From her new sundresses to her recent engagement to Trevor, a young Indo-Trinidadian-Canadian engineer, Valmiki's daughter is finally meeting the expectations of young Indo-Trinidadian womanhood. It seems that she has capitulated, has perhaps decided to follow her father's path. But we discover that, after the wedding, the young couple will live in Canada, the country that throughout the book has been imagined as a place of sexual freedom and self-expression. Viveka opts for both an "appropriate" marriage and fleeing the island, choosing neither submission nor full resistance but, instead, a feminist response.

As Viveka prepares for the wedding, she reflects back on the day when Trevor proposed. As she sits in the car with him discussing their future, she thinks how much easier life will be if she doesn't resist the heteronormative expectations of her mother, her culture, her homeland. But, in the background, threads of her resistance pluck at her senses: the quiet soundtrack of the discussion is a classical cello piece, Anick's favourite music, and outside the car the cane fields burn, reminding her of the history of homophobic colonialism that constricts her: "On either side of two sections of the highway, fields were ablaze. Ribbons of glowing cane leaves spiralled upwards and sailed through the air. They floated back down as grey strands of ash. Although she had the air intake vents closed off and cold-air blower turned on high, the sweet smell of the burning cane fields, the heaviness of the smoke, managed to enter the vehicle" (376). The burning cane seems to symbolize the persistence of colonialism and the inevitability of history's repetition. For centuries the cane has been burned in the same way to kill it off and then renew the fields between growing seasons.[25] We see that colonialism, like the cane smoke, is insidious, creeping into the car despite her best efforts, just as colonial values and attitudes are internalized by the colonized despite efforts to resist them. For Viveka, the burning cane alludes not only to an abstract island or the regional colonial past, but also to her own "sugar Indian" bloodline. This is personal. Surrounded on all sides by flames, breathing in the smoke, haunted by the cello's faint reminder of forbidden passion and elusive fulfilment, she seems to be nothing more than the novel's title suggests: Valmiki's daughter, repeating Valmiki's mistakes.

But Viveka is doing something more. Determined to become neither Merle Bedi (excluded from society because of her open homosexuality) nor Anick (accepted by society only because she closets her bisexuality), Viveka gropes for a third way. Her marriage to Trevor is not, as it first appears, a simple reiteration of her father's decision to mask his homosexuality with heterosexual respectability. Rather, it is "a means to an end" (376), a "descending in order to rise" (389): a way to escape to Canada, where she can someday hope to be free. In Viveka's cunning, courage and imagination, in the *why* of her choices (as opposed to the *what*), loving perception finds neither inaction nor submission, but rather a feminist response.[26]

This complex response to oppression can also be read as echoed by the blazing sugar cane in the background of her decision, for the cane fires evoke not only the colonial history of plunder and exploitation but also the class rebellion with which Trinidadian people responded.[27] Cane fires were at times set to destroy the colonizers' profits and give voice to the workers' outrage and resistance, and they could spread through chain reactions to the entire island and beyond.[28] Crop-burning was "the ultimate act of worker resistance against the plantation crop that created the colonial Caribbean".[29] Therefore, the flames, smoke and ash surrounding Viveka's car suggest not only colonialism and its insidious colonization of the deepest self but also a kind of deep and potentially contagious discontent, even desperation. This juxtaposition, like Valmiki's plate of fried plantains, ties Viveka's oppression as a lesbian to the plight of other historically suppressed classes in

Trinidad – a gesture towards a possible solidarity among sexual minorities and economic and racial underclasses that might enable Trinidad to fully decolonize itself.[30]

SOVEREIGNTY OF THE IMAGINATION

In Trinidad, as elsewhere in the Caribbean and the rest of the post-colonial world, the transition from a *post*-colonial state – in which elites assume the former colonizer's role within oppressive structures of inequality; identity is contingent on differentiation from the former colonial power; colonial-style divide and rule dictates internal power dynamics; and the Independence Pact remains intact – to a *de*colonial state – in which colonial structures of inequality are dismantled; identity is unyoked from the former colonizer; new solidarities upend internal power dynamics; and the Independence Pact is dissolved – could be achieved in part through realignment of the popular classes with same-sex-loving (SSL) individuals and persons of nonbinary gender expression. Such an interruption of the homophobic consensus would empower poor and working-class people to combat their own maltreatment rather than revisiting it upon others. Likewise, it would redirect LGBTQ activists away from the temptation to integrate society via the dominant discursive register of respectability, the very source of their oppression.[31]

The importance of Caribbean homosexual visibility – of not choosing the closet – to the project of full decolonization in the Caribbean cannot be overstated. In his introduction to the 2006 collection *Our Caribbean: A Gathering of Lesbian and Gay Writing from the Antilles*, editor Thomas Glave contends that gay and lesbian writing is desperately needed in the region, "for the expansion of our imagination and our very lives – our survival. It is so very important for us each to know that we are not, no matter what anyone tells us, throughout the archipelago and beyond it, alone."[32] This writing, he insists, must address what it is like to be lesbian or gay and also Caribbean, and all the intersections that necessarily entails. It must treat the difficulty of full self-realization within the archipelago and the role played by histories of colonialism in creating and entrenching homophobia. As the collection's title, *Our Caribbean*, suggests, this writing must assert that lesbians and gays belong to Caribbean lands, cultures and peoples, and that Caribbean lands, cultures and peoples belong to them. Emigration to Canada or other imagined utopias is not enough.

This is particularly important, as Rosamond King argues, because when one is an out homosexual – particularly an out lesbian, an identity with yet another intersectional oppression to contend with, that of gender – others will contest either one's Caribbeanness (one must have been "contaminated" by foreign culture) or the homosexuality (one must be confused). Like the Victorian European colonizers of the past, the black and brown elites of the present day police and erase non-conforming female sexualities. Yet, she continues, Caribbean lesbians do exist, and that existence must be recognized *as such* in order to achieve solidarity and decolonization for all:

> We are seen every day, but we are still invisible *as Caribbean lesbians*. The dream still to be acted on and realized is not only to stand with gay, bisexual, transgender, and all-sexual brothers and sisters, but also with heterosexual sisters and brothers. The dream is to pursue genuine change and acceptance for all Caribbean people, so that we can live and love and work together while acknowledging each other's existence in difference.[33]

According to King, then, validation and visibility for all are foundational to closing colonially inflicted wounds and ushering in a new era of community-building in the Caribbean.

Shani Mootoo's work is particularly important in this project of decolonization through visibility. She says, "Every book and every work is a coming out, as, in my own strategy, my audience is both the like-minded, queer person, and the one who is appalled by my identity of existence."[34] Mootoo's writing breaks the vicious cycle of silence and exclusion around non-heteronormative desire in the Caribbean context. Works such as *Out on Main Street* and *Valmiki's Daughter* help construct a more inclusive and affirmative social imaginary in which "Caribbean" and "queer" are not mutually exclusive categories. Importantly, these texts also interrogate the historical processes and class implications embedded in Caribbean understandings of sexuality. In so doing, they advocate for exposing and changing representations of sexuality as an integral part of decolonization.[35] Echoing Gisèle Pineau's potluck world vision, Edwidge Danticat's prayer for a welcome table and Lakshmi Persaud's meditation on the kitchen as a site of divine connection, Shani

Mootoo's incendiary reimagining brings sexual minorities and economic and racial underclasses together for their mutual liberation. Like Maryse Condé (as we will see in chapter 5), Mootoo calls for a radical redefinition of *us* and *them* and for knocking down all barriers to Caribbean liberation, including homophobia. True sovereignty of the imagination, as her fiction illustrates, will mean that *all* Caribbean people will be free to live, love and express themselves on their own terms.

CHAPTER 5

MARYSE CONDÉ
THE PEN AND THE PAN

Les identités se forgent.[1]

IN 1946, GUADELOUPE AND ITS SISTER island, Martinique, opted to exchange their colonial status for that of French *départements d'outre-mer* ("overseas departments"). The black and mulatto[2] elites favoured cultural and political assimilation with the French, and all sought the protection of France against the growing threat of US interference, which (as we have seen in chapter 2) was devastating the archipelago. Above all, majority Guadeloupeans needed to leverage French national power in order to check the extreme economic dominance of a tiny group of powerful *grands blancs* (known as *békés* in Martinique), descendants of the enslaving families of the past. However, over the next several decades they met with profound disenchantment. Just as abolition in 1848 had not eliminated extreme economic exploitation and hunger, departmentalization did not put an end to the violence of European economic, political and cultural domination, including a forced dependency on the European territory of France, even for food. After decades of lamenting colonial alienation, a dependent mentality and self-negation, in the late twentieth century French Antillean artists and intellectuals began reconceptualizing sovereignty and even freedom itself. Maryse Condé has been one of the leading voices in this endeavour.

In her culinary fiction, Maryse Condé offers a new vision of French Caribbean and post-colonial empowerment through food, holding women up as heroes, telling women's stories that had long been ignored by male cultural theorists and historians. In recent years she has published two novels that connect food to writing and to Guadeloupean culture, history and politics. *Victoire: My Mother's Mother* is a fictional autobiography that fills in the gaps of Condé's maternal grandmother's life. Condé draws upon the sometimes true, the almost true and the half true to tell the true-true story of Victoire's experiences as a black, female, illiterate cook in post-abolition colonial Guadeloupe.[3] *Of Morsels and Marvels*, meanwhile, is a culinary memoir drawn from Condé's life experiences as an activist, scholar and author whose travels have taken her all over the world. Both works use food imagery to show how gender, individual self-actualization and group empowerment operate interdependently in Guadeloupe and throughout the post-colonial world. Moreover, they examine the role of the artist (both literary and culinary) in engendering the ongoing historical process of French Antillean liberation and post-colonial sovereignty. As Condé deliberately associates the literary and the culinary in *Victoire* and *Of Morsels and Marvels*, she emphasizes the interconnectedness and interdependence of psychological and bodily liberation.

NO PRISONER OF HISTORY

Maryse Condé was born in 1937 in Guadeloupe to black bourgeois parents who emphasized the family's connection to mainland France and favoured the French language over Guadeloupian Creole. In 1953 she left Guadeloupe for Paris to complete her university studies. Condé spent the 1960s in politically tumultuous and newly independent Africa, in Guinea, Ghana and Senegal. During that time she came to realize that as a Caribbean person she was an outsider in Africa, despite Négritude's promises of universal black solidarity. In 1970 she returned to Paris and earned her doctorate from the Sorbonne in 1975. Condé worked for many years in the American academy, most notably at Columbia University, where she chaired the Center for French and Francophone Studies until her retirement in 2002. She has continued to write prolifically post-retirement, producing novels, plays, critical essays, children's literature and four works of autobiographical fiction, including two in which cooking is a prominent theme: *Victoire, My Mother's Mother* (2006)[4] and *Of Morsels and Marvels* (2015).[5] Her body of work has won numerous prizes, including the 2007 Prix tropiques for *Victoire* and the 2018 New Academy Prize in Literature (an alternative to the Nobel Prize for literature, which was not awarded that year). In 2015 she was awarded the Légion d'honneur, France's highest honour, and in 2020 she was decorated with the Grand-croix de l'ordre national du mérite by French president Emmanuel Macron.[6]

Condé is an iconoclast, known for both her rejection of linguistic group identification ("I like to repeat that I write neither in French nor in Creole. I write in Maryse Condé")[7] and her insistence on the primordial importance of individual experience over group belonging ("It's more important to be oneself wherever we are. To be oneself. To find one's voice, to find one's way").[8] In this, she is profoundly *fanonienne*.[9] "I am not a prisoner of History", the Martinican psychiatrist Frantz Fanon famously wrote in *Black Skin, White Masks* in 1952. "I must not look for the meaning of my destiny in that direction. . . . I am not a slave to the slavery that dehumanized my ancestors."[10] Like Fanon, Condé refuses to be defined by colonialism's legacy.[11] Rejecting both racism and racial essentialism, Fanon refused the notion of a universal black experience, emphasizing instead the diversity of black lived experiences: "The black experience is ambiguous, for there is not *one* Negro – there are *many* black men."[12] Condé both embraces and expands on Fanon's thinking, bringing the additional dimension of gender awareness to his foundational ideas.

Her writing constitutes keen social critique, lampooning hypocrisy and highlighting the shortcomings of ideology throughout a vast post-colonial space that encompasses the Americas, Europe and Africa. In 2007 she distanced herself from *la Francophonie*[13] and instead contributed to the artistic movement towards a *littérature-monde*.[14] In a 2009 interview she explained that her identity is not based on her country of residence: "I have an American passport. My imagination, my heart, they don't care. Where I live isn't important to them. They are Guadeloupian in their own way."[15] Condé again renounced the notion of origins in a 2011 documentary, *Maryse Condé: A Voice of Her Own*, where she stressed the fluid, changeable nature of so-called French identity.

Condé's penchant for provocation has yielded a rich body of work that engages with lived experience and literary theory in persistently fruitful ways. Over the past four decades her writing has rejected identity politics, tirelessly pushing back at Négritude, *antillanité* and *créolité*,[16] and consistently championed intellectual freedom with regard to post-colonial discourse. These tensions – between the global and the local, between individual character-istics and various forms of group belonging, and most especially between a historically determined trajectory and (especially artistic) self-determina-tion – are among the defining characteristics of Condé's *oeuvre*.[17] In keeping with this spirit, both her food-focused fictional biography *Victoire* and her partially fictionalized culinary memoir *Of Morsels and Marvels* contem-plate the relationship between history and the group imaginary, *Victoire* in post-abolition Guadeloupe and *Morsels and Marvels* in today's post-colonial, increasingly globalized world. Using culinary metaphors and Fanonian logic, both works examine how artists can disrupt historical determinism, heal the Caribbean imaginary and unshackle the individual by using both the pen and the pan.[18]

POST-ABOLITION GUADELOUPE

Victoire is set in late-nineteenth-century and early-twentieth-century colonial Guadeloupe, between the abolition of slavery in 1848 and Guadeloupe's de-partmentalization a century later. It depicts abolition not as a clean-cut end to slavery but as one link in the chain of history. Condé's novel articulates a complicated understanding of slavery's arduous legacy, beginning with the difficult period following abolition.[19] The book's characters, especially Victoire herself, are torn between racially determined forms of belonging, rooted in slavery and ironically magnified by abolition,[20] and the individual longing to be themselves.[21]

In Guadeloupe during the early years of the seventeenth century, black enslaved Africans toiled alongside indentured white *engagés*. Métis – people of racially mixed ancestry – were not only tolerated but free by royal decree. However, over time the white *engagés* gradually disappeared, and enslaved Africans were imported in massive numbers to replace them. As *slave* and *black* became very nearly synonymous, the Métis were reassigned (in accor-dance with the infamous Code Noir of 1685)[22] to their enslaved mothers' status. Despite the abolition of slavery in 1848, at the end of the nineteenth century colour revealed one's origins, and the memory of slavery was shamefully inscribed onto blackness. Both the official documents and the popular literature of the time attest that, a half-century after the abolition of slavery, Guadeloupe remained fundamentally a colour-based society; the lines of filiation between "freed person" and "free person of colour" were fully intact, and servitude was clearly racialized.[23] By the latter half of the nineteenth century, then, the socio-economic system of slavery had engendered a so-cio-racial society in Guadeloupe.

Under slavery a hierarchy of colour had emerged, with terms such as *mulâtre*, *câpre* and *sang-mêlé*[24] dividing enslaved Afro-Antilleans into phe-notypically and genotypically assigned social sub-groups, effectively pitting them against one another. Divisions based on phenotype could create divisions even within the same family, and they were thus a very effective way to prevent organization and revolt. Lighter-skinned enslaved Afro-Antilleans, for example, were preferentially used as house servants and commanded a higher market value, and the light-skinned enslaved house servants were encouraged to distance themselves from the enslaved field workers and attach themselves to the whites, with whom they worked closely. Writes Sainton of the resulting intra-racial animosity, "It is the internalization of the masters' racial ideology by Blacks that marks the complete victory of the ideology of colour."[25]

Within the group imaginary, certain expected behaviours were assigned to each racially determined sub-group. Those expectations endured beyond abolition and were built into the racialized structure of late-nineteenth-century Guadeloupe. In the group imaginary, blacks – who lived under the "curse of Ham" – were made for difficult, degrading work. Blacks themselves interiorized self-loathing and the negative stereotypes. They believed that it was natural for blacks to betray other blacks; that the mulattos mimicked but hated whites, with whom they competed; and that the mulattos looked down on or denied their black relatives, reappropriating the term *nègre* for themselves.[26]

In this society, one's real and knowable genealogy worked in tandem with a powerful "imaginary of origins" in which individuals commonly assigned themselves imagined ancestors, constructing a pyramidal hierarchy based on anteriority. Those with black ancestors who were free before 1848, for example, outranked those with black ancestors who had been freed only after abolition. Among whites, old creole families were preferred to newly arrived white ancestors. This imaginary of origins also took into account the status of one's ancestors. For example, if one's ancestors were enslaved, it was better if they were domestic workers and artisans than if they worked in the fields. While the socio-economic system was becoming more flexible, then, the system of colour remained fixed, and highly subjective (if not totally imaginary) hierarchies from the past played an important role. Therefore, in post-abolition Guadeloupe one's appearance was intimately linked to one's status and ancestry; the past, real or imagined, was constantly at play in the present.[27]

Victoire directly addresses this phenomenon of imagined origins. In *Of Morsels and Marvels*, Condé writes:

> My book *Victoire: My Mother's Mother,* intended to rehabilitate my grandmother, cook to a family of white Creoles, includes a great deal of provocation, which is a dominant feature of my personality. As a rule, people are said to be proud to count as an ancestor a poet, a philosopher, a historian whose lost notes they found in a trunk in the attic, or a brave soldier who died for their homeland. To claim as one's own a *dèyè chez*, a servant who never knew how to speak French, smacks of heresy. (ix)

Victoire violates the integrity of the imaginary of origins by exposing the presence of purely invented elements in our relationship with the past. The novel plays with this tradition of imagined origins as an explicitly imagined story – a fictional history – of the past; it says as much about Condé herself as it does about Victoire, just as the imagined origin stories did for nineteenth-century Guadeloupeans. But Condé's imagined history does not reinforce existing social, economic and racial distinctions. It instead *disturbs* historical hierarchies by elevating Victoire's cooking – usually viewed as menial labour – to a conscious creative, influential art form on a par with literature.

STRANGER THAN FICTION

In *Victoire: My Mother's Mother*, Condé aims to disrupt history by fictionalizing it and recovering the untold story of her maternal grandmother, who worked as a live-in cook for a wealthy white creole family in post-abolition Guadeloupe. Little historical information remains about Victoire, but Condé tells her story as she has imagined, excavated and inherited it. She explains, "It's the story of my mother and of my grandmother but seen and edited by the imagination's eye"[28] – an example of the "true-true" of fiction. Condé's writing puts in order the scattered happenings of Victoire's life, drawing a bold trajectory to connect them and ascribing emotions and motivations to ancestors long gone and never physically encountered.

The artist's ability to contribute to healing the group imaginary resides in her ability to dream a past and a future that go beyond reality. Condé views the writing of *Victoire* as a journey to discover her inner self (17), initially inspired by the discovery that her *noiriste* mother, Jeanne, was brought up in a white household – a reality that Condé sees as stranger than fiction: "*La réalité dépassait la fiction*" (16).[29] Victoire is mostly imagined – a device for Condé to tell her own and her mother's story: "If she [Victoire] has always interested and fascinated me", she clarified in a 2010 interview, "it's because she had such an influence on my mother. . . . I never really understood who my mother was. . . . Victoire is an element that helps me get at the truth about my mother and consequently about myself."[30] According to Condé, she writes in order to understand her mother's stilted relationship to the sensual pleasures in life: her lack of interest in cooking or eating delicious, appealing food and her difficulty in showing or receiving affection. At the same time Condé ostensibly writes to make sense of her own, opposite inclination: her abiding passion for provoking delectation with both the pen and the pan. "What I am claiming", she writes, "is the legacy of this woman [Victoire], who apparently did not leave any. I want to establish the link between her creativity and mine, to switch from the savors, the colors, and the smells of meat and vegetables to those of words" (59).[31]

The story is this: Victoire, born to an unnamed and absent white father and an adolescent black mother who died in childbirth, suffers one betrayal after another at the hands of those who might have protected her. The girl is brought up by Caldonia, her maternal grandmother, in an atmosphere of privation. Perhaps understandably, Caldonia expresses her love through calories: "No egg was fresh enough, no breast of chicken white enough, and no flour light enough for the baby's stomach" (7). Yet she fails to send her granddaughter to school, although education was already freely available at the time, a refusal that changes the course of Victoire's life: despite her very light skin, she will be unable to join the educated class of mulattoes. Instead Victoire goes to work in the sugarcane fields, but the other cane workers reject her because she is too light-skinned for the job; her very presence troubles entrenched societal expectations for the intersections of colour and class. Victoire's position in the Guadeloupean class and racial hierarchies is a complex one, for she is too black for the whites, too white for the blacks, and too poor and uneducated for the mulattoes. Her lack of education keeps her from moving up and her light skin colour keeps her from moving down. She thus lives on the border between different races and economic statuses, and her illiteracy keeps her from crossing that border.

As a teenager, Victoire is sent by her grandmother to work as a domestic for a cousin, Thérèse Jovial, who is one of what Guadeloupeans call the *grands nègres*.[32] In late-nineteenth-century Guadeloupe, the practice of placing a young person with a family of superior colour and property was a relatively common form of colour-barrier transgression. In the best cases it was a source of vertical solidarity, while in the worst cases it was akin to neo-slavery.[33] Victoire's situation with the Jovials is the latter. As *restavec* (a live-in scullery maid), "Victoire was treated like a pariah, like a slave at the Jovials. Never like a relative, not even a poor or disreputable one" (19). Moreover, her light skin (much lighter, in fact, than her bourgeois cousin's) once again defies common assumptions about correlations between colour and class.

The assertion that Victoire is treated "like a slave" echoes through Condé's descriptions of life at the Jovials'. The abuse is not limited to overworking her with menial labour, but it also extends to other kinds of exploitation. Thérèse's socialist fiancé, Dernier Argilius, known as a champion of the people, takes advantage of the very young girl sexually. Argilius, who preaches the importance of self-definition and radical freedom for black people, is known as "an ardent defender of the illiterate oppressed Negroes emerging from the belly of slavery" (30). Yet, as the narrator wryly points out, his theories are not put into practice when it comes to taking advantage of the young black girl who is under the protection of his fiancée. "Theses, monographs, and biographies have been written on the subject of this role model and martyr", writes Condé of Dernier Argilius. "My question, then, is what is an exemplary man?" (30). The sexual abuse leads Thérèse to break off her engagement with Dernier and to evict the teenaged Victoire, her relative, who is pregnant with Dernier's baby. The parallels to slavery are implicit but clear: enslaved Afro-Antillean women were often sexually abused by their masters, and often blamed and cruelly punished afterwards by the men's wives.

Pregnant and alone, Victoire finds work as a cook with Anne-Marie and Boniface Walberg, a wealthy white creole couple with two children of their own. Decades after the abolition of slavery, Victoire's experience with the Walbergs in some ways also replicates that of her enslaved ancestors. She works in their kitchen, feeding their culinary appetites; she serves as Anne-Marie's constant companion, feeding her social appetites; and she is the object of Boniface's attentions, feeding his sexual appetites. Rumoured to be endowed with a penis that would not be out of place on a bull (56), Boniface "thrust himself into Victoire four to five times a night" (67). The narrator reminds us that "in the Antilles there is a time-honored practice where the white male marries the white female but takes his pleasure with every mulatto or black girl he can lay his hands on. Slavery or no slavery" (61). The Walbergs' rapacious appetites – Boniface's for sex and his wife's for sweets – echo the ravenous colonial appetite for the products of Guadeloupe, for both its sugar and its women.

Though the relationship is founded on a twisted dynamic of dependence and exploitation, the Walbergs seem to be the only people who show Victoire kindness. They treat Victoire's daughter like one of their own, dressing her extravagantly and sending her to the best schools on the island, where the dark-skinned girl is surrounded by white and mulatto classmates. The child, Jeanne (Condé's mother), eventually comes to hate the Walbergs and resent Victoire. She joins the educated black elite of the island and shields – or perhaps deprives – her children, including little Maryse, from the truth about their familial past.

COOKING AND WRITING

Victoire has access only to the pan, not to the pen. Her lack of formal education is thematized throughout the novel and the narrator returns to it often, always blaming the people who could and should have helped Victoire get an education but did not. She blames Caldonia, who spoils Victoire with luxurious food but never sends her granddaughter to school – a decision that the narrator identifies as an act of neglect, for her lack of education condemns Victoire to life as a *femme à mouchoir*,[34] a life of labour, servitude and dependence. She blames Thérèse Jovial, who is not only an employer but a family member, Victoire's godmother, and an avowed feminist who has an exceptional education yet never teaches Victoire a single letter of the alphabet. Free evening classes for adults were taught by the Brothers of Ploërmel at the time (27), but the Jovials never attempt to send Victoire there. Thérèse exploits Victoire's body for the labour it produces, just as Dernier exploits Victoire's body for his sexual pleasure. If Thérèse had instead fed Victoire's mind, teaching her to read and to write, "[s]he would have removed her from the obscurantism in which Victoire lived all her life. She would have opened the doors to another future for her. We can even imagine that her entire existence would have changed" (27).

Victoire's daughter, Jeanne, is highly educated and uses the pen as her weapon, while, as we have seen, Victoire is not educated at all and her only weapon is the pan – but it is a formidable one. In the Walbergs' kitchen she enjoys the creative freedom she will never experience in the realm of writing, but she is a creative genius with the pan. Some passages in *Victoire* suggest that there is an artistic empowerment of sorts in its protagonist's cooking. Her education in the kitchen seems to take the place of her education in the classroom, and her brilliance in the kitchen seems to make up for her illiteracy. Her cooking is shown as artistic, inspired, creative – as genius – and Victoire becomes well-known throughout Guadeloupian high society for her skill and creativity. In this passage, for example, which describes Victoire's cooking in her early years at the Walberg home, cooking is posed as a creative outlet, one that the narrator makes equivalent to the joy and empowerment of writing: "It was her way of expressing herself, which was constantly repressed, prisoner of her illiteracy, her illegitimacy, her gender, and her station as a servant. When she invented seasonings or blended flavors, her personality was set free and blossomed. Cooking was her Père Labat rum, her ganja, her crack, her ecstasy. She dominated the world. For a time, she became God. Once again, like a writer" (71). Yet Victoire cannot write. And once again the people in her life fail her. Like her grandmother Caldonia and her godmother, Thérèse, the Walbergs do not give Victoire access to education, to the pen. Indeed, despite their kindness to her, they provide her with no money or property of her own that might enable her to trade the security of their home for the sovereignty of her own. She is framed as a possession – a treasured possession, to be sure, but owned body and soul, like a favourite enslaved woman.

There are many reminders that both Victoire herself and her culinary art belong to the Walbergs. At first, "[s]ince neither Anne-Marie nor Boniface entertained at home, folk in La Pointe for a long time knew nothing of the jewel they possessed" (60). Later, Anne-Marie uses Victoire and her cooking as a weapon: "She wanted to thumb her nose at the narrow-mindedness and arrogance of polite society. 'I'll make them drool,' she was heard to say" (70). Eventually "Anne-Marie was bombarded with requests. . . . Could she loan Victoire for a christening, a birthday, or a wedding? Each time she had great pleasure replying in the negative" (71). Victoire is a valuable object, but an object nonetheless. The most eminent families "coveted her and dreamed of appropriating her for themselves" (71). Again and again throughout the novel, people fail to provide Victoire with an education; they deny her access to the pen in addition to the pan. They reduce her to her body and to the material products of her physical labour: the dishes that feed other people's physical appetites.

While certain passages of *Victoire* inject an author-like autonomy into Victoire's experiences as a cook, when those passages are placed in the context of the rest of the novel – and with the fact in mind that social critique is a cornerstone of Condé's writing – another reading emerges. The first reading suggests a kind of inevitable causal relationship between Victoire's autonomous culinary creativity, asserting itself even in the most unlikely of circumstances, and Condé's own life as a writer. However, that hopeful reading is continually haunted by a second interpretation. In this shadow reading, Victoire's lifetime of culinary labour has only transient rewards; it is difficult labour that simply feeds the appetites of others. As we have seen, throughout the novel her cooking is exchangeable with her body, and we are shown how both her food and her body become fodder to satisfy the appetites of others. Indeed, Condé uses metaphors of cannibalism throughout.

A good deal of recent scholarship has focused on Condé's use of this trope, epitomized in *The Story of the Cannibal Woman* (2003), and her use of the technique of "literary cannibalism", as demonstrated in works such as *Windward Heights* (1995), her Caribbean take on *Wuthering Heights*, and *Crossing the Mangrove* (1990), in which she puts her own spin on *In Praise of Creoleness*.[35] *Victoire* is another iteration of cannibalism, for when people are eating Victoire's cooking, they are eating not only her labour but her body – and, indeed, herself, since cooking is her creative outlet. Her food metonymically stands in for her identity, her self.

ESKLAVAJ PA MÔ![36]

Condé traces Victoire's ancestry (and, by extension, her own) into Guadeloupe's colonial past, back to the enslaved Afro-Antilleans on Antoine de Gehan-Quidal's sugar plantation. In the final decades of the nineteenth century, Condé muses, the post-abolition condition of this particular branch of her family was perhaps even worse than under slavery: "As slaves, these men and women were less destitute. In their servitude, a master provided them with a roof over their heads and enough not to starve to death. As free men, what did they own except their poverty?" (8). For them the price of freedom was an empty stomach. Real progress, as *Victoire* (and later, *Of Morsels and Marvels*) shows, comes not from theoretical victory but from concrete, material improvements in everyday life. Although Victoire's grandfather is a fisherman, he has to sell all or most of his catch, leaving the family to eat scanty meals of *kassav* soaked in *tchòlòlò* (10)[37] or cheap ingredients such as roots, hot pepper and pig tail (32).

Condé's fictional account mirrors the historical reality. In the years following abolition, poor black rural workers generally ate only one real meal a day. They consumed very little meat and used sugar and alcohol as a caloric substitute for meals. In many cases poor rural blacks were malnourished and underfed, paid so little that they had to supplement their diet by growing their own food, fishing and hunting. Meanwhile, the upper and middle classes, along with their kitchen servants, enjoyed elaborate meals and sweets, even publishing their banquet and party menus in the press.[38]

This is a stark contrast with how the *blancs pays*, such as the Walbergs, eat. Victoire's menus are more than a testament to her talent; they are also an indictment of insatiable capitalist appetites. While the poor eat little or no meat, the Walbergs' guests enjoy sausage, lobster, pork and rabbit, followed by both cake and sorbet (70). Anne-Marie benefits from her place in the system; her access to luxurious desserts makes her look richly appealing – the narrator calls her "a genuine Rubens, blonde and pink" (88). However, at the end of her life, her colonialist appetites destroy the body that houses and sustains them. She grows very fat in her old age, her body displaying the rot inherent in decadence. Anne-Marie suffocates under her own voracious appetite for sugar: "She could no longer get downstairs. Folds of fat prevented her from wedging her viola under her chin. Her pudgy fingers could no longer handle her bow. She apparently owned an old phonograph and listened to operas from morning to night while tirelessly nibbling on *rahat-loukoum*, stuffed dates, *grabyo koko*, grilled peanuts, and candies such as *douslets* and *sik a koko têt roz*[39] (100).

This inequity is keenly felt by Jeanne, Victoire's daughter and Condé's mother, who grows up in the Walbergs' house. Jeanne reverses the pattern of her mother's life, rejecting the material, the physical and the sensual – the pleasures and power of the pan. She instead focuses purely on the intellect, the part of life that her mother was denied. It is this quirk in her mother's personality that Condé seeks to explore with this novel. In *Victoire*, as in other Condé works, this Spartan attitude towards food also entails emotional alienation and a rigid adherence to ideology, to theory over practice.

Jeanne, like Victoire, falls between the cracks of black and white identities in Guadeloupe. She is emotionally isolated from the white people she grows up with, for while in private she is treated practically like the Walbergs' own daughter, in public, especially in the company of other *blancs pays*, Jeanne is like a performing pet – the black maid's amusingly accomplished daughter. Her distaste for her mother's affair with Boniface increases her distaste for white people in general, and she adopts strong *noiriste* politics.[40] At the same time, Jeanne is distanced from poor blacks, including her own mother, by her education and mastery of French and her superior social caste. Yet the haunting reminders of her poor, illiterate black ancestors, including her own mother, prevent Jeanne from full psychological integration into the black bourgeoisie. She is utterly and painfully alone.

Jeanne's ascetism – her rejection of physical appetites and her privileging of mental ones – is obvious: she "had no palate and was notoriously incapable of boiling an egg" (2) and prefers "hard-boiled eggs and tomato salad with one or two sardines in oil as a bonus" (164) to her mother Victoire's rich and varied cuisine. She dissociates herself from both the sensual pleasures of food and the affective and emotional pleasures of motherhood, maintaining a cold, strictly intellectual relationship with little Maryse. Jeanne privileges the intellect to the detriment of the heart, even to the exclusion of common sense: "Jeanne, full of modern ideas, ardent reader of the Catholic journal *J'élève mon enfant* [I'm bringing up my child] was of the opinion that babies should be given a strict routine, a bottle of milk every three hours, alternating with a bottle of apple juice or filtered water, and never be taken out of their cradle for the slightest reason" (155).

Thanks to the Walbergs' influence and money and her own intelligence and work ethic, Jeanne has received a top-notch education, outshining her *blancs pays* classmates and earning top marks. She goes on to work as one of the first black elementary-school teachers in Guadeloupe. Thanks to this professional career and her marriage to black businessman Auguste Boucoulon, Jeanne enjoys a rapid and definitive social ascension that is intimately tied to the written word. Therefore, while Victoire has access only to the pan – the sensual, embodied, affective, artistic, creative side of life – Jeanne is entirely wedded to the pen, to the cognitive intellectual life. Each woman lives her life in binary terms: either the pen or the pan. Jeanne espouses the pen in simple rebellion against her mother's lifelong attachment to the pan. Viewing her mother's choices through the lens of what Maria Lugones calls "arrogant perception", she is so focused on the absence of resistance as revolt (a simple no, in fairness, being impossible for Victoire) that she fails to see Victoire's culinary art as a resistant *response*. However, as the narrator's "loving perception" asserts, Victoire's choice to express herself using the only means at her disposal – the pan – is indeed a kind of resistant feminist response. In Maryse the narrator's version of events, Victoire's subversion of the labour she is condemned to do anyway – her reappropriation of cooking as a medium for her intelligence, her passion, her creative genius, her *humanity* – certainly constitutes active subjectivity, if not full-fledged agency.[41] And that's not nothing.

TAUBIRA AND THE MEANING OF MEMORY

"There is before Taubira and there is after Taubira", remarks Maryse Condé, as she talks with Christiane Taubira in the final scenes of *Maryse Condé: A Voice of Her Own*. Both *Victoire: My Mother's Mother* and *Of Morsels and Marvels* belong to that post-Taubira world. *Victoire* was published in 2006, twenty-three years after the 1983 French decree establishing a formal day of commemoration to mark the abolition of slavery in its overseas territories;[42] five years after the passage of 2001's *"loi Taubira"*,[43] which recognized the slave trade and slavery as crimes against humanity; and two years after the establishment of the National Committee for the Memory and History of Slavery, for which Condé served as its first president. But *Victoire*'s publication also came just a few months after the passage of the 2005 *"loi Mekachera"*,[44] whose article 4 required the French school curriculum to recognize the "positive role of French overseas presence". Although this law was aimed at North Africa, its implications affected other formerly colonized spaces, including the French Antilles. It betrayed the French lack of full cognizance of the deep and lasting scars left by colonialism. When the *loi Mekachera's* article 4 was struck down by the Conseil constitutionnel[45] in January 2006, there was resistance: a bloc of UMP[46] representatives demanded that the *loi Taubira* be repealed in the interest of "balance and fairness", and some French historians and teachers – already uneasy about the dangers of an "official" version of history of any kind and dismayed at being held hostage by political interest groups on every side – expressed outrage (if not surprise) that historical reform had so quickly degenerated into historical revisionism.[47]

According to Françoise Vergès, appointed president of the National Committee for the Memory of the Slave Trade, Slavery and Their Abolition in 2017, some believe that including the history of the slave trade in the mainstream French curriculum would be bowing to "communitarian whim". For those people, conversations about the slave trade, slavery, abolition and their legacy belong to the realm of memory rather than history. Memory is seen as emotional and subjective, both *partielle* (only partly true) and *partiale* (biased). History, on the other hand, is seen by them as rational and objective, universally valuable. For others, including Vergès herself, these revisions complete incomplete histories, filling a gap: "Isn't the history of the slave trade the history of France?" she asks in *La mémoire enchaînée* (Shackled Memory). "That is France's history, and it's not the slaves' descendants' fault if France is suffering from amnesia."[48] In the end, although the *loi Taubira* was not struck down, the message was out: like abolition itself, the law was neither a new beginning nor a complete ending.

However, the *loi Taubira* remained a decisive moment in the relationship between slavery and the French imaginary. As Vergès notes, it made "the slave trade, slavery and the different stages of their abolition . . . topics of conversation".[49] In 2008 President Nicolas Sarkozy announced that the history of slavery would henceforth be officially taught in French elementary schools. Meanwhile, Maryse Condé continued to publicly promote education about slavery,[50] arguing that it helps us to understand its legacy, the "link between the suffering of our ancestors and what we experience today". She adds, "Slavery is not dead! It continues in a different form, in a more acceptable form, in a more tolerable form, but it's still there. As long as there is a kind of divorce between yesterday and today, in my opinion, we have not done as much as we should."[51]

Clearly the *loi Taubira* had enormous symbolic importance for the Antilles, and in theory it was anti-racist and anti-colonialist. But it did not create any meaningful change in the actual lived conditions of post-colonial Antilleans. In fact, many Antilleans felt that post-colonial economic conditions were a form of continued economic exploitation, that is, wage slavery. In 2009, popular outrage about the high cost of living in the French Antilles resulted in a general strike in Guadeloupe and Martinique. Demands included a minimum wage based on the local cost of living, price and profit caps on basic needs, and meaningful negotiations with local employers.[52] In the midst of the clash, the documentary film *The Last Masters of Martinique* threw fuel on the fire.[53] The film highlighted the uninterrupted, mindfully preserved bloodline between the enslaving plantation owners of the seventeenth century and the extremely wealthy white creole community in Martinique, known locally as *békés*. The *békés*, according to *The Last Masters*, make up less than 1 per cent of the island's population but command 20 per cent of its wealth. The film revealed their quasi-monopoly on local food production, processing and distribution and their control of the lion's share of food imports and exports. Documentary footage intimated that the *békés* were and always had been in close cooperation with the French Ministry of Agriculture and the president of the republic, and now with strategically placed higher-ups in the European Union. Despite its symbolic importance, the *loi Taubira* had done nothing to change the actual distribution of power. Faced with food prices two and half times those in the European territory of France, Antillean minimum-wage workers, who necessarily constitute a captive market, owed their souls to the company store. "We are slaves", says one worker as he looks straight into the camera. "We are slaves."[54]

Condé's *Of Morsels and Marvels* was published in May 2015 amid a new round of public debate on the subject of slavery; the contentious climate surrounding the so-called memorial laws[55] of the previous twenty-five years, which had given rise to conflict between minority groups and the French majority, seems also to have pitted one minority group against another. On 10 May 2015, French president François Hollande travelled to Guadeloupe to inaugurate the ACTe Memorial, which memorialized the slave trade and slavery in Guadeloupe. Artists, journalists and other public figures asked if it was in fact a form of appeasement. Hollande's January 2015 speech in which he called the Holocaust "the greatest crime ever committed" had deepened resentments in Guadeloupe. Some Antilleans wondered why France had approved the reparations paid to former colonists of Algeria and enslavers of Haiti, Martinique, Guadeloupe, Guyana and the island of Réunion, while rejecting the idea of reparations for the *victims* of their crimes. Days before Hollande arrived in Guadeloupe, the Representative Council of the Black Associations of France announced plans to file a suit in favour of reparations, saying, "Commemoration is good. Reparations are better."[56]

Meanwhile, debate over the fallibility of history was heating up in the European territory of France. The education minister, Najat Vallaud Balkacem, was instituting curriculum reform at the middle-school level, and public discussions asserted that education about slavery (as well as the Holocaust and Islam) had replaced instruction on essential French events and values, such as the Enlightenment.[57] This was seen as a threat to the core French identity. Incendiary comments on the reforms included former education minister Luc Ferry's objections to what he termed "a post–January 11th ideology"[58] in "a repentant Europe", as well as journalist and historian Jacques Julliard's conclusion that the new curriculum "reeked of shame for being French, hatred for being French".[59] A historian and member of the Académie française, Pierre Nora, called the reforms "a sign of the times: a form of national guilt that maximizes Islam, the slave trade, and slavery and tends to reinterpret Western and French development through the prism of colonialism and its crimes".[60] According to Nora, "We are living under the Empire of Memory and even the Tyranny of Memory."[61] These critics objected that Christine Taubira's reforms pushed her personal version of history. Published in May 2015 (the same month as *Of Morsels and Marvels*), the jacket of an unauthorized biography, *Le mystère Taubira: La vérité derrière l'icône* (The Taubira mystery: The truth behind the icon) declared, "Christiane Taubira decides everything. It's her version of history that she wants people to hear."[62]

While *Victoire* contributes to group memory about the legacy of slavery and abolition in Guadeloupe, *Of Morsels and Marvels* treats the aftermath of colonialism in a broader, post-colonial climate where group histories often seem to be mutually exclusive rather than mutually enriching.[63] Using her imagination and what she knows to be true, Condé fills in the gaps of history, directly addressing women's unique perspectives on and experiences with freedom and sovereignty.

A MATTER OF TASTE: AUTHENTICITY AND THE INDIVIDUAL

Of Morsels and Marvels, published nine years after *Victoire: My Mother's Mother*, shifts from a focus on Condé's grandmother's relationship to culinary art to a more direct analysis of the author's own lifelong passions for cooking and for writing – her mastery of both the pen and the pan as tools of feminist change, her synthesis of her grandmother's and mother's approaches to the world. Condé perceives parallels between the freedom offered by both cooking and writing. In an interview about her culinary memoir she says, "The drive to create is the same in the writer and in the cook. The one uses words, the other uses ingredients, flavours and spices to create beauty, pleasure, to take hold of people, give them pleasure. Making a tajine[64] with unexpected combinations and a book with a shocking subject, metaphors, images, it's the same thing."[65] The autobiographical essays in *Of Morsels and Marvels* follow Condé through her travels on five continents, from her early childhood in Guadeloupe to her old age in Paris. From the *flankoko*[66] of her childhood in

Guadeloupe to the delicious Breton cuisine she could never bring herself to attempt at home, in each place and dish Condé finds lessons about history's power to shape destinies, the conformism that seems inherent in human nature and, most important, what it means to tell one's truth.

While Condé's purported purpose in writing this memoir is to understand her own deep attachment to cooking, each chapter reads like an essay in which she contemplates the shortcomings of all kinds of ideology: from sexism to monolithic Feminism, from racism to Négritude, from fascism to communism, from colonialism to post-colonial nationalism. Over the course of the memoir, it becomes clear that while ideology may lose itself in the sweeping generalities of its own detachment, the culinary is necessarily inextricably tied to the real, to the concrete, and to the importance of individual experience. In this way the culinary reflects Condé's approach to the literary, which must never serve ideological interests or conform to group expectations. Rather, it must advocate for social change through an understanding of individual difference. In the final chapter, Condé's grandson tells her he is interested in learning how to cook and then changes his mind. She ends by asking rhetorically if, in the end, she will have neither a literary nor a culinary heir. *Of Morsels and Marvels* is something of a recipe for becoming that heir, and it has lessons for Caribbean feminism in its insistence on individuality, alliance across differences, and rejection of ideology.

One might not ordinarily think of the kitchen, a space traditionally assigned to women, as a site of revolt. However, because Condé's bourgeois mother, Jeanne, disdains cooking, seeing the sensual and the indulgent as signs of weakness, little Maryse must rebel through food, by stealing chocolates and hiding out in the kitchen with the cook. According to *Of Morsels and Marvels*, Maryse's distaste for convention made its appearance at a very young age: "I was not in favour of the traditional dishes whose unchanging recipes seem to come from sacred texts inherited from our ancestors. I liked to create and invent" (6). From her earliest days, this dogged pursuit of self-actualization drives a wedge between Maryse and those closest to her: "My passion for cooking went hand in hand with my dream for freedom. This attraction was an innate part of my personality. Why did my mother want to hurt me? Why did she want to stifle it?" (8). For Condé, cooking is appealing because it allows for unfettered originality, an element she sees as fundamental to the creative process. During her teenage years in Paris, for example, she assures her sister that nobody taught her to prepare her delicious if atypical dishes: "Nobody", she insists. "It came to me in a dream" (11). When her sister tries to claim that people have to learn to cook, young Condé objects. "No. The art of cooking is a gift. Like all the other gifts, nobody knows where it comes from" (12). Some years later, in Africa, she doubles down on her assertion. "Cooking is an art", she insists. "It relies on an individual's fantasy, invention and freedom. Cookbooks are for dummies. There are no such things as rules and directives" (26).

But this attitude causes Condé problems when she cooks other peoples' heritage dishes. People expect "tradition" and "authenticity" – conformism – in their food (a desire that has been a theme throughout this volume). Tradition, as we have seen, is "dangerous, a form of self-destruction, an ossification of culture that aides the ethnocentric racist push towards culture as ornament".[67] This conversion of culinary culture into ideology becomes clear as Condé attempts to cook food from her own culture and that of others. The family cook in Guadeloupe is scandalized by her addition of powdered cinnamon to goat Colombo and refuses to even taste Maryse's concoction: "What kind of pig's swill is this?" (6). A fellow diner in Africa, displeased with a restaurant's interpretation of a classic dish, insists on inviting Maryse to her home, where she will taste "real" *mafé* (26). In South Africa, Condé is not welcome in the kitchen; the servants remind her, "Real ladies don't bother about what to cook" (223). Even Condé's British mother-in-law, who accepts Maryse into the family with open arms, can't tolerate the substitution of pork for leg of lamb with mint sauce (200). Maryse's North African friend is sorry to see her eating mullet and couscous with utensils: "Too bad you don't know how to eat with your hand", he tells her. "It would taste even better" (202). And in Australia, the French cultural service seems to have no problem with her pro-independence politics, but her refusal to eat the best raw oysters in the world is "an unheard of scandal" (215).

These conservativisms about food reflect and give rise to other types of conservativisms, insists the author; they end up producing the same kind of ideological purism and rigidity that Condé sees in her mother, Jeanne. People's behaviour around the table consistently reveals an urge, even among the downright revolutionary, to police divergence of all types. *Of Morsels and*

Marvels suggests that feminism in particular (like other movements whose purported end goal is individual self-actualization) has become mired in ideology, leaving little room for individual tastes and preferences. "I want to squash the too-common argument that women should be in the kitchen", declares her Tunisian friend Zineb, while Condé asks, "Why can't a doctor in philosophy or a Nobel Prize winner in chemistry treat their guests to a delicious meal?" (71). Indeed, Condé's passion for cooking feels for her like a rebellion against feminist orthodoxy: "To be considered an excellent cook", she claims, "also helped me change my image as the militant feminist intellectual I was too often stuck with" (ix). Her kitchen is a site of rebellion against the restrictions of a reified feminist ideology that leaves no room for the individual, for particularity, for context, for the local. "Perhaps that's what 'rebellious' means?" muses the author. "To tell one's truth come what may" (191).

But, like her literary rebellions, Condé's kitchen rebellions continually run up against others' desire for purity, rigidity, tradition and "authenticity". In midlife, Maryse and her then-partner (later second husband) Richard, a white British man, return to Guadeloupe, where they find that her friends and family have limited palates and narrow minds. Her friend José and his wife, for example, cannot understand either the mixed relationship of Maryse and Richard (José deems Richard, as a white man, personally responsible for colonialism's crimes) or the mixed dish of conch and haddock that Maryse prepares for them: "It's a bit unusual", murmurs José's wife, and José himself labels it "nouvelle cuisine" (53). As for Maryse's family, although they are perfectly capable of deviating enough from standard Guadeloupian fare to eat one cheese pizza after another, they too are turned off by Maryse's unconventional combinations. "Never mix sweet and savory. Never mix meat and fish; nor meat and shellfish", declares Condé's sister. "Tuna fish in a curry is unthinkable" – as is the combination the woman is really complaining about: the relationship between a black woman (Maryse) and a white man (Richard, whom Maryse has brought home for the first time) (80). Condé sees her home island as too mired in convention to value her nonconformist approach to both Caribbean food and Caribbeanness: "I had learnt my lesson. Just as my cooking was not genuine Guadeloupean, I too would never be a genuine Guadeloupean. But what does the word 'genuine' mean? Nobody has been able to explain it to me. In this age, where everything is interconnected and exchanged, is it possible or even desirable?" (59).

Condé decides that authenticity is for the birds. Her rejection of the orthodoxy of authenticity encompasses her reactions to theories of postcoloniality, which do not accord with her lived experience. When, as a student, Maryse learns from Marxist historians that she is "colonized", it makes her feel inauthentic, an adopted Guadeloupean rather than a native daughter: "The language I had spoken since childhood, the religion that my mother had inculcated me with and the habit I was wearing, they said, were all borrowed. The truth lay elsewhere. All that was highly complex. I felt like a child who suddenly finds out she is adopted. What kind of attitude should I take with my biological parents?" (15). Many years of trying to answer that question bring Condé to the conclusion that all of us have the right to be our own person without regard to whether or not a tradition "belongs" to us. The conclusion plays out in both the kitchen and in literature. Condé says, "Whatever one's origin, one always has the right to appropriate a dish. Either you reproduce it faithfully or you add variations of your own invention. Dishes have no nationality" (66), and "It is neither possible nor desirable to complete with traditional cuisines, *stricto sensu*. We should invent, reinvent according to our taste, and recreate according to our imagination. In cuisine, every daring invention is permitted" (111). For her, cooking is a totally free form of transaction in which, unlike literature, there is no such thing as plagiarism (229). Instead, cooking is what writing should be: a way to take in, digest, transform and produce new ideas.

Literature and cuisine are identified as points of contact, parallel forms of exchange in which we come to a deeper understanding of the world around us. Maryse's first taste of tajine, a North African dish that combines savoury ingredients with sweet fruits, is enough to make her feel far less alone in the world. Reflects Condé, "I had often introduced dried fruit in my culinary compositions. When it was a question of fish especially, I got the impression I was breaking a taboo, of offending, of committing a fault. That evening I learnt that other people were doing the same" (72). "What might have seemed a personal eccentricity", she continues, "was closely akin to the taste of other human beings. In a certain way, I had invented the tajine" (73). A complementary instance of contact and exchange occurs through literature and history during a trip to Japan: "We carried out a transfer of identity. These young Japanese, spoilt children of the Pacific, set their pride to one side and emerged from their splendid isolation. Their shoulders bore the triple weight of dispossession, dispersion and exile of the people from the Caribbean. They discovered the plantation system where they were whipped by their cruel masters. They became the wretched of the earth" (116).

At times Condé acknowledges that cuisine is not solely fertile terrain for individual expression; it is also a way of representing a people's past. Like Gisèle Pineau (as we have seen in chapter 1), she understands that food, like the stories passed down from generation to generation, can act as a historical archive. In the mid-1970s, for example, she teaches an ethno-cuisine course in which she strives to communicate Antillean history to her students in Paris: "I worked hard, consulting books by travellers and missionaries, genuine scriveners on the life and food of the slaves . . . I made an effort to keep to tradition: no cinnamon in the curried goat Colombo which Adélia used to reproach me for, and no aged rum in anything" (46). While cooking for some acquaintances in Guadeloupe, people who consciously embody Guadeloupean history through traditional dress and dancing the *gwo ka,* she says, "In order not to scare these palates unaccustomed to culinary eccentricities, I toned down my passion to invent" (56). Echoing in her own way their passion for Guadeloupean history and cultural continuity, Condé feeds them black pudding and cucumber salad, breadfruit soufflé and tuna stew (into which she can't resist slipping a few Chinese eggplants). Pleased with the connection she's made with her guests, she reports, "In spite of these small caprices, the guests devoured my dishes and asked for more" (57). With outsiders, at least, she seems like "real" Antillean – and she feels like one.

Condé's health begins to decline, and she and her husband decide to spend Christmas in Guadeloupe with her children and her grandchildren. In a sudden reversal of roles, it is now Maryse who insists on native Guadeloupean – not global, not imported – cuisine:

> Without bothering about their preferences, I insisted on making a traditional meal. I spurned the smoked salmon and oysters that were easily available in the shops in Pointe-à-Pitre and insisted on having black pudding made with pig's blood and not the conch or codfish imitations now in fashion. I had to have

Creole ham, pakala yams and fresh-picked pigeon peas. The only concessions
I made were Bollinger champagne and the Yule log. (205)

A certain heartache inhabits *Of Morsels and Marvels*. Some part of Condé,
despite (or because of) her wanderings, culinary and otherwise, yearns to
be accepted and appreciated, just as she is, in her own Guadeloupe. Indeed,
in the last chapters of *Of Morsels and Marvels*, as Condé's mortality begins
to weigh upon her, one gets the sense that, in the end, if ever she can close
old wounds and make peace with her island, it will be at the table.

THINGS WE CANNOT SWALLOW

Although for Condé food can be a form of positive exchange, a way to understand and immerse herself in other cultures while remaining her stubbornly
individual self, the novel also acknowledges food's power to separate people,
its power to represent other, uglier cultural traditions and beliefs, such as
the racism and forced assimilation that are themes in every chapter of this
book. Food is a double-edged knife, for it can individuate and affiliate, bind
and exclude.

For example, Condé's first attack of indigestion – the literal inability to
take something in and digest it easily and without discomfort – occurs not
at home in Guadeloupe but in Paris, where she has moved to attend second-
ary school. In Condé's recollection of those years, France is where people
eat "hard to swallow dishes like cauliflower au gratin, mashed potatoes or
braised endive" or "boiled potatoes, every variety of cabbage, green cabbage,
red cabbage, cauliflower, Brussels sprouts, always overcooked, and tasteless
breaded fish" (10). Alternating between bitter and bland, French foods (like
France itself) fall far short of the comfort foods, sweet and spicy, that she
enjoys in an Antillean restaurant in Paris: "codfish cakes, chicken Colombo,
Creole rice. For dessert the unavoidable coconut flan" (9–10). Among the
teenager's worst experiences with Parisian French food are lunches at her
sister's place, where instead of comforting Guadeloupean food she is always
served a horsemeat steak, which she eats alone in the kitchen while her sister
busies herself with other things: "I had a lot of trouble swallowing what I
had been served" (10). Her inability to swallow the meat emblematizes her

inability to swallow the assimilation being forced upon her, the demands
that she erase her Guadeloupean heritage and fit into the mould of the
Parisian woman. These attempts to force Condé to assimilate into mainstream
European French culture and leave behind the traditions of Guadeloupe
play out not only at the table but in language as well: in Guadeloupe, Jeanne
and Condé's father forbade her to speak Creole, and the family spoke only
French at home. Condé imagined that this rehearsal for assimilation would
make her transition to life in the European territory of France relatively easy,
but her disgust at the food of Paris exposes both the centrality of culture
to culinary pleasure and the cultural rift between Guadeloupe and Paris.

A similar shock awaits Condé in India, where culinary difference also mirrors cultural difference. Condé had eaten Indo-Caribbean food as a child and
had enjoyed many pleasant Indian meals at her friend Raj's home in Paris,
so she was looking forward to her midlife trip to India. But after experiencing overt acts of racism by Indians there, she finds herself unable to enjoy
the food; indeed, she is barely capable of eating at all. Strangers stare at her,
point at her, laugh at her with something "between hilarity and repulsion"
(79) and even go so far as to call her "monkey" (84). In the midst of this
terrible experience, she is served a traditional Indian dish; writes Condé, "I
couldn't swallow it. India remained stuck in my throat" (82).

Of Morsels and Marvels is also a commentary on the unfulfilled expectations
and broken promises of more than a half-century of ideology. This work's
focus on food is a displacement towards the tangible, a shift away from the
realm of ideas and towards lived experience. The proof of the pudding, says
the book, is quite literally in the eating. As she travels the world, Condé's
experiences with food illustrate the disappointed ideals of one revolution
after another. During a trip to communist Poland, for example, she observes
a striking mismatch between the sumptuous theatrics of sporting events,
ballets and operas and the boiled potatoes and sausages served at every meal.
"Was it possible to satisfy the soul with so many marvels, so many cultural
treasures but to leave the body unsatisfied and hungry for more?" she asks.
"Is spiritual munificence enough to compensate for physical inadequacy?"
(17). Likewise, in her memory the *mafé* of newly independent Africa is synonymous with food shortages and destitution (19). Independence, realizes
Condé, is a purgatory that may or may not lead to something better. Cuba's

renowned successes in education and medicine are tarnished by penury in the kitchen. "What did our hosts think of the Revolution? . . . What was it like in daily life?" she wonders. "To dress, drink, eat, invite friends, raise children and spoil them?" (129). Through this disparate collection of half-kept promises and impotent ideologies, Condé sketches the deficiencies of French republicanism, indirectly indicting a long line of failed French ideals, from the Revolution and abolition right up to the *loi Taubira*. There is a clear disconnect between intellectual efforts at memorializing the slave trade, slavery and abolition – by building monuments and holding public ceremonies – and the glaring economic disparities between the descendants of the enslavers and the descendants of the enslaved, still so evident in the 2009 general strike. This discrepancy raises all the same questions: Is it possible to sate the mind and leave the body unsatisfied? Is spiritual munificence enough to compensate for physical inadequacy? What about daily life? What can we swallow and what must we reject?

CULINARY DREAMS

Both *Victoire* and *Of Morsels and Marvels* ask what role the artist can play in healing the group imaginary. The artist can help people imagine history, and the way we imagine the past is the key to growth and healing for the future. "I am not a prisoner of History", writes Franz Fanon. "I must not look for the meaning of my destiny in that direction. . . . In the world I am heading for, I am endlessly creating myself."[68] And the artist can also help people imagine their futures: "The fact is that no decree frees a society from its past. The society *frees itself* from sociological continuities, cultural and ideological representations", concludes Jean-Pierre Sainton.[69] "Time plays its role in the healing, but human consciousness, once awakened, has its part to play in the transformation of reality . . . in submission or in action."[70]

Victoire imagines a possible future of reconciliation between the races and classes on Guadeloupe – one that can serve as a goalpost for reality to work towards – in a scene of culinary reconciliation between Victoire, Jeanne and the Walbergs. With Victoire's health declining, Jeanne agrees to allow the Walbergs (whom she continues to resent) into her home for a final meal:

I am going to call this meal "The Last Supper". It could be the subject of a painting with Victoire in the center, surrounded by the people she had cherished throughout her life. But on that particular day she did not simply reunite those who were dear to her before death carried her off. It was her way of writing her last will and testament. One day, she hoped, color would no longer be an evil spell. One day, Guadeloupe would no longer be tortured by questions of class. The white Creoles would learn to be humble and tolerant. There would no longer be the need to set a club of Grands Nègres against them. Both would get along, freely intermingle, and who knows, love each other. (189)

In yet another explicit comparison between cooking and writing, the author claims that the meal is Victoire's "way of writing her last will and testament". Through this metaphor she empowers Victoire, endowing her with a social vision that goes beyond her own narrow life experiences and personal challenges to encompass the broader society and its widespread ills. In this, her final culinary feat, Victoire uses the table to bring together opposing groups, silently calling for a covenant between the past and the future, between black and white, between rich and poor.

Like *Victoire*, *Of Morsels and Marvels* addresses a post-colonial world characterized by persistent socio-economic disparities and ideological entrenchment. As the world moves forward in the aftermath of half-achieved (if not utterly failed) revolutions, this work asks what the role of the artist will be. The chapter titled "Traveling in My Dreams, Dreaming of Traveling" reflects on the various ways in which an artist can engage with an unjust world. Its first pages describe the Guadeloupian tradition of dream interpretation, which promises to tell the future using signs from the past. The dreams that Condé recounts in this chapter – culinary dreams transformed into literary art – are her encoded understandings of the past and the present, as well as her encrypted visions of the future. If *The Key to Dreams*, sold in Guadeloupean shops in Condé's childhood village, could "foresee the future based on past omens", her own art predicts the future of the human liberation project by using clues drawn from the great trajectories of its history.

The narrator casts herself in two opposite roles in relation to dreams. She is Scheherazade ("I found myself in the same position as Scheherazade in the *Arabian Nights*"), who is not disenchanted by the light of morning that ends dreams but uses her dreams to move forward and gain what she needs.

She is also Scheherazade's husband, Shahryar – "I had no control over these nocturnal imaginations. . . . My dream would abruptly come to an end in the morning with the first rays of the sun. I would lie in bed, puzzled and frustrated" – who is always awakened from the dream by morning, but who is so beguiled by those dreams – his wife's suspenseful stories – that he spares her life day after day, wishing always to re-enter the dream (253). In this analogy, the dreamer/Scheherazade/writer's artistic creation represents an ongoing process that has the urgency of life or death, something that has the power to change the future. At the same time, the dreamer/Shahryar's hopes are raised and then dashed time after time as the artist is repeatedly confronted with art's impotence to fully achieve its goals.

In the first of four dreams, the dreamer travels to Indonesia, which she expects to be a magical place. Instead she is greeted by the horrific stench of piles of garbage and the sight of women carrying heavy vessels of polluted water on their heads. This disturbing encounter is quickly forgotten when she accompanies the Sultan of Yogyakarta, who typifies the political savvy with which revolutions of all kinds can be skirted,[71] to his palace. Inside the palace she finds an inversion of the world outside. The stink of rubbish is replaced by the sweet perfume of roses, jasmine and honeysuckle. In place of poorly dressed women drawing dirty water, the dreamer finds richly clad women whose heads bear only their long, silky hair. The Sultan serves the dreamer Indonesia's national dish:

> I tasted it. And, surprise, it seemed succulent to me, the best *nasi goring* one could imagine. I lost all restraint. I helped myself. I helped myself again. In short, I stuffed myself under the indulgent eye of the sultan. "How do you find our cuisine?" he asked me maliciously. "It's the best in the world," I answered, my mouth full. "I have prepared a little surprise for you," he smiled. With those words, he signaled a servant who brought me a silver platter with a parchment, rolled up and tied with a scarlet ribbon. I opened it. It was the recipe for the *nasi goring*. When I lifted my head to thank him, I noticed that the sultan and the whole shining assembly around him had disappeared. (334)

In this sequence, the Sultan encourages the dreamer to indulge her basest desires, to gorge herself and forget the indigent people she has just en-countered. His "malicious" question asks what he already knows: that she has been seduced by pleasure, easily persuaded to dismiss the misery she has seen. The parchment suggests a devil's contract, its ribbon the scarlet of transgression, its silver platter underscoring the dangers of ease. This dream wonders if the pleasures of the table and of fiction distract us from the world's very real problems, whether they use energy that could or should be used in action.

The second dream, which seems to respond to the first, takes place in Chile, where a trip to Pablo Neruda's house is followed by a Chilean meal eaten below Salvador Allende's portrait. Neruda, emblematic of the engaged artist, emphasized the complementary functions of the concrete and the imaginary in changing the conditions that surround mankind. Interestingly, like Condé, Neruda believed that the kitchen offers a poet's education, affirming in his Nobel lecture, "I have often maintained that the best poet is he who prepares our daily bread: the nearest baker who does not imagine himself to be a god. He does his majestic and unpretentious work of kneading the dough, consigning it to the oven, baking it in golden colors and handing us our daily bread as a duty of fellowship."[72] This daily effort towards making the world better seems to answer Condé's first dream, about the pleasures and problems of escapism. For Neruda, the products of mankind are a perfect mix of the spiritual and the material: "bread, truth, wine, dreams".[73] As she drives around Santiago, a city whose complacent neoliberal crowds seem to have no demands at all, the dreamer searches for any sign of the "spirit of Allende" (337), the figure of revolution forced underground, any sign that the Chilean people remember and believe, as Allende once said, that "social processes can be arrested neither by crime nor force. History is ours, and people make history."[74] This dream wonders if the engaged artist, no matter how committed, can leave any lasting mark at all.

The dreamer continues on to Madagascar, where, "blinded" by the island's poverty (260), she attempts to distract herself with the "dazzling beauty of nature" (341) and stop thinking about the sickly, malnourished children who fill the streets. Haunted by the misery she has witnessed, deeply touched and inspired by a local priest's efforts to care for Madagascar's orphans, the dreamer returns to the United States determined to do something about the situation herself. Her ineffective article in the Columbia University newspaper earns her no more than an angry letter from the Madagascan

Students Association. Thinks the dreamer, "I, nevertheless, had relieved my conscience" (263). Circling back to and reiterating the first dream, this one asks if writing – even writing journalism rather than fiction – is enough in a world where real poverty and problems exist.

In the fourth dream, the dreamer shares a meal in China with Piu Dong, an author whose work is unpublishable in China because her husband is a political dissident. "Before we start to eat the dishes we have prepared for you, let us drink a toast to the freedom of expression which does not exist here", suggests Dong (270). This writer, a great admirer of Condé's work, treats the dreamer to an extravagantly varied, sumptuous meal that celebrates Chinese aesthetics and creativity. "Piu Dong was sitting on my right", recalls the dreamer. "Sometimes we squeezed each other's hand affectionately. I don't know why that was my last dream of a meal" (271). In this, the dreamer's final vision, Condé realizes that a lifetime of tensions between individual freedom and group solidarity has been a mirage. Daring to be oneself, to find one's voice, to find one's way, is itself an act of solidarity – one that is contagious.

OF FREEDOM AND SOVEREIGNTY

In *Victoire: My Mother's Mother* and *Of Morsels and Marvels*, as Condé engenders the ongoing Guadeloupean experience with freedom and sovereignty, she also conceptualizes and disseminates wider truths about the Caribbean. Despite the tendency (including among Guadeloupeans themselves) to talk about Guadeloupe as an incongruous aberration, the island is neither a paradox nor an exception in the contemporary Caribbean, where most societies are non-sovereign, including territories, departments, protectorates, municipalities and commonwealths. Besides, islands with flag sovereignty such as Haiti have endured neocolonial oppression in all its forms, right alongside all the others. "Representations of non-sovereign societies as sites of paradox and exception", argues Yarimar Bonilla, "have only served to occlude these repetitions, masking the larger sociohistorical processes that shape the question of sovereignty in the region as a whole".[75]

Likewise, in her interlocking works of culinary fiction, Condé's intentional coupling of the inequalities, constraints and contradictions faced by women in post-abolition Guadeloupe and the post-independence formerly colonized world encapsulates the disappointments, setbacks and pitfalls of the freedom struggle throughout the Caribbean. Meanwhile, her other calculated pairing – of cooking and writing – advocates for a desperately needed reintegration of the theoretical (the view from above) and the material (the reality on the ground) across the archipelago. Over the past century and a half, throughout the region, newly emancipated Afro-Caribbean peoples were channelled into the emerging wage economy by abstract promises of freedom; then newly independent nations (or, in the case of Guadeloupe, newly departmentalized regions) were guided into a series of institutions, from the International Monetary Fund (IMF) to the United Nations, by theoretical guarantees of equality.[76] But as Condé's fictionalized historical accounts so aptly illustrate, in reality both formerly enslaved people and former colonies nonetheless found themselves living within systems of intrinsic inequality. By focusing on the particularities of individual Guadeloupian women's tangible circum-stances – the forces that limited her grandmother's life possibilities and the very real obstacles Condé faced in her own self-actualization – she fills in the gaps of a much broader Caribbean history, dismantling the myths surrounding abolition and political sovereignty throughout the region in relatable and accessible ways.

Condé's engagement with the intersections between gender and racial-ized and nationalized forms of belonging is also both profoundly specific to the Guadeloupean context and emblematic of the Caribbean as a whole. In Guadeloupe, masculinist discourse about competing forms of representa-tion and belonging have raged since departmentalization in 1946, when Guadeloupeans became a permanent cultural, linguistic and racial minority inside the larger political entity of France. In the last decades of the twenti-eth century, as it became clear that French Antillean political independence movements would never gain the momentum needed to achieve political self-determination, the quest for cultural autonomy became paramount. As a result, the question of what qualifies as "authentically" French Caribbean language, culture and art (including literature) dominated what remained a largely male-dominated public debate. It makes sense, then, that in her food-focused fiction Condé engenders the question of whether various forms of belonging can or should be hierarchical, and of whether or not "authentic" racial or national identities even exist. As we have seen, the pressure on Caribbean women to subordinate gender to race and nation and self-actualization to group demands is not unique to the Afro-Guadeloupean context. On the contrary, a preoccupation with these onerous expectations is common to all the Caribbean women's writing brought together in this volume. Throughout this target corpus of culinary fiction, we have found echoes of Condé's depictions of the authentic as a tool for identity construction, one for which women pay the price. Like Condé, Pineau, Danticat, Persaud and Mootoo also depict Caribbean women as assigned to be gatekeepers of legitimacy in the kitchen and in their own bodies and behaviours, as expected to sacrifice their individuality and personal needs to the cause of "authentic" racial, religious, ethnic, class and national identities.

Taken together, *Victoire* and *Of Morsels and Marvels* illustrate Condé's approach to homegrown Caribbean feminisms: her dual commitment to both the writer's vision and imagination and to the quotidian labour of feeding and caring for others, to work that makes the world a better place in very concrete ways. In her culinary fiction, Condé goes beyond the *jamais vu* ("never seen before") straight to *l'impensé* ("the unthought of")[77] – and indeed, it is the role and responsibility of the artist to conceive of and communicate the inconceivable, to dream up a better world for us all.

Condé's worldview and the importance of the *jamais vu* and *l'impensé* in constructing positive social change may have been most clearly articulated in the realm of modern Guadeloupean politics. In her 2015 study of Guadeloupean labour activism during the 2009 general strikes, Yarimar Bonilla distinguishes between two ways of thinking about post-abolition Guadeloupe: emancipation (the "freedom project") required the new working class to buy into the logic of a free market and activity in exchange for money, erasing hidden forms of resistance that were born under slavery, while decolonization (the "sovereignty project") demanded that post-colonial peoples internalize the idea of nation-states as discrete, necessary and eminently desirable units of political and economic organization, while also silencing and foreclosing other forms and alignments. According to Bonilla, true liberation means freeing the mind of all of these constraints; abolition must be dissociated from freedom, and political sovereignty from societal transformation. During an era of "postcolonial disenchantment" and "exhausted political options and vocabularies",[78] the objects of Bonilla's study managed to imagine something new – both the *jamais vu* and *l'impensé*. The Liyannaj kont pwofitasyon (LPK) did not confine itself to a single nationalist ideal. Instead it asserted a new vision of social and political organization in which the *nou* ("us") is not a non-sovereign nation but a diverse alliance of everyday people who have inherited a legacy of colonialism and slavery (including patriarchy) and who together face the contemporary effects of neoliberal economics (including sexism). Meanwhile, the *yo* ("them") is all those who reap profits from the abusive colonial relationship today as well as all those who, through either action or inaction, allow this *pwofitasyon* ("exploitation") to continue.[79]

When we read Condé's culinary fiction, including its gaps and spaces, we can observe that it models precisely this kind of movement. And we find in her writing the very radical conceptual framework that homegrown Caribbean feminisms (and, indeed, all manner of twenty-first-century liberation movements) need: to change who is *nou* and who is *yo*, to ally with others who are not like us but share our interests. By broadening conventional definitions of freedom and challenging customary forms of belonging in *Victoire: My Mother's Mother* and *Of Morsels and Marvels,* Condé rethinks existing "unifying" ideologies from Négritude to socialism, from feminism to post-colonialism. As she does so, she advocates for her own version of *liyannaj kont pwofitasyon,* a loose but powerful alliance of very different people against all forms of exploitation. As she writes about the abuse, isolation, betrayal and abandonment of women, at the hands of both *yo* and *nou* – the very groups we might expect to be a source of support – she elucidates the need for unexpected forms of solidarity to combat unanticipated forms of oppression. Condé's depictions of Caribbean women who long for individual autonomy, uneclipsed by group demands, cry out for societies in which everyday people stand up with and for each other. Her homegrown Caribbean feminism yearns for a world in which women are neither prisoners of history nor enslaved to "authenticity", but totally free to express themselves as artists and as human beings. And as we have seen throughout this volume, although Condé may often feel like a lone dreamer, she most certainly is not.

WORLD TRAVELLING

By traveling to other people's "worlds" we discover that there are
"worlds" in which those who are the victims of arrogant perception are
really subjects, lively beings, resisters, constructors of visions.[1]

AS I LAID OUT IN THE introduction, contemporary Caribbean culinary fiction is a
compelling form of what decolonial feminist philosopher María Lugones calls
"world" travelling, providing insight into Caribbean women's perspectives,
subjectivity and creativity. For Caribbean women, this can mean a window
onto past generations, neighbouring islands or the diaspora, other racial or
ethnic groups, social classes, religious affiliations, sexual orientations or
gender identities. And for American women like me, who live in a sustained
state of unequal relationship with Caribbean peoples, it is an invitation to
reject wilful ignorance and look the "true-true" of fiction in its face.

As I followed these fictional Caribbean women all over the world and deep
into their own worlds, I was repeatedly confronted by the US government's
role in a deeply violent global capitalist world order. Maryse took me to the
Chile of her dream, where the CIA had killed the spirit of Allende. Sophie,
Amabelle and Freda showed me the rape, murder, mutilation and torture
Caribbean women have suffered at the hands of US-backed dictators. I
watched over little Félicie as she played with Barbie, whose blonde locks were
no more innocuous than the American GIs who, it seemed, just wouldn't
go home. I accompanied Kamla to the Hollywood movies that flooded her
childhood, where she identified not with the cowboy but with the American
Indian, one of the original casualties of US imperialism. And beyond the

twinkling lights of Luminada Heights, Viveka gestured towards the shadowy offshore rigs where even now Shell Oil is pumping out climate death day and night. Such is the power of fiction to personalize and connect that, after visiting those fictional worlds, there was simply no denying, as Danticat writes, "You are – we are all implicated in this."[2]

Among and beyond these literary worlds, US imperialism in all its forms also perpetrates slow violence, for it profoundly impacts Caribbean people's access to food. The region imports 80 per cent of its food, most of it from the United States. And in the simplest of terms, that imported food is paid for through travel and tourism, often also from the United States. As early as April 2020 the COVID-19 pandemic had renewed fears about the risks entailed in such heavy dependence, from potential disruptions of shipping lines and supply chains to possible agricultural labour shortages in the United States. And by June 2020 tourism had come to a virtual standstill. Moreover, because of the economic downturn in the United States, concerns had arisen about the sustainability of remittances, a substantial part of many Caribbean economies.[3] By July the number of food-insecure people in the region had jumped from 1.2 million to 2.9 million, with the extremely food insecure holding steady at 400,000. Many of those surveyed by one relief agency[4] reported having changed their diets, from eating less to skipping meals or even going a day without eating. Unsurprisingly, the impacts on eating habits were most widespread among low-income families.[5] It had never been so clear that the United States has the power to decide what and even whether most of the Caribbean eats.[6]

The COVID-19 crisis intensified (pre-existing) calls for homegrown solutions to this dangerous food dependence. Agricultural economists called for regional leadership to achieve food security, "to tear down the barriers and expedite inter-island food trade".[7] The agricultural ministers of CARICOM countries stepped up and pooled resources, taking measures to boost domestic food production.[8] However, as social movements such as La Campesina have pointed out, unless plans to achieve Caribbean food security include increased Caribbean food sovereignty, they will achieve limited success in the long run. Caribbean peoples need democratically determined, people-centred trade and agricultural policies that integrate small farmers' social, environmental and economic interests, increasing their competitiveness and supporting their long-term success.[9] Equally important, Caribbean consumers need to know that, once food is being produced locally, they will be able to afford it. In all of this, intra-regional solidarities across all manner of divides are and will continue to be key, and Caribbean women's lived experiences will be the best yardstick for measuring success.

As I write this final note, I want to conclude, with a conciliatory broad stroke of the pen, that this visionary group of Caribbean women authors has, like Glissant's "open boat",[10] something to teach the whole world. But clearly not all of us are in equal need of the lesson. And so I will conclude instead that these constructors of vision have something to offer those of us, both within the Caribbean and beyond its borders, who are still learning to live in solidarity, reciprocity and unity in diversity. If ever there was an occasion for everyday people to completely rethink *nou* and *yo*, if ever there was a time to attempt the *jamais vu* and *l'impensé,* that time is now.

NOTES

INTRODUCTION

1. Condé, *Of Morsels and Marvels*, xi. The original French-language *Mets et merveilles* (2015) was translated into English as *Of Morsels and Marvels* in 2020 by Richard Philcox. All translations are his.
2. Ibid., viii.
3. Wilk, *Home Cooking*, 4.
4. I take these metaphors from, respectively, Munasinghe's *Callaloo or Tossed Salad?* and Khan's *Callaloo Nation*.
5. Wilk, *Home Cooking*, 14.
6. Gadsby, *Sucking Salt*.
7. Shahani, *Food and Literature*, 16.
8. Gilbert, *Culinary Imagination*, 6.
9. Loichot, *Tropics Bite Back*; Githire, *Cannibal Writes*.
10. Mintz, *Sweetness and Power*.
11. Moore, "Sugar".
12. For the purpose of this exercise, I examined Palmié and Scarano's edited collection *The Caribbean: A History of the Region and Its Peoples* (2011), Higman's *A Concise History of the Caribbean* (2011), and Heuman's *The Caribbean: A Brief History* (2014).
13. Twenty-first-century "general" histories of the Caribbean conscientiously reject history's role as an accomplice in subjection. Instead they pursue something akin to a "people's history" (to borrow the term from Howard Zinn in *A People's History of the United States*) that acknowledges the creativity and resilience of the oppressed and, by extension, asserts the imminent possibility of a more just future. The question remains as to whether or not this shift in perspective adequately accounts for the role of gender systems and relations in that "people's history".
14. Chamoiseau, *Texaco*, 122.

15. Mohammed and Shepherd's multidisciplinary edited collection *Gender in Caribbean Development* (1988) marked a shift in historical thinking about the Caribbean, for it moved from using women as a category of analysis to using gender. Gender history, including metadisciplinary examinations of methodology, epistemologies, paradigms and representations, has continued to proliferate and diversify; see Mohammed, *Gendered Realities* (2002) and Bailey and Leo-Rhynie, *Gender in the 21st Century* (2004), among others. By reading sources against the grain and insisting on different perspectives, gender historians have fundamentally changed Caribbean historiography; see Brereton's reflections on twenty-five years of engendering Caribbean history in "Women and Gender".

16. Glissant, *Discours antillais*, 132.

17. Ibid., 33.

18. See Edward Saïd's *Orientalism* (1978) and Edouard Glissant's "History and Literature", in *Le discours antillais* (1981).

19. Arnold, "Erotics of Colonialism", 6.

20. Ibid., 7.

21. Ibid., 8.

22. Ibid., 15.

23. They are among those Haitian women writers whom Myriam Chancy, in *Framing Silence*, calls revolutionary.

24. Pirbhai, "Jahaji-Bhain Principle", 53.

25. Ibid., 12.

26. Davies and Fido, "Women and Literature", 11.

27. In 1980, at Audre Lorde's suggestion, the Black lesbian feminist Barbara Smith created the activist Kitchen Table: Women of Color Press in order to publish without being at the mercy of white-dominated presses. Kitchen Table published a number of works on Black feminism, including Smith, *Home Girls*.

28. Marshall, "From the Poets in the Kitchen", n.p.

29. Ibid.

30. Adisa, "Senses Related to the Nose", lines 21 and 23.

31. One might argue that Opal Palmer Adisa is a contemporary of, not a predecessor to, the group of authors I treat here. However, owing to the difference in genre and above all the absence of the uniting trope of a shared meal, I have classed her among these first-wave "kitchen talk" writers instead of with the second-wave authors of *The Pen and the Pan*.

32. Torres-Saillant, *Intellectual History*, 214.

33. Puri, *Caribbean Postcolonial.*
34. Ferly, *Poetics of Relation,* 53.
35. Garth, *Food and Identity;* Goucher, *Congotay!*
36. Beushasen, "Caribbean (on the) Dining Table", 19.
37. Allen and Sachs, "Women and Food Chains", 15. The more we understand about the relationship between women and food, the better we can understand how women use food to reproduce, resist and rebel against gender constructions in a variety of contexts; see Avakian and Haber, "Feminist Food Studies", 2. Moreover, because food practices and their representations are part and parcel of daily life, they are especially revelatory of the particularities of time, place and culture (7). As such, they provide an excellent means for contextualizing women's liberation struggles in the Caribbean.
38. For such an overview, see Mohammed's "Women's/Feminist Activism". Mohammed separates feminist and women's activism into three distinct yet overlapping categories: self-defined feminist and non-governmental women's organizations, the state machinery and gender, and tertiary-level teaching and research in gender studies. I contend that women's creative writing is its own form of activism, overlapping in some ways with gender studies yet able, perhaps, to reach a broader, less self-selected audience.
39. Ashcroft, Griffiths and Tiffin, "Feminism and Post-colonialism", 250.
40. Mohanty, "Under Western Eyes", 261.
41. Narayan, "Essence of Culture", 88.
42. Ibid., 92.
43. Ibid., 94.
44. Ibid., 96.
45. Basksh-Soodeen, "Issues of Difference", 72.
46. Ibid., 79.
47. Ibid., 80.
48. MacKinnon, "Intersectionality as a Method", 1019.
49. Ibid., 1026.
50. Ibid., 1028.
51. McDonald, "What Is This T'ing", 47.
52. I have drawn on Vivian May's *Pursuing Intersectionality* for an understanding of and terminology for intersectionality as it is depicted in the target corpus.
53. Mohammed, "Towards Indigenous Feminist Theorizing", 8.
54. Ibid., 13.
55. Ibid., 16.

56. Ibid., 24–25.

57. Reddock, "Diversity, Difference", 1.

58. Ibid., 13.

59. An iconic figure and trailblazer in Caribbean feminism, Andaiye died in 2019 after half a century of feminist scholarship and activism at the intersection of gender, race and labour, authoring such works as *The Valuing of Women's Unwaged Work* (1984) and *The Angle You Look from Determines What You See: Towards a Critique of Feminist Politics in the Caribbean* (2002).

60. Andaiye, "Angle You Look From", 11.

61. Barriteau was and remains a giant in Caribbean feminist scholarship and gender studies, having made decades of key contributions to the core canon of feminist scholarship from the Caribbean. Barriteau's copious body of work includes such writings as *The Political Economy of Gender in the Twentieth-Century Caribbean* (2001) and numerous edited volumes, including the influential *Love and Power: Caribbean Discourses on Gender* (2012) and *Confronting Power, Theorizing Gender* (2003).

62. Barriteau, "Issues and Challenges", 39.

63. Mohammed, "Like Sugar in Coffee", 23.

64. Paravisini-Gebert, "Homegrown Roots", 4.

65. Ibid., 12.

66. See Sanatan, "Homegrown Feminism".

67. Hosein has been an influential figure in articulating Indo-Caribbean feminist perspectives on gender and feminism, including *dougla* (mixed black and East Indian women) feminisms. See, for example, her ground-breaking 2016 co-edited collection, *Indo-Caribbean Feminist Thought*, which crystallizes a quarter-century of Indo-Caribbean feminist scholarship. As we will see, her work on Indo-Caribbean femininity and creolization informs chapter 3, "Lakshmi Persaud: Forbidden Fruit".

68. "Edwidge Danticat and Victoria Brown: Caribbean Feminisms on the Page", Barnard Center for Research on Women, 17 September 2015, https://bcrw.barnard.edu/videos/edwidge-danticat-and-victoria-brown-caribbean-feminisms-on-the-page/ and http://bcrw.barnard.edu/event/caribbean-feminisms-on-the-page-edwidge-danticat-victoria-brown/.

69. hooks and Mesa-Bains, *Homegrown*.

70. With the exception of Peepal Tree, the very small press (twenty books a year) that published Persaud's novels, thanks to a grant from the British Arts Council, and Press Gang Publishers, the similarly sized Toronto-based feminist coopera-

tive that published Shani Mootoo's *Out on Main Street and Other Stories*, all the publishers of the target corpus are divisions of huge publishing conglomerates.

71. Lugones, *Pilgrimages/Peregrinajes*, 98.

72. Ibid., 218.

73. Ibid., 29.

74. Ibid., 18.

75. Ibid., 97.

76. Ibid., 161.

77. *Errance* ("errantry") is Edouard Glissant's term for navigating and acknowledging multiplicities of cultural influences. It might also be translated as "wandering". See Glissant, "Errantry, Exile", in *Poetics of Relation*.

78. This phrasing was inspired by Roy's "Reading Communities", 484.

CHAPTER 1

1. "God help us get back to Guadeloupe!" (my translation). See Pineau/Spear, "5 questions".

2. Bureau pour le développement des migrations dans les départements d'outre-mer, an institution whose purpose was to facilitate movement between the French overseas departments (Martinique, Guadeloupe, French Guyana and Réunion Island) and mainland France.

3. For a complete history, see Constant, "Politique française".

4. The thirty years of French economic expansion that followed World War II.

5. Edouard Glissant contends that the "myth of non-separation from France" is a defining characteristic of French Antilleans, making them wildly different from their Haitian cousins, who have been independent since 1804 and are indeed unique in the Caribbean. See Dash, *Edouard Glissant*, 6.

6. Constant, "Politique française", 17.

7. This term, still in use in the 1990s when Pineau wrote *L'Exil selon Julia* and *Un Papillon dans la cité*, has largely been replaced by others such as "Afro-French", "Afro-pean" or even just "Afro". See, for example, Amandine Gay's documentary *Ouvrir la voix* (Arte, 2017).

8. Recall that this is Edouard Glissant's term for an empowered, conscious, active engagement with difference. See Glissant's "Errantry, Exile" in his *Poetics of Relation*.

9. See Glissant, *Intention poétique*; *Discours antillais*; and *Poetics of Relation*.

10. Bernabé, Chamoiseau and Confiant, *In Praise of Creoleness*.

11. Ibid., 13.

12. See Hall, "Creolization, Diaspora, and Hybridity".

13. *Habitations de loyer modéré*, French state-subsidized low-income housing.

14. Suburbs commonly associated with lower incomes in Greater Paris. I use the untranslated French term throughout this chapter, as it entails socio-economic and cultural realities that don't necessarily translate to suburbs elsewhere.

15. This is *verlan*, or backwards slang, for *Arabes* and generally used to refer to persons of North African descent in the Parisian *banlieues*, roughly equivalent to "North African in the city". *Verlan* itself is a product of these multicultural *banlieue* neighbourhoods and is characteristic of them, just as Creole is emblematic of the Caribbean.

16. Murdoch, *Creolizing the Metropole*, 17.

17. This is a term the French routinely attach to any form of self-identification or community attachment that might supersede being "French". According to republican universalism, one must always identify as French *before* (and preferably instead of) identifying as black, Catholic, gay, female and so on.

18. Murdoch, *Creolizing the Metropole*, 255.

19. Hargreaves, "Translator's Introduction", xix–xx.

20. I use *History* in place of *history* here in order to emphasize its monolithic nature and totalitarian bent.

21. Glissant, *Discours antillais*,

22. Ibid., 133. Like Glissant, the *créolistes* feel it is urgent to restore collective memory in the Caribbean and advocate erasing the separation between literature and history. History, they assert, is less equipped than the creative writer to penetrate certain aspects of Caribbean experience and memory. According to them, the Caribbean writer must expose and valorize every aspect of life in the Caribbean, however insignificant. See Lewis, *Race, Culture and Identity*, 102.

23. Loichot, "Devoured by Writing", 335.

24. Pineau/Veldwachter, "Interview", 181.

25. Pineau/Spear, "5 questions".

26. Pineau/Veldwachter, "Interview", 182.

27. Pineau/Jurney, "Entretien", 108.

28. Île-de-France (literally "Island of France") is the region that encompasses Paris and its suburbs.

29. Women of the French Caribbean: Traces and voices; 150 years after the abolition of slavery (my translation).

30. Pineau/Makward, "Entretien", 1202; Pineau/Spear, "5 questions"; Pineau/ Veldwachter, " Interview", 180.

31. Durmelat, "Narrative"; Fulton, "Disengaged Immigrant".

32. Mehta, "Culinary Diasporas".

33. Githire, "Horizons Adrift"; Gyssels, "Exil selon Pineau"; Pineau "Reconstruire dans l'exil"; Loichot, *Tropics Bite Back*; Murdoch "Negotiating the Metropole".

34. Thomas, "Transgenerational Trauma" and "Gisèle Pineau".

35. Haigh, "Migration and Melancholia".

36. Pineau/Veldwachter, "Interview", 183.

37. Pineau/Makward, "Entretien", 1204, 1207; Pineau/Jurney, "Entretien", 112.

38. Pineau/Spear "5 questions"; Pineau/Makward, "Entretien", 1203; Pineau/Veldwachter, "Interview", 185.

39. Pineau/Jurney, "Entretien", 109.

40. Loichot, "Devoured by Writing", 334.

41. Pineau/Veldwachter, "Interview", 184.

42. For a thorough treatment of Caribbean diasporic writers and filmmakers working in major Western cities, see Murdoch, *Creolizing the Metropole*.

43. Pineau/Makward, "Entretien", 1203.

44. Ibid., 1203 (my translation).

45. See Loichot, "Devoured by Writing".

46. The Creole term for Afro-Caribbean fugitives from slavery ("runaways"), The nèg mawon is a French Caribbean symbol of revolt, self-reliance and a superior ability to adapt and survive in extremely hostile conditions.

47. The *classe de mer*, a school trip to the ocean, is a type of field trip in the French education system, organized and executed in a spirit of republican *égalité*. These entirely state-sponsored trips grant all French children access to nature and the knowledge and pleasure it affords, regardless of socio-economic standing or urban residence. In locating the *classe de mer* in Guadeloupe, Ms Bernichon valorizes the island, counting it among France's diverse sites of natural beauty. In this way she leverages her privilege as an agent of the French state to act as an ally and advocate for a pluralistic vision of Frenchness.

48. Anselin, *Emigration antillaise*, 100.

49. Ibid.

50. Ibid., 191–92 (my translation).

51. Ionesco, "Ici-là", 6.

52. Ibid., 8, 10.

53. Ibid., 5, 11, 12.

54. Ibid., 2.

55. Wilk, "Home Cooking", 49.

56. Pineau, "Reconstruire dans l'exil", 26 (my translation).

57. Mehta, "Culinary Diasporas", 59.

58. Pineau, *Papillon dans la cité*, 66–67. All citations taken from *Papillon* are my translations. Subsequent references to this novel appear parenthetically in the text.

59. Valérie Loichot asserts that cooking, relegated to women and domestic space, tells the story of a people's history just as well as a historical log. See Pineau, "Reconstruire dans l'exil", 36.

60. Brinda Mehta contends that the pig is part of a "politics of corporeal control based on unhealthy eating" and "Europe's credo to maintain the colonizing imprint on the Americas through the long-term consequences of lard consumption". See "Culinary Diasporas", 110. However, this reading assumes that Europeans actually considered pork to be unhealthy, which they likely did not. As it was also consumed by Europeans in the colonies, even those of the planter class, it seems unlikely to have been conceived of at the time as a biological weapon.

61. See Brinda Mehta's assessment of the importance of the yam as a West African culinary retention, in "Culinary Diasporas", 100.

62. Pineau, *Exile According to Julia*, 27–28. All English language quotes and page numbers are taken from Betty Wilson's translation. Subsequent references to this novel appear parenthetically in the text.

63. Knowing his death is imminent, Jesus commands his disciples to keep him alive by using food and memory: "And he took bread, gave thanks and broke it, and gave it to them, saying, 'This is my body given for you; do this in remembrance of me'" (Luke 22:19).

64. Joan Dayan identifies the zombie as a lingering memory of slavery: "The phantasm of the zombie – a soulless husk deprived of freedom – is the ultimate sign of loss and dispossession" (*Haiti, History and the* Gods, 37).

65. Michael Pollan points out that cuisines tend to resist change: "It is often said that the last place to look for signs of assimilation in an immigrant's home is the pantry." See *In Defense of Food*, 174.

66. Loichot, "Devoured by Writing", 328.

67. By the power of the written word, Africans were enslaved (the Black Code of 1685), freed a first time (by Revolutionary decree in 1794), re-enslaved (under Napoleon in 1802), and freed again (definitive abolition, associated with Victor Schoelcher, in 1848).

68. Valérie Loichot notes that one of the fundamental themes of both *Un papillon dans la cité* and *L'exil selon Julia* is the rewarding process of becoming a writer.

The protagonists, she claims, transform themselves from mere consumers to producers of discourse. See Pineau, "Reconstruire dans l'exil", 35.

69. Glissant, *Poetics of Relation*, 7.

70. Loichot, "Devoured by Writing", 334–35.

71. Pineau, *Exile According to Julia*, 16.

72. Brinda Mehta notes that Félicie's relationship with her mother suffers because of Aurélie's rigid commitment to assimilation. Félicie wonders if her mother has "abdicated all rights to their Caribbean identity"; "Culinary Diasporas", 98.

73. Loichot, *Tropics Bite Back*, 63.

74. An iced cake in the form of a yule log, part of the traditional French Christmas dinner.

75. Regional products or products of the local land.

76. The average French reader would recognize cider, milk and *rillettes* as typical products representative of the Sarthe region.

77. See Revel's "From Cuisine to Gastronomy".

78. A person who lives in northwest France's Sarthe region.

79. "Zouk la Sé Sèl Médikaman Nou Ni", a 1984 song by the Guadeloupean band Kassav', was enormously popular in the European territory of France at the time and remains widely recognizable today.

80. The traditional French wedding cake.

81. Turkish delight.

82. These young people are, as Brinda Mehta puts it, exploring "the possibility of creating diasporic solidarities within and beyond the Caribbean"; "Culinary Diasporas", 89.

83. See "Le Canari: Héritage amérindien", *Patrimoines de Guadeloupe*, 28 October 2009, http://patrimoines-de-guadeloupe.over-blog.com/article-heritage-amerindien -le-canari-38365605.html.

84. In 2012, for example, there were almost twice as many people of French Antillean descent or birth currently living in European France (heavily concentrated in Paris) than made up the entire population of either Guadeloupe or Martinique; Murdoch, *Creolizing the Metropole*, 8. Many second- and third-generation immigrants to Paris identify as Antillean, even if they were not born in the Caribbean and even if they have never visited the Caribbean; ibid., 123.

85. In *Creolizing the Metropole*, H. Adlai Murdoch writes: "In seeking to integrate patterns of ethnic identitarianism with national ones, the challenge for such groups will be to recognize and come to terms with the arc of transformation

that has accompanied their dis-location and to develop an articulative context that will give expression to this new positionality" (14).

86. Ibid., 26.

87. Ibid., 259.

88. The French department of Seine-Saint-Denis consists of the most multicultural Parisian suburbs, and most French Antilleans in the European territory of France live there.

89. Durmelat, "Narrative of 'A Return'", 109.

90. Murdoch notes that it is in exile on the mainland that many Antilleans first learn to value and practise their *antillanité; Creolizing the Metropole*, 63. Richard Wilk observes a similar phenomenon among Belizeans in the United States: "When I interviewed Belizeans who had lived in the United States, one of the most common things they said was that they did not discover their identity as Belizean until they lived abroad ... In Belize they would rather drink rum from Barbados or Jamaica instead of the local stuff, but a Belizean party in Chicago would not be complete without Caribbean, One-Barrel or Traveler's from home"; *Home Cooking*, 170.

91. Pineau, "Écrire en tant que Noire", 290.

92. "The tale of errantry is the tale of relation", writes Glissant in *Poetics of Relation* (18). "Whereas exile may erode one's sense of identity, the thought of errantry – the thought of that which relates – usually reinforces this sense of identity" (20).

93. Pineau, "Écrire en tant que Noire", 295.

CHAPTER 2

1. Danticat/Gonzalez, "Dominican Republic's 'Ethnic Purging'".

2. Guerra Vilaboy and González Arana, *Dictaduras del Caribe*.

3. In Guerra Vilaboy and González Arana's *Dictaduras del Caribe*, see "Introducción" (1–8) for a thorough explanation of the ways in which US economic and political intervention undermined Caribbean economies and development and led to the rise of dictators in the region, and "Dictaduras caribeñas: Una comparación final" (131–41) for insight into what Trujillo's and Duvalier's dictatorships had in common, including their relationship with the United States.

4. Schoenhals, "Trujillo Molina", 144.

5. Wilson, "Duvalier", 883.

6. For a succinct account of Trujillo's and Duvalier's respective rises to power and

regimes, see Schoenhals, "Trujillo Molina", and Wilson, "Duvalier". For an examination of US relations with the Dominican Republic, see Roorda, *Dictator Next Door*. For a consideration of US relations with Haiti, see Gerlus, "Effects of the Cold War", and Guerra Vilaboy and González Arana, "Los regímenes dictatoriales Duvalieristas en Haití (1957–1986)" in *Dictaduras del Caribe*.

7. In "War and Political Violence", Kalisa categorizes all three novels as belonging to the post-colonial woman's war story, loosely defined (167). Writing about women's experiences resists war's destruction, she argues, because it documents the past (165). For her part, Vargas classifies Danticat's *Farming of Bones* as part of a Latin American tradition of *testimonio* that uses fiction to remember and testify against state violence; "Novel Testimony", 1162. While my own analysis contextualizes Danticat's writing mainly within a Caribbean context, it is useful to keep these multiple circles of belonging in mind as one considers her work.

8. Trouillot, *Silencing the Past*, 6.

9. Ibid., 2.

10. Ibid., 19–21.

11. Ibid., 25.

12. Ibid., 26.

13. Chancy, *Framing Silence*, 5.

14. Ibid., 6.

15. Ibid., 12.

16. Ibid., 17.

17. Sarthou, "Unsilencing Défilé's Daughters", 101.

18. Ibid., 99.

19. Mishrahi-Barak, "My Mouth Is the Keeper", 156.

20. Ibid., 162.

21. Bellamy, "Silence and Speech", 207, 210.

22. Danticat/Chancy, "Recovering History", 122.

23. Literally "people outside", the rural peasantry is more closely associated with a traditional way of life. Their access to power and resources, both of which are heavily concentrated in the capital, is severely limited.

24. Danticat/Smith, "Splintered Families", 21.

25. Martin Munro brings together these various observations, by Evelyne Trouillot, himself and Nick Nesbitt respectively, in "Borders", his introduction to *Edwidge Danticat*. All emphases are mine.

26. Mirabal, "Dyasporic Appetites", 34–35.

27. Danticat, "We Are Ugly".

28. See Marshall, "From the Poets".

29. Danticat, "All Geography". Valérie Loichot has emphasized this literary lineage in her readings of metaphors of consumption in Danticat's *Krik? Krak!* and *Breath, Eyes, Memory*. See Loichot, "Edwidge Danticat's Kitchen History" and "Kitchen Narrative: Food and Exile in Edwidge Danticat and Gisèle Pineau", in *Tropics Bite Back*, where she groups Danticat's early writings with Pineau's culinary fiction, dubbing both "kitchen narratives" in which the association of cooking and writing "transforms the daily gestures of women into political acts and home and kitchen into sites of political resistance"; *Tropics Bite* Back, 65. See also Githire, *Cannibal Writes*.

30. See Alexis, "Du réalisme merveilleux".

31. Clitandre, *Edwidge Danticat*, 5; Dash, "Danticat and Her Haitian Precursors", 28–29.

32. See Alexis "Du réalisme merveilleux".

33. Trouillot, "To the Text", 183.

34. In an open letter/New Year's address, Alexis urged artists not to give in to the temptation to make art for art's sake, or to fall into disillusionment and depict human beings only at their most depraved. Instead he called for 1957 to be a great year of *"la belle amour humaine"*, in which art lifts up humanity to its highest and best and paves the way to a better world for all.

35. Mirabal, "Dyasporic Appetites", 38.

36. Danticat, "Plantains Please", 180.

37. Danticat, "This Is My Body".

38. Mirabal, "Dyasporic Appetites", 39.

39. Gadsby's *Sucking Salt* draws on this metaphor for Caribbean women's endurance.

40. Danticat, "All Geography".

41. Danticat, *Create Dangerously*, 40, 36.

42. Danticat, "Grain of Comfort". Danticat revisits these memories in *Brother I'm Dying*.

43. See Munro, "Borders".

44. See Loichot, *Tropics Bite Back*, 94.

45. Danticat, "Price of Sugar".

46. Ibid.

47. Danticat, *Farming of Bones*, 1. Subsequent references to this novel appear parenthetically in the text.

48. Danticat/Chancy, "Recovering History", 122.

49. In recent years the Kreyòl *zo* has come to mean "money". If we consider this

alternative meaning of the word, *travay tè pou zo* becomes "working the land for money", a phrase that contrasts with "working the land for sustenance" or even "survival", emphasizing agricultural workers' very different and extremely precarious relationship to the land within a global capitalist system.

50. "First-class people" who profited from the growing sugar economy and dominated the republic's commercial ties, also the chief concern of US capital. See Roorda, *Dictator Next Door*, 15.

51. Sugar is an especially powerful symbol of destructive addiction; between its introduction to Europe in the time of the Crusades and the seventeenth century, sugar became associated with a number of other addictive substances that included coffee, tea, chocolate and alcohol. See Mintz, *Tasting Food*, 70–71.

52. As Elizabeth McAlister has noted, the muzzle is a powerfully symbolic device that makes material the silencing of both women and blacks. "One only has to remember the torture of the slave masks, modeled on the 'scold's bridle', placed over women's mouths to prevent them from speaking and often eating"; McAlister, "Caribbean Women's Fugitive Speech Traditions", 32.

53. Errol D. Alexander notes that within a few generations of abolition, many people were told not to "rattle the chains of slavery" – not to talk about the days when their ancestors were enslaved. See the foreword to *The Rattling of the Chains*.

54. Danticat/Chancy, "Recovering History", 110–11.

55. Loichot, *Tropics Bite Back*, 87–88. See also Chancy, *Framing Silence*, 125.

56. Danticat, *Breath, Eyes, Memory*, 4. Subsequent references to this novel appear parenthetically in the text.

57. McAlister, in "Caribbean Women's Fugitive Speech Traditions", 32, includes other women among those who silence Caribbean women. In her critique of "the code of silence women share", she points out that when women repress one another's speech with a meaning-heavy *mmm* that moves everyone on to new subjects and other tasks, would-be speakers feel pained, isolated and punished.

58. In "War and Political Violence", Kalisa points out the strong connections that Danticat draws between militarized and gendered violence in *Breath, Eyes, Memory*. The state's use of military and paramilitary forces to control its people, she explains, is closely linked to patriarchal domination. Kalisa also identifies the parallel between the police use of rape to control and terrorize the people and families' policing of young girls' sexuality in the home; ibid., 179. See also Loichot, "Kitchen History", 93.

59. Trouillot, "Tonton Macoutes", 103.

60. See the marketplace scene, 96.

61. "You look a lot like your mother and her mother before her", writes Danticat in "Women Like Us", the epilogue to *Krik? Krak!* "It was their whispers that pushed you, their murmurs over pots sizzling in your head. A thousand women urging you to speak through the blunt tip of your pencil. Kitchen poets . . . they asked for your voice"; *Krik? Krak!*, 222.

62. Danticat, "This Is My Body".

63. The Vodou pantheon includes a number of powerful spirits, or *lwa*, who are distinct from *Bondye*, or the *Gran Met*, the one God. Whereas *Bondye* does not interfere directly in earthly matters, the *lwa* help with everyday problems from love to finance. See Michel, "Bondye".

64. "All people are people", declares the Haitian proverb, "but not all people are the same".

65. Eileen Burchell asserts that the novel "explores the centrality of the mother-daughter relationship to self-identity and self-expression"; "As My Mother's Daughter", 60.

66. Writes Danticat in "Women Like Us", the epilogue to *Krik? Krak!*, "Are there women who both cook and write? Kitchen poets, they call them. They slip phrases into their stew and wrap meaning around their pork before frying it. They make narrative dumplings and stuff their daughter's [*sic*] mouths so they say nothing more"; *Krik? Krak!*, 219–20.

67. Loichot suggests that cooking has healed Sophie because it has helped her "erase the personal boundaries between herself and her mother, the boundaries that kept her mother alien from her, the boundaries that prevented her from caring in an engaged way for her mother"; "Edwidge Danticat's Kitchen History", 107. I'm arguing here that the *lack* of boundaries between mother and daughter is the very source of Sophie's suffering. As bell hooks puts it, the denial of a daughter's identity, as separate from that of her mother, is more likely to "alienate and/or violate than to enhance growth". This unhealthy lack of boundaries is part of what hooks terms "maternal sadism"; *Communion*, 85. Chancy analyses this lack of boundaries in terms of the Vodou *marassa*; *Framing Silence*, 124.

68. "It's an expression, *choukèt lawoze*; it really means somebody who breaks or shakes the dew", explained Danticat in a 2004 interview with Robert Birnbaum (*Morning News*, 20 April 2004, reproduced in Montgomery, *Conversations*, 7–20). "There is also an expression on the other side, *gouverneurs de la rosée*, people who govern the dew, who are kinder people, people of the land who nurture the land and try to control their destiny through the land." Thus Danticat's

The Dew Breaker was designed to function in tandem with Jacques Roumain's seminal *Gouverneurs de la rosée* to depict Haiti's failings, its greatness, and what lies in between.

69. Danticat, *Dew Breaker*, 131. Subsequent references to this novel appear parenthetically in the text.

70. The relationship between the Volontaires de la sécurité nationale (*miliciens*) and the Tonton Macoutes was that the official, public, mainly symbolic *miliciens* provided cover for the unofficial, behind-the-scenes, exceedingly violent Macoutes. See Trouillot, "Tonton Macoutes", 104.

71. In the collection's climactic scene, as the Dew Breaker reflects on his own ever-increasing brutality, he borrows a phrase from Jacques Stephen Alexis: "Tu deviens un véritable gendarme, un bourreau" (198). Alexis's second-person familiar *tu* intimates that this could, even would, happen to you, or to anyone – but it doesn't. In Danticat's polyvocal narrative, some die, others flee and still others actively resist, sometimes in heroic ways. And somewhere between recognition of their resemblances and accountability for their differences lies the truth.

72. This paragraph and the one that precedes it first appeared in my "Scattering and Gathering".

73. The title for this section was inspired by Shemak's "Re-membering Hispaniola", in which she classifies *The Farming of Bones* as *testimonio*, an eyewitness account that foregrounds the voices of the oppressed.

74. Shiva, "Development, Ecology, and Women", 337–42.

75. See Loichot, "Kitchen History", 92, in which she argues that in *Breath, Eyes, Memory* food is important "to remember the past and heal the self and communities in the aftermath of diaspora, immigration, and exile".

76. Loichot invokes Wendell Berry's *Unsettling of America* in her analysis of the disconnect between people and the land in industrialized foodways, as depicted in *Breath, Eyes, Memory; Tropics Bite Back*, 80.

77. Loichot, *Tropics Bite Back*, 93.

78. This paragraph and the one that precedes it first appeared (with some small changes) in my "Scattering and Gathering".

79. Mirabal, "Dyasporic Appetites", 37.

80. "By overthrowing me, you have only cut down in Saint Domingue the trunk of the tree of the liberty of the Blacks", famously proclaimed Toussaint Louverture to his French captors; "it will grow back by the roots, which are deep and numerous" (my translation).

81. Published by the Bruderhof movement, *Plough Quarterly*'s stated goal is to "inspire faith and action".
82. Danticat, "This Is My Body".
83. Insisted Danticat in a 2017 interview, "I don't like the word 'victimhood'. The word 'victim' has become so trite in our culture. Amabelle and the others are survivors of this massacre"; Danticat/Adisa, "Up Close and Personal", 45. In Haiti, she explains, "The women may not be labeling themselves feminists or womanists, but they're doing the work. They're keeping the children alive. They're keeping the family going"; ibid., 42.
84. Trouillot, *Silencing the Past*, 18.

CHAPTER 3

1. Persaud, *Butterfly in the Wind*, 178. This refers to Indian independence and its psychic importance to East Indians in Trinidad. Subsequent references to this novel appear parenthetically in the text.
2. Van der Veer and Vertovec, "Brahmanism Abroad", 150.
3. Singaravelou, "Indians in the Caribbean", 27.
4. Bernabé, Chamoiseau and Confiant, in *In Praise of Creoleness*, for example, term Césaire "ante-Creole", not "anti-Creole".
5. Mariam Pirbhai points out, for example, the implicit call to black consciousness and black power in Edward Kamau Braithwaite's creolized "nation-language"; "Indo-Trinidadian Fictions", 131.
6. "The Hindus who replaced the black slaves in the plantations of Trinidad", write the authors of *In Praise of Creoleness*, "adapted their original culture to new realities without completely modifying them". These Hindus, the *créolistes* explain, are therefore American – "a migrant culture in splendid isolation" – but not creole; Bernabé, Chamoiseau and Confiant, *In Praise of Creoleness*, 30.
7. Puri, *Caribbean Postcolonial*, 172.
8. Ibid., 84.
9. Brereton, "History of Modern Trinidad", 106.
10. Singaravelou, "Indians in the Caribbean", 29
11. Brereton, "History of Modern Trinidad", 107–8.
12. Singaravelou, "Indians in the Caribbean", 30.
13. Ibid., 31.
14. Brereton, "History of Modern Trinidad", 113.
15. See Mohammed, "Gender as a Primary Signifier".

16. Uma Narayan notes that India's "huge array of linguistic, religious, and cultural differences" is such that it is sometimes easier to define a religion in terms of what it is *not* rather than in terms of what it is. See *Dislocating Cultures*, 169.

17. Van der Veer and Vertovec, "Brahmanism Abroad", 153–54.

18. Brereton, "History of Modern Trinidad", 108.

19. While indentured to sugar estates, Indo-Trinidadians concealed their daily devotional rites. The early twentieth century saw racist evolutionary models mutate into the realm of religion, with non-Christians seen as being in a primitive state of development. "Hinduism/Indians invited criticism with polytheism (whose differentiated deities certainly had to be evidence of barbarism), arcane rituals (distinguished from the notion of Christian prayer), and mysticism." See Khan, *Callaloo Nation*, 21, 33, 37.

20. Brereton, "History of Modern Trinidad", 112.

21. Van der Veer and Vertovec, "Brahmanism Abroad", 154.

22. Uma Narayan claims "Hindus coexist more easily with the gods of others than with their food"; *Dislocating Cultures*, 171.

23. Chatterjee, "Nationalist Resolution", 239.

24. Literally "black waters", the *kala pani* is roughly the Indo-Caribbean equivalent to the Afro-Caribbean Middle Passage. Like the Middle Passage, the *kala pani* has both a literal physical meaning – the transport of over a half a million East Indian indentured servants to the Caribbean – and a symbolic spiritual one – a moment of profound loss and a point of no return. Proscribed by Hindu law, travel overseas would have entailed significant negative social and spiritual consequences not only for those who embarked upon the journey, but for their descendents as well.

25. See Persaud's website, http://www.lakshmipersaud.com/author.html; "UWI St Augustine Names Six Honorary Graduands", *UWI St Augustine Campus News*, 11 June 2013, https://sta.uwi.edu/news/releases/release.asp?id=1101.

26. Pirbhai, "Jahaji-Bhain Principle", 53.

27. Persaud/Baksh, "Compelled to Write".

28. Writes Persaud in the autobiographical *Butterfly in the Wind*, "The presence of such an inner voice is not the sort of thing you would wish to speak about, and I had no way of knowing whether anyone I knew had one. So, unwillingly, I carried mine in silence" (52).

29. Khan, *Callaloo Nation*, 74, 87.

30. Ibid., 92.

31. Ibid., 95.

32. Persaud, *Sastra*, 56. This is chief among the master Hindu chef Draupadi's culinary "commandments", all of which are metaphors for larger social realities. Subsequent references to the novel appear parenthetically in the text.

33. "There had to be first times", concludes Persaud's Sastra, then wonders, "Could I be a first timer?" (58).

34. When Sastra finds it more difficult to defy her family and tradition than does her love interest, Rabindranath, the young man speculates, "Perhaps because you are a daughter and not a son, you feel this way. There is something about domesticity; it clings on, encourages you to comply with the tradition that has created it. Perhaps this is why people say women are the custodians of culture" (105).

35. Persaud describes *Butterfly* as a collection of childhood remembrances that she later structured into a novel. See Persaud/Baksh, "Compelled to Write".

36. See Mehta, "Colonial Curriculum".

37. See Mehta, "Indo-Trinidadian Fiction", 151.

38. Shani Mootoo (see chapter 4) uses this word in order to communicate the fact that the terms are inseparable from one another.

39. The tacit understanding among groups such as Jews, Muslims and Hindus, asserts Mary Lukanuski, is that without dietary regulations, the community would fall victim to its individual appetites and would disintegrate; "Place at the Counter", 113.

40. Mannur, "Culinary Nostalgia", 17, 14.

41. Mehta, "Indo-Trinidadian Fiction", 153.

42. Mannur, "Culinary Nostalgia", 15.

43. In "Indo-Trinidadian Fiction", Mehta reads this scene as an erotic form of self-expression for women whose sexuality has been repressed. "Food-based Krishna consciousness offers a creative outlet for women's sexual energies" (159) and "the women in Persaud's novels dramatize their powers of seduction in the kitchen, under the guise of religious devotion" (160). Women's sexualizing of kitchen space, she argues, constitutes "invisible feminism" (160), a "subversive affirmation" of their own sexuality (161).

44. Miriam Pirbhai disagrees. She declares Persaud's work "devoid of the postmodern strategies of irony and metafiction which evoke the fallibility of memory or the distorting effects of nostalgia" (137), faulting her for what Pirbhai reads as "awkward silences" regarding the rum-shop owners' complicity in social dysfunction; "Indo-Trinidadian Fictions", 145.

45. Pirbhai sees Kamla's attitude as naive, pointing out that "her unqualified celebration of Indian nationalism glosses over its dominant Hindu discourse;

oversimplifies an otherwise complex group of stratified religious, political, ideological, and class interests"; "Indo-Trinidadian Fictions", 143.

46. Adlai Murdoch underscores the fact that Indo- and Afro-Caribbean peoples did not identify with one another because European colonialist thinking had driven them to have a low opinion of one another; "Writing India", 119.

47. Mohammed, "Asian Other", 67.

48. Khan, *Callaloo Nation*, 12–13

49. Mehta, "Indo-Trinidadian Fiction", 158.

50. Ibid., 162.

51. Ibid., 159.

52. Higman, *Jamaican Food*, 28.

53. Mehta, "Indo-Trinidadian Fiction", 163.

54. Higman, *Jamaican Food*, 27.

55. Appadurai, "Gastro-Politics", 496.

56. Miriam Pirbhai objects to Persaud's characterization of the Muslim Mrs Hassan, claiming that the author "simplifies the latter's position as an unbending orthodoxy which contrasts radically with the more accommodating Hindu doctrine. It is not her presence as a minor character that renders Mrs Mohammed [*sic*] a problematic archetype, therefore, but the deployment of her character and values as contrast and foil"; "Indo-Trinidadian Fictions", 142. However, read in the context of Persaud's entire *oeuvre*, Mrs Hassan becomes one rigidly orthodox woman among many, most of whom are actually Hindu.

57. An East Indian syrup-soaked sweet.

58. See Sutherland, "Sita and Draupadi".

59. Mehta, "Indo-Trinidadian Fiction", 151.

60. Ibid., 165.

61. Roy calls this "nation-making through commensality"; "Reading Communities", 484. Mannur terms this "multicultural eating", noting its possibilities for overcoming racial and ethnic differences; "Culinary Nostalgia", 27.

62. My readings of Persaud in this chapter have been generally informed and shaped by Hosein and Outar, *Indo-Caribbean Feminist Thought*.

63. Hosein, "Modern Navigations", 9.

64. Ibid., 10.

65. Ibid., 20.

66. See Mahabir and Pirbhai, "Introduction".

67. Mehta, "Colonial Curriculum", 112

68. Khan, *Callaloo Nation*, 12–13.

CHAPER 4

1. Mootoo, *Out on Main Street*, 48. As this short-story collection is discussed in detail, subsequent references appear parenthetically in the text.
2. Girvan, "Assessing Westminster", 95–96.
3. Lindsey, "Myth of Independence", 94.
4. Girvan, "Assessing Westminster", 97.
5. Lamming, *Sovereignty of the Imagination*, 7.
6. Gaskins, "Buggery", 434–35.
7. Han and O'Mahoney, *British Colonialism*, 105.
8. See, for example, Kizito, "Bequeathed Legacies", 567–72, or Srivastava, *Sexual Sites*.
9. Wahab, "Homophobia", 487.
10. Ibid., 484–85.
11. For middle-class elites in Jamaica, observes David Scott, building the post-colonial nation has meant imposing a single vision of the national good and the national citizen-subject on the diverse segments of the popular masses. Sexual mores have had a significant role to play in that project. While "middle-class modern" conflates respectable citizenship and reproductive heterosexuality with legitimate power, "popular modern" adheres to reputational discourse and profligate heterosexuality as an alternative form of self-fashioning. The failure to impose that single vision, observes Scott, produces deep anxieties among middle-class elites about the fragility of post-colonial sovereignty. See Scott, "Fanonian Futures?" 190–93.
12. Wahab, "Homophobia", 485.
13. Surtees, "Homophobic Laws".
14. In order to increase visibility and encourage more social contact, insists Jackman, legislation outlawing anti-gay bullying would be needed; "Protecting the Fabric", 102. While the High Court has proven effective in eliminating existing laws that criminalize homosexuality regardless of public sentiment, it is well beyond judicial reach to pass legislation against anti-gay bullying. Without a shift in public perception and a concomitant shift in political will, it is easy to see how the vicious cycle of ignorance and repression could be reinforced and perpetuated despite this important court victory. In fact, the Coalition Advocating for Inclusion of Sexual Orientation (CAISO), an important local and regional advocate for LGBTQ/SSL people, has long prioritized the fight against discrimination and differential treatment over decriminalization. See Gaskins, "Buggery", 446.

15. However, literary scholars have generally sought not to follow her desire to deconstruct categories but instead to categorize her, to define her in terms of one or another of her intersecting identities: as a woman writer of colour (Tagore, *Shapes of Silence*), an anglophone Caribbean writer (Valovirta, *Sexual Feelings*), a lesbian writer (Mootoo/Hall, "Interview") or a queer writer of the Caribbean diaspora (Pecic, "Shani Mootoo's Diasporas"). Similarly they have tried to pigeonhole her work in the context of Indo-Caribbean women's writing (Mahabir and Pirbhai, "Tracing an Emerging Tradition"), Indian diasporic women's writing (Helff, *Unreliable Truths*), South Asian writing (Selvadurai, *Story-Wallah*) or diasporic Canadian or North American writing (Aziz, *Confluences 2*). But as Narain, Donnell and O'Callaghan insist, Mootoo's fiction is fundamentally Caribbean – that is to say, fundamentally hybrid, intersectional and creole. See Narain, Donnell and O'Callaghan, "Shani Mootoo".

16. Mootoo, "On Becoming an Indian Starboy", 167–68.

17. Ibid., 168.

18. Mootoo/Hall, "Interview", 110.

19. Just as other Indians seem to judge her (at least, as she perceives them doing so), the narrator judges her girlfriend, Janet, whom she sees as not Indian enough. Though Janet is dark-skinned and dark-haired, her mother named her for the pretty little blonde, blue-eyed girl from the colonial primary school readers she studied as a child, and the family's last name, Mahase, has "no association with Hindu or Indian whatsoever" (47). Janet is arguably more completely colonized than the narrator, more assimilated, more lost to her former culture. For Janet, the sacred Hindu festival Diwali has lost all religious significance; it is reduced to decorative lights and the eating of special dishes such as *burfi* and *prasad*, dishes she had eaten with her Hindu neighbours. And the narrator recalls that Janet's family was one of the first to convert "from Indian to Presbyterian" (46). Note that in these examples the narrator conflates Indianness with being Hindu. The Hindu faith is tightly bound with "authentic" South Asian culinary traditions and, not surprisingly, Janet's family is even further removed than the narrator from this tradition. Perhaps Janet cannot even be said to be a "kitchen Indian". In some ways, she is a tourist in Indian culture. Just as a mainstream Canadian might enjoy an Indian restaurant, Janet eats Indian food simply because it tastes good and satisfies her hunger. In fact, to the narrator's great embarrassment, she attempts to order *prasad* – a dish with great spiritual significance that is prepared only for Diwali – for dessert in an Indian restaurant. "Since den I never go back in dat restaurant", confesses the narrator, "I embarrass fuh so!" (47).

20. Mootoo, *Valmiki's Daughter*, 9. Subsequent references to this novel appear parenthetically in the text.

21. In *Sovereignty of the Imagination*, Lamming acknowledges the role that Afro-Caribbean people, particularly the black middle classes of Trinidad and Guyana, have played in portraying the East Indian as "alien and other, a problem to be contained". At the same time, he points out, Indians who identified "too readily" with the creolizing process were mocked and treated as inauthentic (33). Therefore, the East Indian's only route to Caribbean belonging was through shaping the land itself, "inscribing their signatures on a landscape that will be converted into home" (33).

22. Writes Lamming, "Men do not simply say, 'We are in power because we feel we have a right to be and that's the end of that. There's nothing you can do about it.' They never say that. They believe they represent and are the guardians of some social order, which is in the interest of all, and then they will hire a variety of intellectual mercenaries to argue that this is true. This social order is usually supportive of the material interest in the dominant ruling group and they translate these interests as being identical with the interest of the total society"; *Sovereignty of the Imagination*, 16.

23. I borrow this term from Zoran Pecic, "Shani Mootoo's Diasporas".

24. Recall that I draw this framework for feminist solidarity and understanding from Lugones, *Pilgrimages/Peregrinajes*.

25. Pre-harvest firings, sometimes known as "cool burns", have been a normal part of sugarcane production in Trinidad for more than a hundred years, a reminder that "the crop" – *the* crop – is underway. See Richardson, *Igniting the Caribbean's Past*, 100, 112, 101.

26. Lugones, *Pilgrimages/Peregrinajes*, 29, 98, 219.

27. Throughout the Caribbean, fire carries a strong social connotation: insurrections have often been associated with fire or threats of fire. See Richardson, *Igniting the Caribbean Past*, 6.

28. Ibid., 119.

29. Ibid., 125.

30. In "Cannes Brûlees", Elder explains that burning cane plays a mythical role in Trinidad, where the *canboulay* (from the French *cannes brûlées*, "burnt canes") procession is an integral part of all-important Carnival celebrations. *Canboulay* celebrates emancipation and embodies Afro-Trinidadians' "aspirations for true liberty, the freedom to pursue their own goals as human beings" (38). In essence, *canboulay* is "a duel between the European moral codes and the

African canons of freedom" (39). Moreover, as re-enactments of the *canboulay* riots of the late nineteenth century remind us, the "decadent" and "unsavory" masses have always been a threat to the hegemony of "respectable" society, and respectable society has always been prepared to leverage the power of the state to enforce its brand of morality.

31. Wahab, "Homophobia", 499.
32. Glave, "Desire", 4.
33. King, "More Notes", 194–95.
34. Mootoo, "On Becoming an Indian Starboy", 172.
35. Pecic, "Shani Mootoo's Diasporas", 3.

CHAPTER 5

1. From *Victoire: Les saveurs et les mots*. Translated by Richard Philcox as "Identities are forged" in *Victoire: My Mother's Mother*.
2. In the context of the French Caribbean, this term is used to denote a very specific group of people whose social privilege is historically and presently drawn from a combination of colourism and longstanding economic advantage.
3. See Chamoiseau, *Texaco*, 122, for an explanation of the "*vrai-vrai*" one obtains by braiding together the "half-true", the "sometimes-true" and the "almost-true".
4. Originally published as *Victoire: Les saveurs et les mots* in 2006, then translated into English by Richard Philcox in 2010. All translated quotes from *Victoire* are from the latter. Subsequent references to both versions of this novel appear parenthetically in the text.
5. Originally published as *Mets et merveilles* in 2015, then translated into English by Richard Philcox in 2020. All translated quotes from *Morsels* are from the latter. Subsequent references to both versions of this novel appear parenthetically in the text.
6. Spear, "Maryse Condé".
7. Condé, "Liaison dangereuse", 205.
8. Sesquin, *Voix singulière*. Translated as *Maryse Condé: A Voice of Her Own*, with subtitles by Richard Philcox. All translated quotes taken from *Une voix singulière* are from the latter.
9. In fact, she says so herself in *Maryse Condé: A Voice of Her Own*.
10. Fanon, *Black Skin*, 204–5.
11. This is not to say by any means that she denies colonialism's impact. In fact, she

served as the first president of France's National Committee for the Memory and History of Slavery.

12. Fanon, *Black Skin*, 115.

13. In theory, French-speaking countries and peoples, which would include France. In practice, "francophone" and "French" have often constituted complementary categories. Although of French nationality, Antillean writers such as Condé have been categorized primarily as francophone, thereby disputing or displacing their French identity.

14. "World literature". This new appellation was intended to address and move beyond the artificial division between "French" and "francophone" literature. See Condé, "Liaison dangereuse"; Thomas, "Maryse Condé".

15. Condé/Benali and Simasotchi-Bronès, "Rire créole", 22.

16. *Antillanité* and *créolité* appeared in the 1960s and 1989, respectively. While the first concept stresses the specificity of the West Indian experience, the second focuses on cultures with common traits (such as a history of slavery, plantations and cultures in contact) around the world.

17. See Vergès, "Singulière Maryse Condé".

18. See Moudileno, "Gastronomie furtive" for a discussion of food in Condé's works before *Victoire*.

19. The history of the slave trade and slavery has in many ways been silenced by abolition, which became part of a narrative of ineluctable progress in human and citizens' rights, a narrative that tended to minimize France's role in the slave trade and slavery. The difficult post-abolition period, like slavery itself, doesn't fit neatly into that narrative. See Vergès, *Mémoire enchaînée*, 74, 111.

20. "Colored society at the end of the nineteenth century", writes historian Jean-Pierre Sainton, "can be perceived as more *racialized*, that is to say more racist than the slave society it inherited from" (my translation); Sainton, *Couleur et société*, 76.

21. Condé's novel speaks to the ways in which individuals experience race as a structure within society – a difficult subject to broach in the French context, where the biological meaninglessness of the concept is often called upon to stifle debate. Sainton asserts that "the mere mention of it makes people tense up intellectually over the insignificance of the word 'race'"; meanwhile, in the French Caribbean "[t]he tendency is to live with (or to submit to) a social and cultural fact that is at the heart of daily collective life while avoiding studying it so that you don't have to face it mentally"; ibid., 38. Refusing to dismiss the word *race* as a lexical residue of false logic, Sainton, much like Condé in *Victoire*,

advocates for understanding race in late-nineteenth-century Guadeloupe in experiential and identity-based terms. He warns that we must avoid diminishing or diluting the problem of race in our approach to a society that, in its daily reality, affirms its raciality both institutionally/systemically and through individual beliefs, discourse and behaviour; ibid., 41, 44.

22. A royal decree defining the conditions of slavery in the French colonial empire. See France, *Code Noir*.

23. Sainton, *Couleur et société*, 12–13, 29–30, 52.

24. Terms referring to varying combinations of white and black ancestry that resulted, presumably, in discernible nuances of skin colour.

25. Sainton, *Couleur et société*, 62.

26. Ibid., 79–86.

27. Ibid., 100–101, 121–22.

28. Condé/Boisseron, "Intimité", 135.

29. Philcox translates this sentence as "Reality was stranger than fiction"; see *Victoire: My Mother's Mother*, 2. However, in the literal translation – "Reality went *beyond/further than* fiction" – we find a hint that the opposite might also be true. The novel is made up not only of *réalité qui dépasse la fiction* (reality that goes beyond fiction) but also of *fiction qui dépasse la réalité* (fiction that goes beyond reality). In *Victoire*, Condé does not insist on unattainable objectivity or verifiable accuracy in her pursuit of truth. She prefers instead to allow her imagination and intuition free rein as she interprets and expands on the established facts available to her. After all, as she learned from her father, "You forge an identity" (16). "A novelist is not a journalist", insisted Condé in an interview with Benedicte Boisseron. "Based on the facts, he embellishes, he makes things up, he imagines"; "Intimité", 138.

30. Ibid., 135.

31. In "The Return to and Beyond the Mother", Laurie Corbin reads *Victoire* in association with two other texts in which fact and imagination work together to shed light on Condé's maternal line. Corbin traces the evolution of Victoire's presence in these *récits* from "historical" to "mythical". Both Sarah Mosher's "(Auto)biographical Victories" and Bonnie Thomas's "The Cook and the Writer" focus on the parallels Condé draws between her own literary production and her grandmother's cuisine. Both critics emphasize the ways in which her version of her grandmother's story empowers Victoire and identifies her creativity in the kitchen as a precursor to Condé's own success as a writer.

32. Members of the black bourgeoisie. Although the Jovial family touts its status

as purely a result of "intellectual and human values, self-pride, respect, and social esteem" (14) and insists that its social position is unrelated to money, economic capital is clearly a factor.

33. Sainton, *Couleur et société*, 74–75.

34. A kerchief-wearing woman, which is to say a woman of the lower social classes. This term is opposed to the *femme à chapeau*, or hat-wearing woman, who occupies a higher social rank.

35. Broichhagen, Lachman and Simek's critical collection, *Feasting on Words*, places Condé's approach to the image of the literal and the literary cannibal in its historical, cultural and literary context.

36. "Slavery is not dead!" Condé declares this to be the case in the film *Maryse Condé: A Voice of Her Own*.

37. Cassava, a staple food in tropical regions, including the Caribbean, and watered-down coffee.

38. Sainton, *Couleur et société*, 134–38.

39. This list includes Turkish delight and the Creole names of a number of traditional Antillean sweets made with coconut or coconut milk, cane sugar, lime, vanilla and cinnamon.

40. Black nationalist.

41. See Lugones, *Pilgrimages/Peregrinajes*, 18, 29, 98 and 218 for explanations of the differences between arrogant perception and loving perception, between resistance as a simple no and resistant response, and between agency and active subjectivity.

42. France, Décret n° 83–1003 du 23 novembre 1983 relatif à la commémoration de l'abolition de l'esclavage, LégiFrance, 26 April 2012, https://www.legifrance.gouv.fr /loda/id/JORFTEXT000000336997/2020-12-21/.

43. Loi reconnaissance de la traite et de l'esclavage crimes contre l'humanité, for which French politician Christiane Taubira was a principal advocate.

44. Loi reconnaissance contribution nationale des Français rapatriés, named after Algerian-born French politician Hamlaoui Mekachera.

45. Constitutional Council, the highest constitutional authority in France.

46. Union pour un mouvement populaire (Union for a Popular Movement), a centre-right political party. In 2015, the UMP was renamed "Les Républicains". From 1981 to 2017, along with the centre-left Parti socialiste, the UMP was one of the two most powerful political parties in France.

47. "Demande de déclassement de la loi Taubira", Liberté pour l'histoire, 8 May 2006, https://www.lph-asso.fr/indexed2e.html?option=com_content&view

=article&id=38%3Ademande-de-declassement-de-la-loi-taubira&catid=5%3A-communiques&Itemid=15&lang=fr.

48. Vergès, *Mémoire enchaînée*, 31.

49. Ibid., 7.

50. See, for example, Ministère de l'Enseignement supérieur et de la Recherche et Alliance française, "Enseigner les traites, l'esclavage, leurs abolitions et leurs héritages" [Teaching about the Atlantic slave trade, slavery, their abolition and their legacy. Sensitive questions, current research], 18–20 May 2011, a conference sponsored by a number of human rights groups and hosted by the French Ministry of Higher Education and the Alliance française, https://www.ohchr .org/documents/events/iypad/eurescl.pdf.

51. Sesquin, *Maryse Condé*.

52. Nedelkovski, "Grève générale".

53. "Un reportage sur les 'békés' enflamme la Martinique", *Le Monde*, 13 February 2009, https://www.lemonde.fr/politique/article/2009/02/13/un-reportage-sur -les-bekes-enflamme-la-martinique_1154769_823448.html.

54. Bolzinger, *Derniers maîtres de la Martinique*.

55. The 1990 Gaysott law (prohibiting Holocaust denial), the 2001 law recognizing the Armenian genocide of 1915, the 2001 Taubira law and the 2005 Mekachera law.

56. "Réparations: Nouvelles actions judiciaires", *Carib Creole News*, 5 May 2015.

57. Vergès points out that despite (and precisely because of) its unique commitment to the natural rights of all human beings, regardless of race, the Haitian Revolution is consistently omitted from the great revolutions of the Enlightenment. The resulting European monopoly on democratic ideals therefore presents an incomplete picture of core French values. *Mémoire enchaînée*, 40–41.

58. The attack on the offices of *Charlie Hebdo* took place on 11 January 2015.

59. "Réforme des programmes: 'Débranchons le déconomètre', implore Luc Ferry", *Le Parisien*, 12 May 2015, https://www.leparisien.fr/societe/reforme-des-programmes -debranchons-le-deconometre-implore-luc-ferry-12-05-2015-4764849.php.

60. Roger-Petit, "Collège".

61. Tremolet de Villers, "Pierre Nora".

62. Vigoureux, *Mystère Taubira*, 2.

63. Simasotchi-Bronès compares Condé's approach to the post-colonial world to Achille Mbembe's description of post-colonial Africa in *De la postcolonie* (2000), which is to say that Condé's writing addresses a world in which the formerly

colonized are pitted not only against their former colonizers and their neo-colonizers, but also against each other. See her introduction to *Maryse Condé en tous ses ailleurs*, 7.

64. A North African stew that often combines meat and fruit.

65. Torregano, "Maryse Condé".

66. A Caribbean dessert made from condensed milk, eggs and coconut.

67. Lugones, *Pilgrimages/Pelerinajes*, 161.

68. Fanon, *Black Skin*, 204.

69. Sainton, *Couleur et société*, 20.

70. Ibid., 156.

71. Remarkably resilient, the sultans of Yogyakarta have managed to retain their hereditary claim to power inside one of the most democratic nations in Southeast Asia. See "Yogyakarta's Sultans, Carrying On", *Economist*, 6 September 2012, https://www.economist.com/banyan/2012/09/06/carrying-on.

72. Neruda, "Towards the Splendid City".

73. Ibid.

74. Allende, "Last Words".

75. Bonilla, *Non-Sovereign Futures*, 10.

76. Ibid.

77. Bonilla uses these terms to describe the successes of the Liyannaj kont pwofi-tasyon (LPK) in its campaign to negotiate directly with the French government; *Non-Sovereign Futures*, 176. The LPK was an umbrella group of labour and social organizations that led the 2009 general strike.

78. Ibid., 3.

79. Ibid., 152–57.

AFTERWORD

1. Lugones, *Pilgrimages/Peregrinajes*, 18.

2. Edwidge Danticat, quoted by Juan González on *Democracy Now!*

3. According to the World Bank, personal remittances in 2018 were equal to 32 per cent of Haiti's GDP, 16 per cent of Jamaica's and 8.9 per cent of Dominica's; World Bank, "Personal Remittances Received (% of GDP)", https://data.worldbank.org/indicator/BX.TRF.PWKR.DT.GD.ZS.

4. Nothing called "charity", "aid", "relief" or even "social services" is a substitute for mutual aid. Whether it is rich people or the government deciding who gets the help, what the limits are to that help, and what strings are attached, none of

this is an acceptable substitute for mutual aid and food sovereignty, in which people are empowered to help themselves and each other in sustainable, non-hierarchical ways. See Spade, "Solidarity not Charity!"

5. "Caribbean COVID-19 Food Security and Livelihoods Impact Survey Regional Summary Report, July 2020", Reliefweb, 27 August 2020, https://reliefweb.int /report/world/caribbean-covid-19-food-security-livelihoods-impact-survey -regional-summary-report-july.

6. Ewing-Chow, "Five Ways".

7. Ibid.

8. See, for example, the Caribbean Agricultural Research and Development Institute's distribution of hundreds of cassava slips to small farmers across the Bahamian state; Forbes, "Caribbean Food Sovereignty".

9. Ibid.

10. "Our boats are open", writes Glissant of French Antillean history, "and we sail them for everyone"; "The Open Boat", in *Poetics of Relation*.

BIBLIOGRAPHY

Adisa, Opal Palmer. "Poui". *Obsidian III* 2, no. 2 (2000): 39.

———. "Senses Related to the Nose". *Frontiers* 17, no. 3 (1996): 176–77.

Alexander, Errol D. *The Rattling of the Chains*. Vol. 1. Alexander, 2015.

Alexis, Jacques Stephen. "La belle amour humaine". *Lettres françaises*, 1957.

———. "Du réalisme merveilleux des Haïtiens". *Présence africaine* 165/166 (2002): 91–112.

Allen, Patricia, and Carolyn Sachs. "Women and Food Chains: The Gendered Politics of Food". *International Journal of Sociology of Food and Agriculture* 15, no. 1 (2007): 1–23.

Allende, Salvador. "Last Words to the Nation". Speech, 11 September 1963. Marxists Internet Archive. https://www.marxists.org/archive/allende/1973/september/11.htm.

Andaiye. "The Angle You Look from Determines What You See: Toward a Critique of Feminist Politics in the Caribbean". Lucille Mathurin-Muir Lecture. Mona: University of the West Indies, 2002.

Anselin, Alain. *L'émigration antillaise en France: La troisième île*. Paris: Karthala, 1990.

Appadurai, Arjun. "Gastro-politics in Hindu South Asia". *American Ethnologist* 8, no. 3 (1981): 494–511.

Arnold, A. James. "The Erotics of Colonialism in Contemporary West Indian Literary Culture". *New West Indian Guide* 68, no. 1 (1994): 5–22.

Ashcroft, Bill, Gareth Griffiths and Helen Tiffin. "Feminism and Post-colonialism: Introduction". In *The Post-Colonial Studies Reader*, edited by Bill Ashcroft, Gareth Griffiths and Helen Tiffin, 249–58. London: Routledge, 1995.

Avakian, Arlene, and Barbara Haber. "Feminist Food Studies: A Brief History". In *From Betty Crocker to Feminist Food Studies: Critical Perspectives on Women and Food*, 1–26. Amherst: University of Massachusetts Press, 2005.

Aziz, Nurjehan, ed. *Confluences 2: Essays on the New Canadian Literature*. Toronto: Mawenzi House, 2018.

Bailey, Barbara, and Elsa Leo-Rhynie. *Gender in the 21st Century: Caribbean Perspectives, Visions and Possibilities*. Kingston: Ian Randle, 2004.

Baksh-Soodeen, Rawwida. "Issues of Difference in Contemporary Caribbean Feminism". *Feminist Review* 59 (1998): 74–85.

Barriteau, Eudine Violet. "Issues and Challenges of Caribbean Feminisms". *African Feminisms* 58 (2003): 37–43.

———. *The Political Economy of Gender in the Twentieth-Century Caribbean.* New York: Palgrave, 2001.

———, ed. *Confronting Power, Theorizing Gender: Interdisciplinary Perspectives in the Caribbean.* Kingston: University of the West Indies Press, 2003.

Bellamy, Maria Rice. "Silence and Speech: Figures of Dislocation and Acculturation in Edwidge Danticat's *The Dew Breaker*". *Explicator* 71, no. 3 (July 2013): 207–10.

Bernabé, Jean, Patrick Chamoiseau and Raphaël Confiant. *Éloge de la créolité/In Praise of Creoleness.* Translated by M. B. Taleb-Khyar. Paris: Gallimard, 1993.

Beushasen, Wiebke. "The Caribbean (on the) Dining Table: Contextualizing Culinary Cultures". In *Caribbean Food Cultures: Culinary Practices and Consumption in the Caribbean and Its Diaspora*, edited by Wiebke Beushausen, 1–20. Bielefeld, Germany: Columbia University Press, 2014.

Bolzinger, Romain, dir. *Les derniers maîtres de la Martinique.* Tac Presse/Canal +/ Planète, 2009.

Bonilla, Yarimar. *Non-sovereign Futures: French Caribbean Politics in the Wake of Disenchantment.* Chicago: University of Chicago Press, 2015.

Brereton, Bridget. *A History of Modern Trinidad: 1783–1962.* Kingston: Heinemann, 1981.

———. "Women and Gender in Caribbean (English-Speaking) Historiography: Sources and Methods". *Caribbean Review of Gender Studies* 7 (2013): 1–18.

Broichhagen, Vera, Kathryn Lachman and Jeanette Simek, eds. *Feasting on Words: Maryse Condé, Cannibalism and the Caribbean Text.* Princeton, NJ: Princeton University Program in Latin American Studies, 2006.

Burchell, Eileen. "As My Mother's Daughter: *Breath, Eyes, Memory* by Edwidge Danticat (1994)". In *Women in Literature: Reading Through the Lens of Gender*, edited by Jerilyn Fisher and Ellen S. Silber, 60–62. Westport, CT: Greenwood Press, 2003.

Césaire, Aimé. *Notebook of a Return to the Native Land.* Translated by Annette Smith. Middletown, CT: Wesleyan University Press, 2002.

Chamoiseau, Patrick. *Texaco.* Translated by Rose-Myriam Réjouis and Val Vinkurov. New York: Vintage, 1998.

Chancy, Myriam. *Framing Silence: Revolutionary Novels by Haitian Women.* New Brunswick, NJ: Rutgers University Press, 1997.

Chatterjee, Partha. "The Nationalist Resolution of the Women's Question". In *Recasting Women: Essays in Indian Colonial History*, edited by Kumkum Sangari and Suresh Vaid, 233–53. New Brunswick, NJ: Rutgers University Press, 1990.

Clitandre, Nadège. *Edwidge Danticat: The Haitian Diasporic Imaginary*. Charlottesville: University of Virginia Press, 2018.

Condé, Maryse. "Intimité: Entretien avec Maryse Condé". Interview by Bénédicte Boisseron. *International Journal of Francophone Studies* 13, no. 1 (2010): 131–53.

———. "Liaison dangereuse". In *Pour une littérature-monde*, edited by Michel le Bris and Jean Rouaud, 205–16. Paris: Gallimard, 2007.

———. *Mets et merveilles*. Paris: Lattès, 2015.

———. *Of Morsels and Marvels*. Translated by Richard Philcox. London: Seagull, 2020.

———. "Le rire créole: Entretien avec Maryse Condé". Interview by Zineb Ali-Benali and Françoise Simasotchi-Bronès. *Littérature* 154, no. 2 (2009): 13–23.

———. *Victoire: Les saveurs et les mots*. Paris: Mercure de France, 2006.

———. *Victoire: My Mother's Mother*. Translated by Richard Philcox. New York: Atria International, 2010.

Constant, Fred. "La politique française de l'immigration antillaise de 1946 à 1987". *Revue européenne des migrations internationales* 3, no. 3 (1987).

Cope, Robyn. "Scattering and Gathering: Danticat, Food and (the) Haitian Experience(s)". In *The Bloomsbury Handbook to Edwidge Danticat*, edited by Jana Evans Braziel and Nadège Clitandre. New York: Bloomsbury, 2021.

Corbin, Laurie. "The Return to and Beyond the Mother: Maryse Condé and Representations of Maternity". *Life Writing* 4, no. 2 (2007): 231–45.

Crenshaw, Kimberlé. "Demarginalizing the Intersection of Race and Sex: A Black Feminist Critique of Antidiscrimination Doctrine, Feminist Theory and Antiracist Politics". *University of Chicago Legal Forum* 1989, no. 1 (1989): 139–67.

Danticat, Edwidge. "All Geography Is within Me: Writing Beginnings, Life, Death, Freedom and Salt". *World Literature Today* 93, no. 1 (2009). https://www.worldliteraturetoday.org/2019/winter/all-geography-within-me-writing-beginnings-life-death-freedom-and-salt-edwidge-danticat.

———. *Breath, Eyes, Memory*. New York: Soho, 1994.

———. *Brother, I'm Dying*. New York: Alfred A. Knopf, 2007.

———. *Claire of the Sea Light*. New York: Alfred A. Knopf, 2019.

———. *Create Dangerously: The Immigrant Artist at Work*. New York: Vintage, 2010.

———. *The Dew Breaker*. New York: Alfred A. Knopf, 2004.

———. "The Dominican Republic's 'Ethnic Purging': Edwidge Danticat on Mass Deportation of Haitian Families". Interview by Juan González. *Democracy*

Now! NPR, 17 June 2015. https://www.democracynow.org/2015/6/17/the
_dominican_republics_ethnic_purging_edwidge.

———. "Edwidge Danticat". Interview by Robert Birnbaum. In *Conversations
with Edwidge Danticat,* edited by Maxine Lavon Montgomery, 37–53. Jackson:
University Press of Mississippi, 2017.

———. *Everything Inside.* New York: Alfred A. Knopf, 2019.

———. *The Farming of Bones.* New York: Soho Press, 1998.

———. "A Grain of Comfort". *O: The Oprah Magazine,* April 2006. https://www.oprah
.com/food/simple-white-rice-edwidge-danticats-simple-meal-with-her-father/all.

———. *Krik? Krak!* New York: Vintage, 1996.

———. "Plantains Please". *Caribbean Writer* 13 (1999): 179–80.

———. "The Price of Sugar". Creative Time Reports, 5 May 2014. https://creativetime
reports.org/2014/05/05/edwidge-danticat-the-price-of-sugar/.

———. "Recovering History 'Bone by Bone': A Conversation with Edwidge Danticat".
Interview by Myriam Chancy. In Myriam Chancy, *From Sugar to Revolution:
Women's Visions of Haiti, Cuba and the Dominican Republic,* 109–30. Waterloo,
ON: Wilfred Laurier University Press, 2012.

———. "Sawfish Soup". *Caribbean Writer* 5 (1991).

———. "Splintered Families, Enduring Connections: An Interview with Edwidge
Danticat". Interview by Katherine Capshaw Smith. In *Conversations with Edwidge
Danticat,* edited by Maxine Lavon Montgomery, 21–36. Jackson: University Press
of Mississippi, 2017.

———. "This Is My Body: Of Food and Freedom". *Plough Quarterly* 20 (2019). https://
www.plough.com/en/topics/justice/social-justice/immigration/this-is-my-body.

———. "Up Close and Personal: Edwidge Danticat on Haitian Identity and the
Writer's Life". Interview by Opal Palmer Adisa. In *Conversations with Edwidge
Danticat,* edited by Maxine Lavon Montgomery, 37–53. Jackson: University Press
of Mississippi, 2017.

———. "We Are Ugly But We Are Here". *Caribbean Writer* 10 (1996). http://faculty
.webster.edu/corbetre/haiti/literature/danticat-ugly.htm.

Dash, J. Michael. "Danticat and Her Haitian Precursors". In *Edwidge Danticat: A
Reader's Guide,* edited by Martin Munro, 26–51. Charlottesville: University of
Virginia Press, 2010.

———. *Edouard Glissant.* Cambridge: Cambridge University Press, 1995.

Davies, Carole Boyce, and Elaine Savory Fido. "Women and Literature in the
Caribbean: An Overview". In *Out of the Kumbla: Caribbean Women and Literature,*
edited by Carole Boyce Davies and Elaine Savory Fido, 1–24. Trenton, NJ: Africa
World Press, 1990.

Dayan, Joan. *Haiti, History and the Gods.* Berkeley: University of California Press, 1995.

Durmelat, Sylvie. "Narrative of 'A Return to the Non-native Land': Gardens and Migration in 'L'exil selon Julia' by Gisèle Pineau". *Journal of Caribbean Literatures* 4, no. 2 (2006): 109–18.

Elder, J.D. "Cannes Brûlées". *TDR* 42, no. 3 (1998): 38–43.

Ewing-Chow, Daphne. "Five Ways that COVID-19 Has Changed What Food Insecurity Looks Like in the Caribbean". *Forbes*, 31 March 2020.

Fanon, Frantz. *Black Skin, White Masks.* Translated by Richard Philcox. New York: Grove, 2008.

Ferly, Odile. *A Poetics of Relation: Caribbean Women's Writing at the Millennium.* New York: Palgrave Macmillan, 2012.

Forbes, Kasmine D. "Caribbean Food Sovereignty during Covid-19". NACLA, 20 August 2020. https://nacla.org/news/2020/08/14/caribbean-food-sovereignty -covid.

France. *Le code noir ou l'édit du roy servant de règlement pour le gouvernement et l'ad- ministration de justice des isles françaises de l'Amérique et pour la discipline et le commerce des nègres et esclaves dans ledit pays.* Versailles, March 1685; reprint, Nîmes: C. Lacour, 2013.

Fulton, Dawn. "The Disengaged Immigrant: Mapping the Francophone Caribbean Metropolis". *French Forum* 32, no. 1/2 (2007): 245–62.

Gadsby, Meredith. *Sucking Salt: Caribbean Women Writers, Migration and Survival.* Columbia: University of Missouri Press, 2006.

Garth, Hanna, ed. *Food and Identity in the Caribbean.* London: Berg, 2012.

Gaskins, Joseph. "'Buggery' and the Commonwealth Caribbean: A Comparative Examination of the Bahamas, Jamaica and Trinidad and Tobago". In *Human Rights, Sexual Orientation and Gender Identity in the Commonwealth: Struggles for Decriminalization and Change,* edited by Corinne Lennox and Matthew Waites, 429–54. London: University of London, 2013.

Gerlus, Jean-Claude. "The Effects of the Cold War on US–Haiti's Relations". *Journal of Haitian Studies* 1, no. 1 (1995): 34–56.

Gilbert, Sandra M. *The Culinary Imagination: From Myth to Modernity.* New York: W.W. Norton, 2014.

Girvan, Norman. "Assessing Westminster in the Caribbean: Then and Now". *Commonwealth and Comparative Politics* 53, no. 1 (2015): 95–107.

Githire, Njere. *Cannibal Writes: Eating Others in Caribbean and Indian Ocean Women's Writing.* Urbana: University of Illinois Press, 2014.

———. "Horizons Adrift: Women in Exile, at Home and Abroad in Gisèle Pineau's Works". *Research in African Literatures* 36, no. 1 (2005): 74–90.

Glave, Thomas. "Desire through the Archipelago". In *Our Caribbean: A Gathering of Lesbian and Gay Writing from the Antilles*, edited by Thomas Glave, 1–11. Durham, NC: Duke University Press, 2008.

Glissant, Edouard. *Le discours antillais*. Paris: Gallimard, 1981.

———. "L'errance, l'exil". In *Poétique de la relation*, 23–34. Paris: Gallimard, 1990.

———. *L'intention poétique*. Paris: Gallimard, 1997.

———. *Poetics of Relation*. Translated by Betsy Wing. Ann Arbor: University of Michigan Press, 1997.

Goucher, Candace. *Congotay! Congotay! A Global History of Caribbean Food*. New York: M.E. Sharp, 2014.

Guerra Vilaboy, Sergio, and Roberto González Arana. *Dictaduras del Caribe: Estudio comparado de las tiranías de Juan Vicente Gómez, Gerardo Machado, Fulgencio Batista, Léonidas Trujillo, los Somoza y los Duvalier*. Monterrey, Mexico: Editorial Universidad del Norte, 2017.

Gyssels, Kathleen. "L'exil selon Pineau: Récit de vie et autobiographie". In *Récits de vie de l'Afrique et des Antilles: Enracinement, errace, exil*, edited by Suzanne Costa, 169–213. Sainte-Foy, QC: GRELCA, 1998.

Haigh, Sam. "Migration and Melancholia: From Kristeva's *Dépression nationale* to Pineau's *Maladie de l'exil*". *French Studies* 60, no. 2 (2006): 232–50.

Hall, Stuart. "Creolization, Diaspora and Hybridity in the Context of Globalization". *Créolité and Creolization*, edited by Okwui Enwezor, 178–98. Ostfildern-Ruit, Germany: Hatje Cantz, 2003.

Han, Enze, and Joseph O'Mahoney. *British Colonialism and the Criminalization of Homosexuality: Queens, Crime and Empire*. London: Routledge, 2018.

Hargreaves, Alec. "Translator's Introduction". In *Ethnicity and Equality: France in the Balance*, by Azouz Begag. Translated by Alec Hargreaves. Lincoln: University of Nebraska Press, 2007.

Helff, Sissy. *Unreliable Truths: Transcultural Homeworlds in Indian Women's Fiction of the Diaspora*. Amsterdam: Rodolpi, 2013.

Heuman, Gad. *The Caribbean: A Brief History*. 2nd ed. London: Bloomsbury, 2014.

Higman, B.W. *A Concise History of the Caribbean*. Cambridge: Cambridge University Press, 2011.

———. *Jamaican Food: History, Biology, Culture*. Kingston: University of the West Indies Press, 2008.

hooks, bell. *Communion: The Female Search for Love*. New York: W. Morrow, 2002.

hooks, bell, and Amalia Mesa-Bains. *Homegrown: Engaged Cultural Criticism.* Cambridge: South End, 2006.

Hosein, Gabrielle Jamela. "Modern Navigations: Indo-Trinidadian Girlhood and Gender-Differential Creolization". *Caribbean Review of Gender Studies* 6 (2012): 1–24.

Hosein, Gabrielle Jamela, and Lisa Outar. *Indo-Caribbean Feminist Thought: Genealogies, Theories, Enactments.* New York: Palgrave Macmillan, 2016.

Ionesco, Mariana. "L'ici-là selon Gisèle Pineau". *Voix plurielles* 4, no. 1 (2007): 2–16.

Jackman, Mahalia. "Protecting the Fabric of Society? Heterosexual Views on the Usefulness of the Anti-gay Laws in Barbados, Guyana and Trinidad and Tobago". *Culture, Health and Sexuality* 19, no. 1 (2017): 91–106.

Kalisa, Marie-Chantal. "War and Political Violence: Nadine Bari's, Edwidge Danticat's and Monique Ilboudo's Literary Responses to Gender and Conflict". In *Violence in Francophone African and Caribbean Women's Literatures*, 151–84. Lincoln: University of Nebraska Press, 2009.

Khan, Aisha. *Callaloo Nation: Metaphors of Race and Religious Identity among South Asians in Trinidad.* Durham, NC: Duke University Press, 2004.

Kincaid, Jamaica. "Girl". *New Yorker*, 26 June 1978. https://www.newyorker.com /magazine/1978/06/26/girl.

King, Rosamond. "More Notes on the Invisibility of Caribbean Lesbians". In *Our Caribbean: A Gathering of Lesbian and Gay Writing from the Antilles*, edited by Thomas Glave, 191–96. Durham, NC: Duke University Press, 2008.

Kizito, Kalemba. "Bequeathed Legacies: Colonialism and State-Led Homophobia in Uganda". *Surveillance and Society* 15, nos. 3/4 (2017): 567–72.

Lamming, George. *The Sovereignty of the Imagination.* Kingston: Arawak, 2004.

Lewis, Shireen K. *Race, Culture, and Identity: Francophone West African and Caribbean Literature and Theory from Négritude to Créolité.* Lanham, MD: Lexington, 2006.

Lindsay, Louis. "The Myth of Independence: Middle Class Politics and Non-mobilization in Jamaica". Kingston: University of the West Indies, Sir Arthur Lewis Institute of Social and Economic Studies (SALISES), 1975.

Loichot, Valérie. "'Devoured by Writing': An Interview with Gisèle Pineau". *Callaloo* 30, no. 1 (2007): 328–37.

———. "Edwidge Danticat's Kitchen History". *Meridians* 5, no. 1 (2004): 92–116.

———. *The Tropics Bite Back: Culinary Coups in Caribbean Literature.* Minneapolis: University of Minnesota Press, 2013.

Lorde, Audre. *Zami: A New Spelling of My Name.* Watertown, MA: Persephone Press, 1982.

Lugones, María. *Pilgrimages/Peregrinajes: Theorizing Coalition against Multiple Oppressions*. Lanham, MD: Rowman and Littlefield, 2003.

Lukanuski, Mary. "A Place at the Counter: The Chaos of Oneness". In *Eating Culture*, edited by Ron Scapp and Brian Seitz, 112–20. Albany: State University of New York Press, 1998.

MacKinnon, Catherine A. "Intersectionality as a Method: A Note". *Signs* 38, no. 4 (2013): 1019–30.

Mahabir, Joy, and Mariam Pirbhai. "Introduction: Tracing an Emerging Tradition". In *Critical Perspectives on Indo-Caribbean Women's Literature*, edited by Joy Mahabir and Mariam Pirbhai, 1–21. New York: Routledge, 2012.

Mannur, Anita. "Culinary Nostalgia: Authenticity, Nationalism and Diaspora". In *Culinary Fictions*, 27–49. Philadelphia: Temple University Press, 2010.

Marshall, Paule. "From the Poets in the Kitchen". *New York Times*, 9 January 1983. https://www.nytimes.com/1983/01/09/books/from-the-poets-in-the-kitchen.html.

May, Vivian. *Pursing Intersectionality: Unsettling Dominant Imaginaries*. New York: Routledge, 2015.

Mbembe, Achille. *De la postcolonie: Essai sur l'imagination politique dans l'Afrique contemporaine*. Paris: Karthala, 2000.

McAlister, Elizabeth. "Caribbean Women's Fugitive Speech Traditions". Women in French Studies International Conference, 8–10 February 2018: "Le bruit des femmes", 25–35. Tallahassee: Florida State University, 2019.

McDonald, Ellie. "'What Is This T'ing T'en about Caribbean Feminisms?': Feminism in the Anglophone Caribbean, circa 1980–2000". *Caribbean Review of Gender Studies* 10 (2016): 43–66.

Mehta, Brinda. "The Colonial Curriculum and the Construction of 'Coolie-ness' in Lakshmi Persaud's *Sastra* and *Butterfly in the Wind* and Jan Shinebourne's *The Last English Plantation* (Guyana)". *Journal of Caribbean Literatures* 3, no. 1 (2001): 111–28.

———. "Culinary Diasporas: Identity and the Language of Food in Gisèle Pineau's *Un papillon dans la cité* and *L'exil selon Julia*". *International Journal of Francophone Studies* 8, no. 1 (2005): 23–51.

———. "Indo-Trinidadian Fiction: Female Identity and Creative Cooking". *Alif* 19 (1999): 151–82.

Michel, Claudine. "Bondye". In *Encyclopedia of African Religion*, edited by Molefi Kete Asante and Ama Mazama, 136. Thousand Oaks, CA: Sage, 2009.

Mintz, Sidney. *Sweetness and Power: The Place of Sugar in Modern History*. New York: Viking, 1985.

————. *Tasting Food, Tasting Freedom: Excursions into Eating, Culture and the Past.* Boston: Beacon, 1996.

Mirabal, Nancy Raquel. "Dyasporic Appetites and Longings: An Interview with Edwidge Danticat". *Callaloo* 30, no. 1 (2007): 26–39.

Mishrahi-Barak, Judith. "'My Mouth Is the Keeper of Both Speech and Silence . . .' or the Vocalisation of Silence in Caribbean Short Stories by Edwidge Danticat". *Journal of the Short Story in English* 47 (2006): 155–66.

Mohammed, Patricia. "The Asian Other in the Caribbean". *Small Axe* 13, no. 2 (2009): 57–71.

————. "Gender as a Primary Signifier in the Construction of Community and State among Indians in Trinidad". *Caribbean Quarterly* 40, nos. 3/4 (1994): 32–43.

————. "Like Sugar in Coffee: Third Wave Feminism and the Caribbean". *Social and Economic Studies* 52, no. 3 (2003): 5–30.

————. "Towards Indigenous Feminist Theorizing in the Caribbean". *Feminist Review* 59 (1998): 6–33.

————. "Women's/Feminist Activism in the Caribbean". *Wiley Blackwell Encyclopedia of Gender and Sexuality Studies*, April 2016. https://doi.org/10.1002/9781118663219.wbegss412.

————. "Writing Gender into History: The Negotiation of Gender Relations among Indian Men and Women in Post-indenture Trinidad Society, 1917–47". In *Engendering History: Caribbean Women in Historical Perspective*, edited by Verene Shepherd, Bridget Brereton and Barbara Bailey, 20–47. New York: St Martin's, 1995.

————, ed. *Gendered Realities: Essays in Caribbean Feminist Thought*. Kingston: University of the West Indies Press, 2002.

Mohammed, Patricia, and Catherine Shepherd, eds. *Gender in Caribbean Development*. Kingston: University of the West Indies Press, 1988.

Mohanty, Chandra Talpade. "Under Western Eyes: Feminist Scholarship and Colonial Discourses". In *The Post-Colonial Studies Reader*, edited by Bill Ashcroft, Gareth Griffiths and Helen Tiffin, 86–106. London: Routledge, 1995.

Montgomery, Maxine Lavon, ed. *Conversations with Edwidge Danticat*. Jackson: University Press of Mississippi, 2017.

Moore, Jason. "Sugar and the Expansion of the Early Modern World-Economy: Commodity Frontiers, Ecological Transformation and Industrialization". *Review* 3 (2000): 409–33.

Mootoo, Shani. "An Interview with Shani Mootoo". Interview by Lynda Hall. *Journal of Lesbian Studies* 4, no. 4 (2000): 107–13.

———. "On Becoming an Indian Starboy". In *The Cross-Dressed Caribbean: Writing, Politics, Sexualities*, edited by Maria Cristina Fumagali, Bénédicte Ledent and Roberto del Valle Alcalá, 167–73. Charlottesville: University of Virginia Press, 2013.

———. *Out on Main Street and Other Stories*. Vancouver: Press Gang, 1993.

———. *Valmiki's Daughter*. Toronto: House of Anansi, 2008.

Mosher, Sarah. "(Auto)biographical Victories: An Analysis of the Culinary and the Literary in Maryse Condé's *Victoire: Les saveurs et les mots*". *Journal of Haitian Studies* 18, no. 2 (2012): 150–66.

Moudileno, Lydie. "La gastronomie furtive de Maryse Condé". *Romanic Review* 94, no. 3/4 (2003): 421–27.

Munasinghe, Viranjini. *Callaloo or Tossed Salad? East Indians and the Cultural Politics of Identity in Trinidad*. Ithaca, NY: Cornell University Press, 2001.

Munro, Martin. "Borders". In *Edwidge Danticat: A Reader's Guide*, edited by Martin Munro, 1–12. Charlottesville: University of Virginia Press, 2010.

Murdoch, H. Adlai. *Creolizing the Metropole: Migrant Caribbean Identities in Film and Literature*. Bloomington: Indiana University Press, 2012.

———. "Negotiating the Metropole: Patterns of Exile and Cultural Survival in Gisèle Pineau and Suzanne Dracius-Pinalie". In *Immigrant Narratives in Contemporary France*, edited by Susan Ireland and Patrice J. Proulx, 129–39. Westport, CT: Greenwood Press, 2001.

———. "Writing India in the West Indies: Indo-Caribbean Inscriptions in Trinidad and Guadeloupe". *CLR James Journal* 9 (2009): 116–46.

Narain, Denise Decaires, Alison Donnell and Evelyn O'Callaghan. "Shani Mootoo: Writing, Difference and the Caribbean". *Journal of West Indian literature* 19, no. 2 (2011): 1–8.

Narayan, Uma. *Dislocating Cultures: Identities, Traditions and Third-World Feminism*. New York: Routledge, 1997.

———. "Essence of Culture and a Sense of History: A Feminist Critique of Cultural Essentialism". *Hypatia* 13, no. 2 (1998): 86–106.

Nedelkovski, Eddy. "Grève générale en Guadeloupe contre la vie chère". *Le Monde*, 24 January 2009. https://www.lemonde.fr/societe/article/2009/01/24/greve-generale -en-guadeloupe-contre-la-vie-chere_1146035_3224.html.

Neruda, Pablo. "Towards the Splendid City". Nobel lecture, 13 December 1971. https://www.nobelprize.org/prizes/literature/1971/neruda/lecture/.

Palmié, Stephen, and Francisco Scarano. *The Caribbean: A History of the Region and Its Peoples*. Chicago: University of Chicago Press, 2011.

Paravisini-Gebert, Lizabeth. "Decolonizing Feminism: The Home-Grown Roots of

Caribbean Women's Movements". In *Daughters of Caliban*, edited by Consuelo Springfield, 1–17. Bloomington: Indiana University Press, 1997.

Pecic, Zoran. "Shani Mootoo's Diasporas". In *Queer Narratives of the Caribbean Diaspora: Exploring Tactics*, 36–101. Houndmills, UK: Palgrave Macmillan, 2013.

Persaud, Lakshmi. *Butterfly in the Wind*. Leeds: Peepal Tree, 1990.

———."'Compelled to Write': An Interview with Lakshmi Persaud. Interview by Anita Baksh". *SX Salon* 4 (April 2011). http://smallaxe.net/sxsalon/interviews /compelled-write-interview-lakshmi-persaud.

———. *Daughters of Empire*. Leeds: Peepal Tree, 2012.

———. *For the Love of My Name*. Leeds: Peepal Tree, 2000.

———. *Raise the Lanterns High*. London: Arcadia, 2004.

———. *Sastra*. Leeds: Peepal Tree, 1993.

Pineau, Gisèle. "5 questions pour Île en île". Interview by Thomas Spear. Video, 33 min. Île en île, 11 June 2009. http://ile-en-ile.org/gisele-pineau-5-questions -pour-ile-en-ile/.

———. "Écrire en tant que noire". In *Penser la créolité*, edited by Maryse Condé and Madeleine Cottenet-Hage, 289–95. Paris: Karthala, 1995.

———. "Entretien avec Gisèle Pineau". Interview by Christine Makward. *French Review* 76, no. 6 (2003): 1202–15.

———. "Entretien avec Gisèle Pineau: Réflexions sur une oeuvre ancrée dans une société mondialisée". Interview by Florence Ramond Jurney. *Nouvelles études francophones* 27, no. 2 (2013): 107–20.

———. *Exile According to Julia*. Translated by Betty Wilson. Charlottesville: University of Virginia Press, 2003.

———. *L'exil selon Julia*. Paris: Stock, 1996.

———. *Fleur de Barbarie*. Paris: Gallimard, 2007.

———. "An Interview with Gisèle Pineau". Interview by Nadège Veldwachter. *Research in African Literatures* 35, no. 1 (2014): 180–86.

———. *Un papillon dans la cité*. Saint-Maur-des-Fossés: Sépia, 1992.

———. "Reconstruire dans l'exil: La nourriture créatrice chez Gisèle Pineau". Interview by Valérie Loichot. *Études francophones* 17, no. 2 (2002): 25–44.

Pineau, Gisèle, and Marie R. Abraham. *Femmes des Antilles, traces et voix: Cent cinquante ans après l'abolition de l'esclavage*. Paris: Stock, 1998.

Pirbhai, Mariam. "Indo-Trinidadian Fictions of Community within the Metanarratives of 'Faith': Lakshmi Persaud's *Butterfly in the Wind* and Sharlow Mohammed's *The Elect*". In *Mythologies of Migration, Vocabularies of Indenture: Novels of the South Asian Diaspora in Africa, the Caribbean and Asia-Pacific*, 127–54. Toronto: University of Toronto Press, 2016.

————. "The Jahaji-Bhain Principle: A Critical Survey of the Indo-Caribbean Women's Novel, 1990–2009". *Journal of Commonwealth Literature* 45, no. 1 (2010): 37–56.

Pollan, Michael. *In Defense of Food: An Eater's Manifesto*. New York: Penguin, 2008.

Puri, Shalini. *The Caribbean Postcolonial: Social Equality, Post-nationalism and Cultural Hybridity*. New York: Palgrave Macmillan, 2004.

Reddock, Rhoda. "Diversity, Difference and Caribbean Feminism". *Caribbean Review of Gender Studies* 1 (2001): 1–24.

Revel, Jean-François. "From Cuisine to Gastronomy". In *Culture and Cuisine: A Journey through the History of Food*, translated by Helen R. Lane, 149–67. Boston: Da Capo, 1984.

Richardson, Bonham C. *Igniting the Caribbean's Past: Fire in British West Indian History*. Chapel Hill: University of North Carolina Press, 2004.

Roger-Petit, Bruno. "Collège: Quand Nicolas Sarkozy s'attaque à Najat Vallaud-Belkacem". *Challenges*, 7 May 2015. https://www.challenges.fr/politique/college-pourquoi-nicolas-sarkozy-declare-la-guerre-scolaire-a-najat-vallaud-belkacem_83464.

Roorda, Eric Paul. *The Dictator Next Door: The Good Neighbor Policy and the Trujillo Regime in the Dominican Republic, 1930–1945*. Durham, NC: Duke University Press, 1998.

Roy, Parama. "Reading Communities and Culinary Communities: The Gastropoetics of the South Asian Diaspora". *Positions: East Asia Cultures Critique* 10, no. 2 (2002): 471–502.

Saïd, Edward. *Orientalism*. New York: Pantheon, 1978.

Sainton, Jean-Pierre. *Couleur et société en contexte post-esclavagiste: La Guadeloupe à la fin du XIXe siècle*. Pointe-à-Pitre: Jason, 2009.

Sanatan, Amílcar. "Homegrown Feminism in the Caribbean". *Telesur*, 20 September 2016. https://www.telesurenglish.net/opinion/Homegrown-Feminism-in-the-Caribbean-20160920-0004.html.

Sarthou, Sharrón Eve. "Unsilencing Défilé's Daughters: Overcoming Silence in Edwidge Danticat's *Breath, Eyes, Memory* and *Krik? Krak!*" *Global South* 4, no. 2 (2010): 99–123.

Schoenhals, Kai P. "Trujillo Molina, Rafael Leónidas (1891–1961)". In *Encyclopedia of Latin American History and Culture*, edited by Jay Kinsbruner and Erick D. Langer, vol. 6, 143–46. 2nd ed. New York: Scribner's, 2008.

Scott, David. "Fanonian Futures?" In *Refashioning Futures: Criticism after Postcoloniality*, 190–219. Princeton, NJ: Princeton University Press, 1999.

Selvadurai, Shyam. *Story-Wallah: A Celebration of South Asian Fiction*. New York: Houghton Mifflin, 2005.

Sesquin, Jérôme, dir. *Maryse Condé: Une voix singulière [Maryse Condé: A Voice of Her Own]*. Jaraproductions, 2011. Subtitles by Richard Philcox.

Shahani, Gitanjali. *Food and Literature*. Cambridge: Cambridge University Press, 2018.

Shemak, April. "Re-membering Hispaniola: Edwidge Danticat's *The Farming of Bones*". *Modern Fiction Studies* 48, no. 1 (2002): 83–112.

Shiva, Vandana. "Development, Ecology and Women". In *Cooking, Eating, Thinking: Transformative Philosophies of Food*, edited by Deane W. Curtin and Lisa M. Heldke, 83–112. Bloomington: Indiana University Press, 1992.

Simasotchi-Bronès, Françoise. "Introduction". In *Maryse Condé en tous ses ailleurs*, edited by Françoise Simasotchi-Bronès. Paris: Improviste, 2014.

Singaravélou, Pierre. "Indians in the Caribbean". In *Les Indes Antillaises: Présence et situation des communautés indiennes en milieu caribéen*, edited by Roger Touson, 27–34. Paris: Harmattan, 1994.

Smith, Barbara, ed. *Home Girls: A Black Feminist Anthology*. New York: Kitchen Table/Women of Color, 1983.

Spade, Dean. "Solidarity Not Charity!" In *Mutual Aid: Building Solidarity During this Crisis and the Next*, 21–30. London: Verso, 2020.

Spear, Thomas. "Maryse Condé". Île en île, 11 January 2021. http://ile-en-ile.org /conde/.

Srivastava, Sanjay. *Sexual Sites, Seminal Attitudes: Sexualities, Masculinities and Culture in South Asia*. New Delhi: Sage, 2004.

Surtees, Joshua. "Homophobic Laws in Caribbean Could Roll Back in Landmark Case". *Guardian*, 7 April 2017. https://www.theguardian.com/world/2018 /apr/07/caribbean-anti-gay-law-ruling-high-court-trinidad-tobago.

Sutherland, Sally J. "Sita and Draupadi: Aggressive Behavior and Female Role-Models in the Sanskrit Epics". *Journal of the American Oriental Society* 109, no. 1 (1989): 63–79.

Tagore, Proma. *The Shapes of Silence: Writing by Women of Colour and the Politics of Testimony*. Montreal: McGill-Queen's University Press, 2009.

Thomas, Bonnie. "The Cook and the Writer: Maryse Condé's Journey of Self-Discovery". *Portal* 10, no. 2 (2013): 1–12.

———. "Gisèle Pineau: Writing as Therapy". In *Connecting Histories: Francophone Caribbean Writers Interrogating Their Past*, 50–75. Jackson: University Press of Mississippi, 2017.

———. "Maryse Condé: Practitioner of Littérature-Monde". *Small Axe* 14, no. 3 (2010): 78–88.

———. "Transgenerational Trauma in Gisèle Pineau's *Chair Piment* and *Mes Quatre Femmes*". *International Journal of Francophone Studies* 13, no. 1 (2010): 23–38.

Torregano, Jacques. "Maryse Condé: 'Ma relation avec l'Afrique s'est fondée sur un mensonge'". Jeune Afrique, 21 May 2015. https://www.jeuneafrique.com/232197 /culture/maryse-cond-ma-relation-avec-l-afrique-s-est-fond-e-sur-un-mensonge/.

Torres-Saillant, Silvio. *An Intellectual History of the Caribbean*. New York: Palgrave Macmillan, 2006.

Tremolet de Villers, Vincent. "Pierre Nora: 'La France vit le passage d'un modèle de nation à un autre'". FigaroVox, 25 May 2015. https://www.lefigaro.fr/vox/societe /2015/05/25/31003-20150525ARTFIG00134-pierre-nora-la-france-vit-le-passage-d -un-modele-de-nation-a-un-autre.php.

Trouillot, Lyonel. "To the Text". In *Edwidge Danticat: A Reader's Guide*, edited by Martin Munro, 180–86. Charlottesville: University of Virginia Press, 2010.

Trouillot, Michel-Rolph. *Silencing the Past: Power and the Production of History*. Boston: Beacon, 1995.

———. "Tonton Macoutes". In *Encyclopedia of Latin American History and Culture*, edited by Joy Kinsbruner and Erick D. Langer, vol. 6, 103–4. 2nd ed. New York: Scribner's, 2008.

Valoverta, Elina. *Sexual Feelings: Reading Anglophone Caribbean Women's Writing through Affect*. Amsterdam: Rodopi, 2014.

Van der Veer, Peter, and Steven Vertovec. "Brahmanism Abroad: On Caribbean Hinduism as an Ethnic Religion". *Ethnology* 30, no. 2 (1991): 149–66.

Vargas, Jennifer Harford. "Novel Testimony: Alternative Archives in Edwidge Danticat's *The Farming of Bones*". *Callaloo* 37, no. 5 (2014): 1162–80.

Vergès, Françoise. *La mémoire enchaînée: Questions sur l'esclavage*. Paris: Albin Michel, 2006.

———. "Singulière Maryse Condé". In *Maryse Condé en tous ses ailleurs*, edited by Françoise Simasotchi-Bronès, 169–78. Paris: Improviste, 2014.

Vigoureux, Christine. *Le mystère Taubira: La vérité derrière l'icône*. Paris: Plon, 2015.

Wahab, Amar. "Homophobia as the State of Reason: The Case of Postcolonial Trinidad and Tobago". *GLQ* 18, no. 4 (2012): 481–505.

Wilk, Richard. *Home Cooking in the Global Village: Caribbean Food from Buccaneers to Ecotourists*. Oxford: Berg, 2006.

Wilson, Larman C. "Duvalier, François (1907–1971)". In *Encyclopedia of Latin American History*, edited by Jay Kinsbruner and Erick D. Langer, vol. 2, 882–84. 2nd ed. New York: Scribner's, 2008.

Zinn, Howard. *A People's History of the United States*. New York: Harper and Row, 1980.

INDEX

CPSIA information can be obtained
at www.ICGtesting.com
Printed in the USA
JSHW021503190822
29483JS00002B/115